Orlando

by Nat Gabriel
illustrated by Mike Reed

Scott Foresman

Editorial Offices: Glenview, Illinois • New York, New York
Sales Offices: Reading, Massachusetts • Duluth, Georgia
Glenview, Illinois • Carrollton, Texas • Menlo Park, California

Salvador was upset. He told
Mama he was going out. He didn't
want her to be worried or sad. He
just needed to be alone.

He hurried across the cornfield.
He turned the corner of the fort and
ran through the door. No one
would see or hear him cry.

The floor was just dirt, but
Salvador liked his fort. He had
made it himself the year before. He
had brought wood scraps from the
old barn behind his house.

Salvador lay down on the dirt floor. He closed his eyes. He had a picture in his mind of his mama. He thought about what had happened at home before he left. He cried some more.

"We have to sell Orlando," Mama had said.

Salvador had put down his fork. "What did you say, Mama?"

Mama tried to explain. But she could not bring herself to say more. She just looked away.

"Why would we sell Orlando?"
Salvador had asked.

"You know we are moving,
Salvador. And we will not have room
for him at our new place. I know he
is a fine pig," Mama had said.

"Orlando is more than a pig!"
Salvador had shouted. "He is
family."

"I know, son," Mama had said.
"If anyone tries to take poor
Orlando, I won't let them!" Salvador
had shouted. Then he had hurried
from the house to his fort.

Salvador adored Orlando.
Orlando was four years old.
Salvador had named him after a
place in Florida he had read about.
There could not be a more perfect
pet for Salvador.

As Salvador lay in the fort crying, it began to rain. At first it was only a light rain. Then it began to pour. Next there was lightning and thunder. It was a very bad storm!

Next Salvador heard a loud
crack! Lightning had struck a tree in
the forest. The tree was on fire!

Salvador got up and ran out of
the fort. It was dark! He couldn't see.
He did not know which way
was home.

Before long Salvador heard a
snorting sound. It was Orlando!
Orlando had come to find him!
Salvador reached out for Orlando.
He felt the pig's ear. He held on.

Orlando led Salvador home. They ran through the cornfield as fast as they could go. Mama stood by the door on the porch.

"Oh, Salvador. I was so worried!" she cried.

"Orlando saved me," Salvador said.

"Yes, I know," said Mama. "He is family! We will just have to find room for him at our next place."

This brought a smile to Salvador's face. Orlando was saved!

"Now he really is a member of our family!" said Salvador.

Wanted
To Tell
You

ALSO BY ANNA MANSELL

How to Mend a Broken Heart
The Lost Wife

anna
mansell

I
Wanted
To Tell
You

bookouture

Published by Bookouture in 2018

An imprint of StoryFire Ltd.
Carmelite House
50 Victoria Embankment
London EC4Y 0DZ

www.bookouture.com

ISBN: 978-1-78681-558-3
eBook ISBN: 978-1-78681-557-6

For Mum

Prologue

My love,

It's cold. Really cold. Like that January we had back when we first met, do you remember? The roof leaked and I couldn't light the fire, so I suggested we wrap up in every jumper we each owned instead. You laughed, told me I was an idiot. But we did it, layer upon layer. Then we sat on the old mattress in the corner of our bedsit, blankets tucked beneath our chins, arms and bodies entwined. We listened to the radio. They talked about childhood sweethearts and I pulled you in close, my own childhood sweetheart, and I promised you we wouldn't be cold forever.

I only wish I knew then what I know now. Maybe things could have been different…

From,

The love you wished I could be.

Chapter One

'So there I was, alone on the moor. The sun was super low and I could barely see a thing. I mean, how long have I been driving those roads?' I ask best friend Claire as she licks her finger to pick up the final crumbs from our third packet of Quavers. Grab bag size. 'I know every hamlet. Every drystone wall. Every village green and remote barn conversion. And it was at its bleakest most beautiful best too; I love this time of year. Maybe that's why I was distracted, I just misjudged it totally.'

The memory of how close vehicular metal came to kissing Yorkshire stone makes my belly do that weird panicky thing when you wish you could go back in time and change something. Like the angle I took that corner. 'Anyway, thankfully, I missed the corner and needn't have worried. But that's when I found it.' Claire is mildly interested, though I know she is actually waiting for the lowdown on the flowers I was given today, not the notebook I found. 'It was just sort of lying there in the corner by the steps, sort of wedged by the bus door,' I say. 'I was getting off to check the damage, thanking my lucky whatsits that I'd no passengers on at the time.'

'What? Not even James?' Claire knows all about the homeless guy I let on for free most days.

'He got off up Micklethwaite today.'

'Right.'

'So there it was. Waiting for me.'

'Waiting for you? Did it have a note on it? To Helen, from… the universe.' She says it in that deadpan way that suggests she thinks my finding the notebook was less about fate and more a simple case of lost property on public transport.

'Well… you know.'

'So whose is it?'

'I don't know! I mean, obviously I looked.'

'Sure!'

'To try and find out who it belonged to, that's all.'

'I hear you.'

I want to pick the book out of my bag, run my fingers down its pages, place a hand on the heart of it and feel the energy that pulses from within… actually she might have a point about fate vs lost property. I might be romanticising. But I don't want her to pick it up and flick through it. I don't want her to shatter the illusion I'm enjoying. I feel protective of its beautiful, looped handwriting. The memories captured in chosen words. Letter after letter to the love of someone's life.

'So did you find out who it belongs to? This magical mystery book?'

'No idea.' I sigh. 'The signature just says, "*The love you wished I could be.*"'

'That is so romantic.' Her tone is filled with faux dreaminess. And the following pause is, I know, for nothing more than dramatic effect because she wants to move the conversation on to the subject of her particular interest. 'Like those flowers, Hel. Those flowers are romantic.'

'Those flowers are the reason I misjudged the corner in the first place. If it hadn't been for his declaration of love, I'd have got that bus back in one piece. I wouldn't mind, but Mr Ali found out about James when he did a mystery shop thingy and already has my card marked. I said to Janice—'

'Janice?' checks Claire, growing impatient because I keep going off-piste.

'Janice!' I repeat. 'My line manager. Do you remember? She's the one who… you know…!' I wink and nudge, trying to jog her memory.

'Your line manager… right…' she drawls, clearly not remembering at all.

'She's the one who reads *Cosmo* over her husband's shoulder when he's… you know…' I wink again but throw in an added cuckoo whistle for clarity. The penny drops, and Claire's eyes widen with recollection.

'Oh! *That* Janice!' she says, grinning.

I try (and fail!) to avoid the image forming in my mind: my boss letting her husband get his conjugal rights whilst she completes a quiz on the multiple orgasm. Apparently, she's mostly A's. I have no idea what that means. 'So anyway, I said to Janice, "Look, James is homeless!"'

'We're back to James.'

'He's cold! Surely we can manage a bus fare once in a while?' I check if Claire's left any Quaver crumbs, which was optimistic at best. Is a fourth bag too much?

'I guess reading it over his shoulder is better than whilst she's on all fours… you know… for example,' says Claire, lost in thought. 'He'd see her flick the pages if he was coming from behind… as it were.'

'Oh God.' I scrunch up my eyes at this new mental image.

'What! Like you've never done it that way?' I roll my eyes at her but she goes on. 'Do you remember, I had that boyfriend who wouldn't do it any other way, but his peni—'

'STOP!' My hands fly up in submission. 'I do not need to hear about your bruised cervix again!'

'Oh my God, Helen, you're such a prude!'

'I am not!'

'Sex is great! Even if that particular experience can still make my eyes water at the memory.'

'Clemmie is barely four weeks old; how can you *possibly* be up for it?'

Claire looks down at her beautiful sleeping baby, nestled in a car seat beneath the sticky, mahogany pub table. We could be forgiven for forgetting she's even there. Not only is she fast on sleeping, but also she's Claire's fourth, which means she's pretty relaxed about motherhood. I wonder if I'd have achieved that status if Alex and I had had siblings for Tom.

'To be fair,' Claire says, 'I'm really not up for it at the moment. It all still smarts a smidge, feels like I've only just stopped pouring the witch hazel.' I recoil, the words witch and hazel bringing back my own memories of childbirth and stitches. 'Doesn't stop me thinking about it though, does it? And anyway, it's not exactly "once in a while" is it?'

'What isn't?' I'm still with the witch hazel.

'Letting James on the bus. You said it's only "once in a while", but isn't he freeriding practically every day at the moment?'

'Oh! Well... yeah... I guess so.' I gaze into the belly of my gin and tonic glass, relieved she's picked up on that story and not yet gone back to the flowers and declaration of love I received this morning. It's true to say that I've been letting James on for free for the last few months, as I have done each winter for the last couple of years. 'It's cold, he'd freeze. Even you, Bingley's answer to Narnia's Ice Queen, has to admit that January has started out pretty bloody northern! It's not like he'd pay to come on if I didn't.'

'It is cold, I'll give you that. I'm getting through my back stash of kiln dried logs at an alarming rate.' She looks up at my face, the face I'm giving of *gee, life's tough*. 'Too middle class?' she asks.

'Little bit!' I grin.

'Anyway,' she flicks her hand as if Tinder swiping left on the subject, 'never mind James and Janice. We have more important subjects to tackle. Like, what are you going to do about those?' She nods towards the bunch of wilting carnations that lie, limply, on the seat beside me. A tiny part of me dies inside.

'Oh God, Claire. It's so ridiculous!' I pick them up for closer inspection and one of the frilly pink heads drops off. I should probably have put them in water. 'I was SO embarrassed. I mean, he just got on the bus with them. I said something like, "Who's the lucky lady?" and he handed them over, saying it was me. I didn't know what to do. There was one of those embarrassing pauses, which he filled by telling me that he'd fancied me for ages and would like to take me out for lunch.' I grab the neckline of my work-issue, polyester jumper, wafting static air across my neck and chin.

'Take you out for lunch? Not dinner! How very cosmopolitan.' Claire is all pouty and giddy with the detail. Vicarious living will do that to a person. 'Does he not know you're married then?'

'Oh I told him, straight away… well, as soon as I could find the words in my brain and get my mouth to function. He was looking at me with such intensity, it was quite arresting.'

'I'll bet it bloody was. God, to have someone arrest me with a look.' She drifts off again before eventually saying, 'You need to claim on the insurance for your wedding ring, that'd sort it.'

'I can't bear to. It has to be somewhere. I cannot have lost it…' It's been missing a year now. It may be time to admit it's not just going to *turn up eventually*. I just know that a replacement won't be like the real thing. It was Alex's grandma's. It has history and meaning and a long and happy marriage in its past. It's just not replaceable.

'So, was he gutted when you told him? Did you break his actual heart?'

'Gutted is a bit of an oversell. More like mild surprise.' I scrunch my eyes up. 'Oh God, I can't remember. I just tried to get him to sit down so we wouldn't hold the bus up. I told him I had a timetable to stick to.'

'It's quite romantic really. Public displays of affection like that.' I turn my nose up at the idea. Probably because I'd love any affection from husband Alex, public or otherwise. 'It is though! And whilst, obviously, I don't condone extra-marital anything, Alex is lovely and you two are life goals. Inspiration. The epitome of happy ever after, BUT...'

I chase the ice in my glass again. If only she knew the truth about the state of my eighteen-year marriage right now. I tell the girls everything, but that subject has been trickier to approach somehow.

'... you must have felt pretty flattered?'

'Well... I don't know... it was okay, I suppose.' I did feel flattered. I still do. I probably shouldn't, but I definitely do... I might even go as far as to say it was a long overdue boost of confidence. Alex might not 'see' me any more, but at almost forty, well, thirty-eight, it is sort of nice to think that maybe I've still got it. Whatever 'it' is.

'Flattered enough to have kept the flowers.' She fixes me with a look that suggests she has totally caught me out.

'What else could I have done with them and, besides, I do love a carnation. They remind me of my grandad. He used to—'

'Don't you try changing the subject again! Okay, here's a question: if you weren't married, would you?'

'No! I am not now, nor will I ever be, somebody's Mrs Robinson,' I declare.

'Mrs Robinson? Christ, how old is he?'

'Well, I don't know really but he doesn't look very old. Early twenties? Maybe? He could be older, I'm rubbish with age.'

'And what's he called?' Claire asks.

'Martin.'

'Nice?'

'Nice, but young. And though it may have been a lifetime since anyone paid me such attention, I basically wanted the bus floor to open up and swallow me whole.'

'With or without the carnations?'

'CLAIRE!'

She cackles, which wakes Clemmie up. As she bends down to calm her back to sleep, I catch sight of myself in the tinsel bedecked mirror behind her. Who knew a human face could take on the purple hue of a hazelnut caramel wrapper, commonly found in a box of Cadbury Roses. The colour worsens, so I waft my jumper a little harder.

Claire sits back up, spying me from beneath her Dawn O'Porter fringe, the Quant bob one, not the Sassoon crop. 'Jesus, Helen, look at the state of you! Come on, give yourself a break; we're old, the attention is nice. Bet you thought about it! I bloody would've. Is he a regular then?'

'He's been getting on the bus for years, he lives up Crossflatts. I bet I've been picking him up for the last five.' Claire mouths 'Oooh matron' and makes me giggle. 'Pack it in. It's not like I've led him on or anything. Not that that matters because apparently he can't stop thinking about me.'

'Fit?'

'Barely out of his teens!'

'You don't know that as fact.'

'He's young.'

'Young is good. Young is keen, eager. Young is—'

'Stop!' I hold my hands up before necking the warm remains of my drink. 'Young is not that much older than Tom! I had Tom at twenty remember, I could probably be Martin's mother for Christ's sake!'

'Young could give you Janice's multiple orgasms!' Claire adds.

'Look, if I was remotely up for any of that stuff, Alex would be the only man to give it to me. Multiple or otherwise. If either of us could be bothered, that is!' I can't actually remember the last time we had sex. He's just not been in the mood and that's been cool with me. All these extra hours whilst he's out of work, I'm knackered. 'No, it was very sweet and, okay, yes, a teensy bit flattering, but I think it was mostly just excruciatingly awful.'

'Aye, I s'pose it would have been. Still…' she draws a long breath '…you can't blame me for wanting the detail. Whilst Gary is keen to point out how much he fancies me and my "baby belly" because, yes, that is what he's calling it now, there's a part of me that wonders if I've still got it, you know? Time marches on… mostly all over my face.'

I shake my head at her. She's always self-deprecated. Among the four of us, my dearest friends, she's the one that not only still has it, but probably looks better now than she did when we were all teenagers. We've regularly told her how much we hate her because of it. Particularly as I, on the other hand, resemble something of a polyester-clad frump with hair in need of attention and a face I don't clear of make-up as religiously as I might. 'Chuffin' baby belly! Tell him from me, he's punching well above his weight with you! Always has been.'

Claire grins, sipping at her Diet Coke. She gazes around the pub, then into her glass with disgust. 'Bloody breastfeeding! What I wouldn't give for a stiff one!'

'Claire!' I warn. Because I've met her before.

'Gin! I meant gin!' She winks, mischievously.

I roll my eyes as if I don't believe her, but all the while I wonder if she can tell that I have caught myself fantasising over Martin's proposition. I mean, I wouldn't, ever. I couldn't, obviously, but God it was nice to feel admired... maybe even momentarily objectified – despite that going against every feminist bone in my body. I guess, being with your other half since you were nowt but kids yourselves, the dynamism is bound to subside. Which is fine, totally fine.

I wonder if that's what happened to the people in the notebook I found; the love and the love they wished they could be.

My phone pings with a text message. Alex – which is something of a novelty these days. 'Oh!'

'What?'

I read. Then read again. 'It's Alex.' My brow crumples, confused.

'Okay... and that's surprising because?'

'He says...' I look up at Claire. 'He says he's going away.'

Chapter Two

Geoff placed the last of the decorations in the old shabby box they'd stored them in for something close to forty years. The silver-coloured tinsel tree, now more bare wire than fire risk tinsel, was packed away. Connie had always wanted a real tree and Geoff sometimes wished he'd let her. Before it was too late. Then there was the old polystyrene carol singers, their felt coats faded from age, their heads glued back on every year for as long as he could remember; the baubles; the fairy lights; the unrecognisable clay Mary and Joseph made by the grandchildren when they were four or five; each item packed away. This, all of this, was Connie's job before. She packed Christmas away, she always had. Two weeks after unpacking and carefully putting each item in its rightful place. Perhaps, that's why it frustrated him now, not because he had to do it – Connie no longer being well enough – but because there was no order to the packing. No sense of where things should go or how they should be wrapped, perhaps to save them being glued again next year. Or so he might know where she'd want them in twelve months' time because his wife of more than seventy years liked their Christmas decorations in a particular way, everything had its place. It didn't matter how she packed things away if she was putting them out the following year, but if trimming up was down to Geoff next year, he'd need to pack things carefully and in order, organised, like all other things he did in life.

He glanced over to her, vacantly staring out of the window as she had been doing for a while now. He dearly wished she were able to pack each item away. He dearly wished that she hadn't looked over at the boxes to ask him what it was all for. 'It's Christmas, love,' he'd answered, several times over, and she'd smiled as if she understood. But he knew better than to believe that.

Does she remember any of the Christmases they've had? The early mornings with their daughter Rosemary, eagerly waking before the sun had come up. The dinners with Geoff's parents and Connie's aunts and uncles. The gifts. The cross words over her feeding a Christmas pudding with his very best whisky. The snatched kisses under mistletoe.

The care workers were right: Connie had been more present last year than this. She'd been more aware. Whether Geoff liked it or not, the last twelve months had stolen more of her. More hours of her. More moments. He'd not noticed, day-to-day, not to begin with. Sometimes she was in, sometimes not. He couldn't quite pinpoint the moment it shifted from often out, occasionally in. The change between how many hours of the day she was present in mind as well as body. The hours grew fewer. Life was getting harder. For more and more hours in the day, more days in the week, Connie wasn't there. She'd all but left her body. It was like a shell that hid the woman sucked up by the disease. He cherished those glimmers when she'd return, as if she'd simply shaken it off. Like dementia hadn't ravaged every corner of her brain. And as if to prove the fact, she'd return with an acute memory. Something from their early years, often one he couldn't recall himself. She'd repeat his army number with clipped precision. She'd recite the recipe for Yorkshire puddings, passed down by her aunt and *her* great-aunt before that, mainly so that he might cook them for her. His heart would swell, as did the Yorkshires. Sometimes she'd recite a funny story, telling Geoff it was one from Rosemary, their daughter, except after a while the memories would merge into something from their grandkids, no longer children, often with names muddled up. And then she'd disappear again, the mistakes in the detail sucking her away. The last time their granddaughter came around, new baby in tow, Connie had no idea who either of them was.

Geoff didn't like to admit that caring for her was getting harder. Or that his frustration grew. He didn't like to think about all of the things he'd never said and now probably couldn't say. Because what would be the point if she didn't understand. Things he'd often wanted to talk about and things he'd buried deep because to relive what he'd been through during his nine decades on this earth, well it might hurt, it could undermine his stiff upper lip. She married a man of strength, a man who could provide, who would care for his family. A man that did not wallow in the sorrows of his past. At the end of the day, he'd been one of the lucky ones.

He held the decoration box closed, wrapping tape around it several times, layering new sticky after brittle old. He lugged it onto the sideboard, heaving, ready for the care workers to hide it up in the loft again tomorrow, just as they'd promised. He rubbed at his arm, prickles of discomfort needled their way down to his fingers, which he stretched and curled to try and rid himself of the sensation.

The letter from Social Services taunted him, sitting there beside the decorations. The words within remained unknown, but he knew enough to expect they'd hurt, and he wasn't prepared to let them. Not yet. Not until he was ready. Right place. Right time. This was their home, a home they moved to shortly before he retired at the age of sixty-five. It was a home that played hotel to the grandkids. It was a home open to house guests and neighbours. It was a home that Connie made; it was Geoff's castle.

It was also the first place he'd felt any peace from the memories of his youth. His 'holiday' at the request of Adolf. The horrors he'd seen, horrors that still played out most nights each time he closed his eyes.

This home was their sanctuary. Till death do us part.

'Geoff,' she said, looking up at him, her eyes sparkling. Was she back? 'Do you remember how you'd write to me? In the early days of the war, or later on, when you worked away?' she asked.

Geoff smiled. 'Of course I do.' Though he remembered she wrote to him far more frequently than the other way around and he remembered that he lived for those letters; they were oxygen, a lifeline, a reminder of what he was surviving for.

He moved to crouch beside her, knees cracking as he did so. 'I remember your letters too.'

'Did I write back?' she asked. Geoff nodded, bending to kiss her hand as it rested on the armchair. Connie laid her other hand on the back of his head, stroking gently. And for a second, he was able to forget the reality of their day-to-day. Safe in the knowledge that if nothing else, they were still together. Sweethearts to old age. For all they'd seen, for all he'd struggled with, for all she'd done for him, for their daughter, still together, still in love. Still lucky.

Chapter Three

I read the text message again. Not that there's much to read. 'It's like half a message, like he's forgotten to add in the bit about where he's going, and when he'll be back. Look.' I hand my phone to Claire who scrolls up and down the phone as if there may be more answers in the history of chat. To be fair, I can't remember the last time he texted anyway.

'Is that it?' she says, incredulous.

'I know! I mean, I know he's a man of few words – even fewer since the redundancy, but shit, he could've expanded a little. I'd worry if I didn't think it's just the way things are these days.'

'What's the way things are?'

'This. Basic communications. I don't know. There's not much between us at the moment. It's fine. It's a phase. We've been here before.' Claire looks at me, she knows the ups and downs of our marriage. 'No, I don't mean *there*, we're not *there* again.'

This is a reference to a particularly rocky patch when Tom started school and I went back to work. We were both busy, juggling. We were taking each other for granted. Nothing happened between him and Amanda Hobson, a girl we were at school with. He'd just gone to hers for headspace. And I believed him, he wouldn't have told me where he'd been if it had been more. He wouldn't have come back and confessed everything. He could just as easily have told me nothing;

he could have told me it had been a work trip or something. Mobile phones weren't in everyone's pockets back then, to not hear from him wasn't cause for panic. And if anything had happened, I just don't think he'd have wanted to work at bringing us back together like he did. He made time for us; he made time to be a husband as well as a father. And I'm certain that's because of Amanda Hobson. But it hurt, the memory of him growing close to someone else when I needed him most. Claire knew.

'Look, we've been together twenty years, Claire. It's just a phase. A patch. We all go through them, don't we!' It's purposefully not a question, but Claire does a funny thing with her mouth and I can't quite work out what she's thinking, which makes me second-guess myself. 'Don't we?'

'Erm… okay. Sure.'

She is unconvincing. 'What! It happens. It'll come to you two, give it time. You might be all newly wedded up, thinking life is roses for ever after.' Claire and her husband have been together for yonks, but only just got married. They've basically re-entered the blissful 'we're a tight team' phase. The one you find just after you marry and realise it's you and your spouse against the world. And it is, for me and Alex too, it's just that we're not quite as in your face about it all these days. That comes with comfort. 'Anyway, at least I can binge watch *Orange Is the New Black* if he's not around to complain. Stub you!'

'God, you're so mature.' I stick my tongue out to reinforce her opinion and she shakes her head. There's a pause. She studies me. 'So… you're okay with this?' she asks.

'Well… I mean, I might have liked it if he'd talked to me before he left, but, sure, it's fine. We don't have to live in each other's pockets, we do have our own lives you know!' It's possible this comes over more defensively than I intended, judging by the rise of Claire's eyebrows. I don't want to feel defensive. I don't want to mind. 'It's fine.' Except, Claire has a look on her face that suggests she doesn't think it is fine and I know that she knows I don't really feel fine about any of it but will wait for me to talk about it when I'm ready. 'A bit of space will do us good. He's lived in his phone since he lost his job. He's permanently laughing at the funny people he follows on Twitter, then palming me off when I ask what's tickled him. He barely moves from his chair and yet he's not present, you know? Today was the first day he left the house. I dropped him off in town so he could go to the Jobcentre. Maybe it didn't go so well. Maybe getting away is exactly what he needs right now, and I can see the look on your face, Claire.'

'What look?'

'The one that wonders when I'm going to tell you how I'm really feeling but it's fine. We're fine. He's just… finding life hard at the moment. It'll pass.'

'Nothing on the job front then?'

'Nope. And I guess nothing today either. It's really hurting him.'

I stare back down at my phone. What if Tom asks where his dad is? Maybe I should at least know the answer to that. I tap out a message. *Where are you going? Are you okay?*

'See, look, I've asked him where he's going to. It's fine. And anyway, he's probably told me and I've forgotten. I've been pretty busy with the extra shifts.' I force a smile.

The pub music ramps up and Clemmie gets restless. 'Argh, I think Attila needs feeding again. I swear she's been dictating my life since the second her head was yanked free of my vagina. I'd better go.'

'Go on, I'll see you Friday for Vicky's birthday drinks, yeah?'

'Yes. Defo. Call if you need anything before then, okay?'

'Course.'

She blows me a kiss, then weaves her way out of the pub and into the car park. I should leave, too. I should go home. I check my phone, just in case Alex has messaged back, but there's nothing. Stretching my legs out beneath the table, I knock my handbag. Remembering the notebook is in there piques my interest. The bundle of letters folded between pages, tied up with red ribbon. The swirl of handwritten letters contained, addressed to *My love*. Signed *The love you wished I could be*. And I wonder if it would hurt to have another little look. A tiny read. Maybe I'll work out who it belongs to and I can reunite this beautiful book with its mystery owner.

The spine creaks as I open it. The letters wedged in tight so they don't move. My hands tingle to touch them. Who is *My love?* Who is *The love you wished I could be?* And why not names? Are the letters intentionally secret? Did the person they were written for ever see them? Are they kept by the love or the love they wished they could be? I sniff at the creamy paper, a page falls open and my heart spikes a little. Then a familiar waft of sweet yet smoky aftershave passes my nostrils. 'Helen,' says a voice from behind me and I snap the book shut.

Chapter Four

My love,

Sometimes I wish I could find a way to talk. To really be honest with you, with those around us. With myself. Perhaps if I could, things would be different. We wouldn't have ended up in this place.

I see couples in the street sometimes. You can tell at what stage they are at in their relationship. I want to tell them to be kind to each other. To themselves. To be patient. To find ways to talk through the hardest things because that is what will keep them together. Of course, who listens when they're young and in love anyway? We didn't.

I didn't.

How I wish I could turn back time.

From,

The love you wished I could be.

Chapter Five

'Martin!' My temperature catapults in time with my heart rate and I drop the book on the table in front of me as if I wasn't really about to take out a letter and read it word for word. I don't care what the doctor says, I've defo started perimenopause.

He nods down at the flowers, still on the chair beside me. 'They need some water,' he says, simply, fixing deep green eyes back on me and I wonder why I can't tear mine away.

'Yeah, I know I was... I was just... leaving.' I'm suddenly – and frankly, ridiculously – nervous. I'm a thirty-eight-year-old woman, nearly thirty-nine, basically I'm kissing forty; nerves have no place in my emotional quiver.

'Shame.'

'What is?'

'That you're leaving.' He watches me get my things together. Not in a predatory way, just in a he's stood next to me and I'm fumbling like an idiot way. 'I thought serendipity was at play.'

He winks. I laugh. Probably louder than I need to. Then I fumble again and drop my coat, which he promptly bends down to collect and offers it back to me. I'm glad I didn't go to pick it up too or we'd have had one of those stupid filmic moments where our eyes met over a North Face all-weather jacket. Okay, maybe the specificities of coat

are irrelevant. Did she have a coat in *Brief Encounter*? When they met
at that station? Oh God, this is ridiculous. And what's with the glint
of mischief in his eyes and why do I quickly look away. 'Nope. No
serendipity here, not today. Or any day! No.'

'No.'

'No.' I swallow. Looking back up at him. His eyes have a sparkle.
He reminds me of someone but I can't quite put my finger on who.
He ruffles his hair with his hand, his arms are strong and muscular
and I wonder what on earth he sees in a woman like me or why I've
even noticed his arms being strong and muscular. Christ, I'm definitely
probably old enough to be his mother.

Why am I even thinking that?

'So… you've not had time to think about my proposal and take
me up on the offer?'

Right. I'm pulling myself together. Right now. This minute. 'I
didn't need to think about it, Martin. I'm flattered, truly. You're very…
handsome… and the flirting is… well, it's a novelty, if truth be told,
but you are, I'm pretty sure, young enough to be my son and I already
have one of those. I made him with my husband, who I love very much.
We should very definitely stick with the relationship we have. I'm the
bus driver, you're the passenger.'

'I'm twenty-eight.'

'Wow, really? You look… younger. Twenty-eight?' He gives me a
wry grin and I flick my hair out of my eyes. 'That must be why you're
so confident then. With women, I mean.' Why am I still talking?

'Is confidence a problem?'

'Well, it's not a problem, as such. No. I'm sure it serves you well
in life. Look, over there…' I nod to a gaggle of young girls who I
think have noticed him anyway. 'I reckon that group would love your

confidence. They're gorgeous, and let's face it, much closer to your age. Not to mention, not married. Unlike me.'

'*You're* gorgeous. But okay, I understand you're married. It's just… with you not having a ring on. I didn't realise… sorry. He's a lucky man.'

I swallow, hard, because I feel like I might have a coronary at how fast my heart is racing. I put my coat on by way of distraction and then collect my handbag, looking for my way out.

'Don't forget your book.' He picks it up from the table.

'Oh it's not…' I take it from him. 'Thank you.' We pause. He waits, patiently. 'Look, I have to go. Thank you for these, they're lovely. Carnations are my favourite, my grandad used to grow them. Whoever you buy flowers for next is a very lucky girl.' He goes to speak but this time, I cut him off. 'Goodnight, Martin.'

I leave. But I can feel him watching me across the room. And I wish it didn't feel so nice to be wanted.

Chapter Six

Preparing for his usual Tuesday morning trip, Geoff hitched up his trouser leg, letting out a groan as he strained to tie the lace on his perfectly polished shoes. They were buffed. Regimental. Just as he'd been taught back in 1942 when he was called up, two weeks before his eighteenth birthday. With both hands on his knees, he pushed up, standing as if to attention. For a man of ninety-three, he was fitter than most. Independent. Something he put down to routine, to keeping busy, to retaining control of his life and home. That the same could not be said for Connie was something he lamented daily. Something he hid from everyone but those closest; those being their daughter Rosemary, and their neighbour Val from over the road.

Connie's gaze drifted towards him and she smiled, politely, as if they'd accidentally caught each other's eye in the doctor's waiting room. She'd not been there all morning. He reached for the paper on which he had written her reminder: 9.35 a.m. – Bus to Bingley. Bank. Supermarket. 11.35 a.m. home. He did not give mention to where he really went, or why. The illness had long since taken her faith in God and explaining why it remained important to him would soon be forgotten, so he'd given up.

'Here you go, love.' He tried passing her the note but when she didn't reach for it, he placed it on the glass-topped table to her left instead. He picked up crisp, dropped petals from the past-its-best poinsettia, dropping them in the bin. It was a pink one. Untraditional, some might say, but pink was her favourite colour and it was a gift from Rosemary. 'I won't be long,' he said, as cheerfully as he could muster. 'It's all on there, love. Val's going to drop in on you before she goes out later, okay?'

'Val?' Connie asked.

'Val. You know, over the road.' She'd lived there twenty years.

'Of course I know Val,' Connie snapped, as if he patronised, but Geoff knew better. Connie had no idea who Val was, she'd lost her months ago. Along with the doctor, their social worker; along with friends and family – well, those they had left anyway, given both their ages. Even their daughter Rosemary was long gone. Geoff was going too and though Connie kept trying to hide the fact, Geoff could always tell when she was pretending to know who he was; each time it hurt as much as the last. As much as the first. Maybe more, it was hard to say. He hadn't told anybody that she'd mostly lost him now too and so far nobody had guessed; it suited him to keep it that way.

'Where are you going?' she asked, staring up at him, wide-eyed. She was like a tiny child in an over-sized chair, her ever-decreasing frame swamped by the ageing brown velour; time stealing her body mass, just as it was stealing her life.

Guiltily, he turned away. 'Bingley. To the bank, then the supermarket. I'll be home at eleven thirty-five.' He tapped the paper with her instructions on. 'There,' he said, patiently pointing to the note she'd already forgotten. She looked at it, reading, then nodded. 'And Val will be over later,' he reminded.

'Val?'

'Val.'

Frustrated, but also angry with his own impatience, Geoff lifted closed eyes skyward. Taking a deep breath, he reached down to her shoulder and her tiny hand reached up to pat his in loving return.

He picked up the re-usable shopping bags from their place on the shelf, dropping them into his own bag, along with his wallet. He paused over the letter from Social Services before deciding it was time he faced the contents, placing it carefully in his inside pocket. 'See you in a bit, love,' he shouted over his shoulder, stepping outside as he pulled the door closed with a fidgety relief.

And for the time being, that was that. There ended the ever-decreasing circle of their morning's conversation. The conversation they'd have every time he tried to leave the house. If Social Services had their way, Geoff suspected those conversations would be fewer and fewer, and whilst he grew increasingly tired by them, he couldn't imagine a home without Connie in it. It just wouldn't be a home.

Chapter Seven

My love,

Sometimes I wonder about the life we had together. I wonder if we could have predicted our story. When we were young, did you imagine us growing old? When we married, did you imagine us being parents? Did you imagine the ordinary, everyday stuff? The work we'd both do, the evenings we'd spend deconstructing our days. Did you picture retirement, the years we might come back together to reconnect, to find common interests? The years of just being together, happy.

I think all I ever hoped for was health, peace, for our love to endure even the toughest of dark days. I think I hoped we might learn from our youth, from the follies, from the days when patience was not in our vocabulary, though maybe you were always patient. Maybe that's why it worked for so long? You stood for more than I might ever have. I see that now, more clearly than anything else. How I wish I could have repaid you before it was too late. Or seen for myself what we were doing to each other, what life was offering. When you're in the moment, too close to see, you can be forgiven for making the wrong choices, can't you? How will I ever know now?

From,

The love you wished I could be.

Chapter Eight

Back straight, Geoff looked up and down the road. He sniffed the January cold air that stripped his nostrils. He took a lungful of Yorkshire fresh, replacing the sick-making, latent frustration of his conversations with Connie with the preferred sense of purpose. His job was to provide, to care for, a job he'd been assigned in one form or another since the tender age of thirteen when his father, a survivor of World War One, was unable to work, when he found the role society expected of him too much to bear. Geoff felt a sense of pride in being asked to take over, he felt a sense of purpose. He was important, he was needed. Being the new man of the house was a job Geoff had worn as a badge of honour ever since… even on the days when the badge was too heavy and the honour not quite a big enough price to be paid. Duty was his middle name.

Taking extra care on the frost-covered ground, Geoff unlatched the gate, closing it firmly behind him as he took up his usual position on the corner by their house. There wasn't a bus stop there, there never had been, but Helen, who grew up next door and was now a driver on Mr Ali's buses, always stopped there anyway. She did that for most of her passengers from East Morton, the older ones at least. People she'd known from being a kid. The ones whose doors she'd knock on to carol sing, or trick or treat. Now, she'd drop them at the gates to their front doors because life was too short to rush from one stop to the next, or so she would say. She'd always been thoughtful like that, right back as a girl when they moved in to the terrace and first met her. She must have been in her early teens, Geoff couldn't quite remember. She'd seen the bus drivers from back in the day picking up Mrs Pedley who used to get the bus from that same corner, a few steps from her gate on the opposite corner of the lane. In those days, Geoff would still drive. Nowadays, he felt too old to get behind the wheel and Helen had told him to just wait by his gate, just as Mrs Pedley had, and she'd stop there for him. He was grateful for her generosity of spirit because sometimes his bones just hurt.

Eyes front, arms to the side, Geoff waited his usual three and a half minutes for the bus to arrive. Habit fed muscle memory, pushing him to glance at his watch as the golden hands turned 9.35 across the brown leather face of his Rotary watch; an anniversary gift from back when Connie was still herself and could choose such things. The bus turned the corner in perfect-precision time, Helen at the wheel. He approved, thrusting a straight arm out for her to clearly see. If she was prepared to flounce bus stop rules, he had a duty to be visible and prompt on her arrival.

The bus pulled up, steam dumping as it lowered, the doors bouncing open with a generous flick.

'Good morning, Helen,' he said, with efficient politeness that betrayed the heavy sadness in his heart. He flashed his bus pass. 'How are you today?'

'Very good, thanks, Geoff. Happy New Year to you. Did you have a lovely Christmas? How are you? How's Connie? Did you see Rosemary?'

Geoff liked Helen's chat. The questions she'd ask whilst waiting for him to take up his usual seat on the right-hand side of the bus. It was an opportunity for him to be Mr Geoffrey Steele. Husband. Former officer in the army. Churchgoer. Man of responsibility and status. Helen had no reason to hear of his woes or learn of Connie's. He could be himself around Helen. 'I'm very well, thank you. And you?'

'I'm excellent,' she trilled, just like she always did.

Geoff offered a nod to a few of the other regulars on the bus. They sat dotted about each side, mostly avoiding James, the homeless man who sat on the second row, his arms hanging over the back of the front bench, ready for their regular chat. 'How are you, James?' Geoff asked, taking up the seat before him.

'Aye, ah'm good, thanks,' he said, sitting back in his chair, his accent thick with Glasgow lilt. 'You okay?'

'Of course, never better.' He enjoyed chatting to James, sometimes just passing the time, other times exchanging stories about the people and places around James' home city of Glasgow, the first place Geoff was posted to during the war.

'We've no' seen Connie in a while,' James went on, looking out of the window in the direction of their house.

'I was thinking the same, Geoff,' said Helen. 'If you want me to help you get her on for a day trip, you've only got to say. It'd be lovely to see her.'

'Oh, she's fine, she's just…' Geoff ran out of words, just as he always did when someone showed they cared and threatened to unpick his carefully tailored reserve. 'She's not too fussed about day trips any more.' He gave Helen the nod that she knew meant he was settled for her to move on. She checked her mirrors before signalling to make her manoeuvre.

Geoff mirrored her because he was an advanced motorist and old habits die hard, but also because it gave him time to prepare his usual response to anybody's questions or suggestions for Connie. A response that kept him as husband, not carer. 'That's why I'm left to do all the chores, eh, James.' He grinned at James who smiled right back at him. 'She says it's God making work for idle hands,' he lied, guilt pricking his conscience. And though he smiled brightly as the bus pulled off, a ghost memory picked at his heart. It was Connie at the window waving. He didn't bother turning to see if the ghost was real. The inevitable disappointment was too much to bear. Instead, he fixed his eyes forward on the road up ahead. He waited for James to pass the time as he always would. He settled in for the journey. The free time to do as he pleased. Time he spent the same way he always did, each time he made the break for this guilt-ridden freedom.

Chapter Nine

I wanted to ask him round for dinner. Him and Connie back at ours, enjoying a roast chicken with all the trimmings. I feel like my house is closed, like I can't be the person I always was. I also miss seeing Geoff and Connie just being Geoff and Connie. Standing by their gate, arm in arm. Sometimes, as I drove up the hill, I'd see him lean in to say something to her and she'd let out a coquettish giggle. Or on the bus, after he'd greeted the rest of us, they'd chat between themselves. They were together, tight, in love.

When they moved in next door, I was twelve, maybe thirteen. I was learning about love and relationships; they inspired me. I'd go round to theirs sometimes, dropping something off for my mum, or picking up tickets that she'd ordered from Connie for the little theatre in town. I'd stand in the doorway to their lounge, gazing at the photos they had everywhere: sepia, black and white, a few in colour; their lives together captured and kept for posterity. When Alex and I got together, Geoff and Connie's photos would come to mind. I'd try to catch our own moments on film, pictures of us to keep for the future. Alex didn't understand it, he'd never seen all their photos and he'd only met Geoff and Connie in passing. Maybe because my own parents split up and family wasn't really a thing, that's why I admired theirs. Did I yearn for the same kind of connection as Geoff and Connie? Is that what made me move in with Alex so young? A chance to build a home with the man I loved, covering the walls in our own captured moments. I loved Alex, but I loved love too. The idea of 'together forever' appealed. Would we have made it this far had I not had Geoff and Connie as an example of what might be? Would we have made it this far had I not fallen pregnant so young?

I went round one Christmas, not long after Tom was born. I'd taken him to see Connie because she loved babies and, as soon as she knew I was almost due, she made me promise I would. Mum had moved house, so they were no longer neighbours. I went though, I visited. Connie cooed, she talked about how Geoff had been busy with work when they'd first had Rosemary. He'd just made it to management in the council, after years of moving from one job to another after the war, he had to focus. She never said how that made her feel but I wondered if she'd told me because she saw how I was struggling. Alex busy with work, the dynamic in our relationship having changed. I told her I missed Alex, I missed the relationship we had before Tom. She promised it would come back. Maybe it did, at some point. It must have. It's hard to tell at the moment.

I pull up for another passenger. 'Morning, morning. How nice is this winter sun, eh? On you get, there's room down the back.' I wait for them to sit down. James winks through the mirror at me as he and Geoff chat.

Like them, each time I stop, I chat the small talk like I always have and feel pretty chuffed that I don't think anyone can tell that my husband has gone AWOL or my marriage is on a knife edge, or that I'm prone to moments of melodrama and over-exaggeration. Can you over-exaggerate? Surely to exaggerate you are, by definition, over-ing something? Each time I stop, I glance at my phone, just in case Alex has texted back. Disappointment increases each time I press a button to wake it up and see nothing but him and Tom smiling back at me. I took it on Tom's seventeenth. They were sharing a joke, heads back, laughter, bookends. Tom asked me where Alex was this morning. Sat there with his Honey Loops like a kid. I downed a coffee and said I couldn't remember. Told him I'd accidentally deleted the text that told me and blamed it on the fact I'm getting old and technology is getting harder. I don't think he believed me.

The bus bell goes, and I pull over. 'See you later, Jenny,' I sing-song. 'Give my love to Bill.' Oh God, we might end up like Jenny and Bill. They hate each other. Always have. It's a known fact. She calls him an arsehole and he says he'd have got less for murder but not in the way that people do to try and be funny.

I want to be Geoff and Connie, not Jenny and Bill. Bill had an affair, years ago. Apparently. I mean, I get that it's flattering if someone shows attention. Christ, I never thought anyone would fancy me again. I wouldn't do anything about it though. And I trust Alex, I do. He just couldn't wear that sort of guilt. And I do know that marriage isn't all giddy and passion for eternity, whatever Claire might want me to believe, we're just not like that. Never have been... Alex just needs to talk to me. Let me listen. Let me help him fix things.

I pull up to the Co-operative supermarket on Bingley main road. I put the handbrake on, waiting patiently as people get off. You must wait until all passengers have alighted, my instructor always said. Alight. Funny word. You don't hear people say it much these days. 'Bye, Gill, see you later, Paul, thanks, bye, cheers, see ya.'

The toe of Geoff's military polished shoe doesn't move. 'It's Tuesday, Geoff, are you not getting off here today?'

Chapter Ten

'Geoff?' Helen shouted down the bus, which snapped him out of a daydream. As James chatted, Geoff had been lost in thought since settling down for the thirty-minute journey into town.

Daydreaming was a habit he usually disliked. Sometimes the memories were good, films he and Connie had watched together. Meals they'd had, holidays on the south-east coast, happy times, the grandchildren. But too often, his mind would drift. Sometimes he'd find himself in the darker hours of his days memories vivid with sights, sounds and smells. This morning, the memory was the look on Connie's face as his platoon picked him up before they were deployed to Arnhem. Fresh in his mind because he'd realised it had that similar distance to the face he sometimes sees now, this morning included. Back then it was self-protection as she buttoned up. He knew where he was going, she knew he was lying but like many wives of the men who went to war, she got on with it because she had to. Sometimes he wondered how that felt. Had he asked? If so, he couldn't now remember her answer. Had she ever truly understood what he'd been through? Or how he felt?

'We're here, Geoff,' said James, who'd moved to stand beside him, a look of concern etched beneath his scraggy beard. It was Tuesday. They all knew that Geoff always got off in town on a Tuesday. Same on a Friday too.

'Sorry, I was miles away.' Geoff pulled himself up and into Helen's view. 'Don't know where I'd drifted off to then.' He beat his hands around his coat to check for wallet, keys, the letter.

'Are you okay, love?' Helen asked this time. 'Have you lost something?'

He patted his coat again, feeling the letter this time. 'No, no. I'm fine. Thank you.' He didn't want to admit to having been awake most of the night. Or the stress of this morning as Connie rejected her breakfast because it wasn't in the right bowl. And her tea was too hot, then too cold. Then she didn't know who he was, and then he was back again, and then the carers came to help out and she was lost again. And it was exhausting… as was the guilt he felt at how frustrated he was. And how tired he was. 'Absolutely fine. Mustn't grumble.'

'Of course. I know that feeling. See you in a bit?' asked Helen.

'Yes, see you in a bit. Thank you.'

Helen pulled away, revealing the old market square with its stocks. The church steeple down the road. The row of shops from bus stop to bus stop and beyond. He glanced at his watch, relieved that he was still on time, given that he remembered nothing of the journey here.

Head down, he went to the bank to pay in his pension, the supermarket to collect a few daily supplies. He shared a joke with the man in the bank. He chatted to the lady on the till whom he saw most weeks. He enjoyed the anonymity of it all. Like on the bus with Helen and James. Among these people, in these places, he was Mr Geoffrey Steele. This time a man of integrity. A man of charm and wit. A good man. A husband, a father, a grandfather, a great-grandfather. It was important.

Jobs ticked off, he focused on the road up ahead. He tried not to inhale the petrol fumes that hung heavy amongst the traffic. He caught nobody's eye as he walked. He stepped through the gate into the churchyard. A place of haven, of solace. A place he and Connie would often visit together, back in the day. A place he now relied upon. He needed its peace, he needed its sanctuary. He needed to feel the weight of the heavy door and the change of air as he walked through it. He didn't hear the police car that screamed up the little hill over the road. He didn't notice the freshly laid flowers at headstones in the grounds. He didn't notice the muddied remnants of confetti not yet swept away or eaten by the birds. Instead, he took the path of aged stone flags leading up to the foot of the church. With each step, his breath grew longer and calmer, deeper. He pushed open the door as the bells chimed half past the hour.

All sounds muffled as he stepped inside. Black iron caught against iron as he lifted the latch to shut the door, pausing as the sound echoed then died, leaving Geoff in the heavy calm of silence. Church peace; an all-encompassing sense like no other he'd ever found. It brought him instant distance from his fears, from his waning energy, from his frustrations. It was like a sort of cushion against them. Against time. Cotton wool.

Knowing it was time he faced the truth about Connie's future, he pulled out the letter from his inside pocket. Cruelly, it was addressed to The Carers of Constance Steele, a title he didn't appreciate but he needed to acknowledge the contents, no matter how much he disagreed with them. Standing at the top of the aisle, Geoff took in a deep, restorative breath through his nose and the scent of newly unfurled lilies set in. Groups of the fresh flowers in white and yellow stood grandly beside him. They reminded him of Cherbourg Lilies and the smell of Shirley Tanner, the woman without whom he'd never have won Connie's hand. Connie wasn't interested in Geoff back then. He was too young for her. He wasn't the kind of man she wanted. So he set about becoming that man, with the help of Shirley Tanner. She was the choirmaster's older sister. All high hair and kitten-heeled shoes. At the time, she seemed ancient to his fifteen-year-old self, but she was probably only in her thirties. Thirty-six at best. But Shirley Tanner taught him to dance, despite chiding him each time he let go of her nipped-in waist, forcing his stubbled cheek into hers, her pungent perfume impossible to ignore, hence the lilies. They'd foxtrot across her kitchen until he got the footwork right and only then would she let him leave, leading him to her front door by his tie.

Without Shirley Tanner, this letter wouldn't be in his hands.

He moved down the aisle to take up his usual spot, third pew on the left. A woman he didn't recognise dropped polish and a duster into the pocket of her fading tabard, offering him a smile as she tiptoed down to the vestry.

In spite of this letter, it had been worth those dancing lessons, Geoff thought. And maybe even the rumours that circulated about Shirley and him. He'd assured Connie that they were nothing more than that, just rumours and nonsense. Then he asked her to the dance and finally she said yes. On that day he swept her off her feet, his hand placed firmly on her naturally tiny waist, her neck smelling fresh and clean, like talcum powder.

They didn't think about getting old when they were young.

Placing his own bag and the now full shopping bags beside him, he rubbed at his hands to release the tension in his blue with cold fingers. He placed them in loose prayer, the letter held within. He looked across to the clock, and then up on high, to the dusty rafters. A shaft of light sliced a pathway from stained glass to pulpit and he followed the journey of dust particles that danced in the air to the heady, enveloping silence. His heart slowed further, in chime with his breath as he gave himself up to his faith. A faith he needed if this letter contained what he feared, the choice for Connie's future taken from him. And if that was the case, what would become of him? Who was he without her? What was left for him?

Slowly, he thumbed open the envelope.

Chapter Eleven

My love,

I wish I could share with you the things that I have learnt. That real beauty in life can be found when we make the time to listen. To observe. To learn. The pace of life, the drive for material things, the need for a bigger house, a faster car, for stuff, it's all distraction. It's things. Things. Things that fuel our motivation, things that drive us, push us to do more, be more, achieve more. And yet, those things change nothing. We remain the same with or without them. I now know this is a fact. The cliché is real.

Most people say they know it's superficial. A Band-Aid on their emotions and yet… most people still desire the things. I don't blame them, sometimes I think to the comfort of heated seats, or the pride you would feel driving up to a 'forever' home. It brings joy, no question, the memories might be warm and yet, discomfort follows. The discomfort that comes with knowing…

I have relied on things and status for all my life. They made me worthy. Am I anyone without them? You always said I was and yet your words were never enough. We can't believe that which we don't feel. Maybe if I had, things might have been better for us both.

From,

The love you wished I could be.

Chapter Twelve

The outcome of a recent 'multi-agency' meeting was inside the manila envelope Geoff held in his hand. A meeting in which people who didn't really know Geoff or Connie discussed what should or could happen. The one in which Geoff felt like an old man, a burden, a problem with a problem. His problem being Connie who, it seemed to him, was no longer a person but a prognosis. Something that needed filing under 'nothing more we can do'. A problem that needed managing until her last dying breath.

He held the letter between shaking thumb and forefinger. He looked back up to God in search of strength and guidance. What was best for Connie? What was best for him? What would people think if Connie left their marital home? If he let her go? What would she think, in those moments of lucidity, or would the move in itself absorb any last drop?

Dear Mr Steele,

Following our meeting, we have discussed the new care package we believe is now required for Constance and would like to offer the following, for both your health and well-being, and for Constance.

- *Current one day [Saturday] respite at St Stephen's Court will henceforth increase to full weekends [Friday to Monday], commencing this coming Friday 5th January.*
- *Thereafter a week's respite, every three weeks, at which you may visit should you wish.*

The above is offered as a basis for migrating Constance from her home to a full-time care facility that is well catered to manage her illness. We believe this will be in her best interests and will give you the support you need, as her main carer. She is now on the list awaiting such a suitable place.

We'd be happy to discuss this plan at your next meeting, however, please don't hesitate to call us should you wish to clarify anything before that point.

Yours sincerely, etc. etc. Such perfunctory words to close a letter that brings such change. Geoff reached into his pocket to retrieve a precision-folded handkerchief. He wiped his eyes, salty moisture threatening to undermine his stiff upper-lipped composure. His heart ached just as it had the day she'd been diagnosed. The day Rosemary came around and cried at the sight of her mother, still able to process, and weeping over the news. The day Geoff wrapped her up in his arms and cradled her to sleep because she was frightened and he said he'd always be there for her. The day he hid his own fears because they weren't relevant in that moment. Not valid. Not appropriate to be shown as the man of the house, as her husband. Where once Connie had unknowingly saved him from the weight of household responsibility – something he'd never truly shared because to tell her would suggest he hadn't coped – now, that weight returned, tenfold.

And, like the little boy whose father was declared unfit to head up the house, the same little boy who would hear his father's cries in the dead of night, who would see fear or emptiness in the man he looked up to, the little boy whose mother required him to step up and be the man, Geoff felt leaden heavy with it all.

A low hum from the church organ began. Normally this was Geoff's favourite part of a Tuesday visit, but he knew that this time, it was about to unpick him. Yet he was helpless. He was rooted to the spot. Left-hand pew. Third row back. Perfectly placed to feel the bass and tone as it vibrated around the stone walls. It crawled inside him and pierced his heart. It was choir singing, it was prisoner of war. It was singing for the guards and singing for her love, quietly, in her ear, as they foxtrotted across the dance floor. It was 1938 when to be this old wasn't even a thought. It was December 1944, on a hidden wireless in a German camp. It was his officer in the Girl's Brigade, typist in an office, his Constance Hall; his girl about town, with a crinkling nose and a soloist's voice. It was her love of music and his love of her. The organ played on and he re-read the letter and the music played and the memories rolled and waved, old with new, playing on a loop. Respite. *They'd ride bikes with friends.* Health and well-being. *They'd survive against the odds.* Migration. *Their love would conquer all.* Best interests. *They'd be together forever.*

The reality. And the pain. And the fear and the hurt and the hate. And the guilt. He looked up again once more to God, in whom his confidence was failing. Her first session was on Friday. Three days away. A precursor to everything changing. The very last thing Geoff had ever wanted.

He just wasn't ready to let her go.

Chapter Thirteen

'Well, that wasnae too bad a day, aye?' James shuffles down the aisle pulling the filthy mac around him that I picked up at the Heart Foundation. It wasn't filthy when I bought it, four or five months ago. Apart from maybe a suspect stain on the back flap but I think I got that out on a boil wash. I bought it for Alex actually, something to help him keep warm as he went to meetings and interviews. He asked me what the point was, he'd already had ten, maybe twelve rejections by then. We rowed. He threw it in the bin. I was so angry, I told him he was being ungrateful then dug it out of the bin and brought it in for James. He was thrilled, it was the response I'd wanted from Alex all along.

'You away home now?' James asks.

'I guess so.'

Maybe if I gaze out of the window for long enough, an alternative might present itself. A knight, on a horse – colour unimportant – arriving at the bus door, ready to whisk me away to a foreign land in which real life is but a dream and a diet of gin and cigarettes isn't actually bad for you... for example.

'Helen?'

A better alternative would be Alex coming home. No matter how frustrated I am, I think that really is my preferred option. I go for my phone just in case but change my mind. Every time I've looked today to see no message, it's given me a wave of sickness and fear followed by irritation. Irritation at me being impatient when clearly he needs space and irritation at him for his total lack of communication. I tried calling, I've texted again. I still don't know where he is or how long he's going to be away, and what I wouldn't give for one of those jokes he used to send, or a kiss out of the blue. *Pinky promise we'll always talk*, that's what we used to say to each other. *Pinky promise.*

Pinky chuffing promise. I'll pinky promise him when I see him next.

James clears his throat to remind me he's still there. 'Shit! Sorry, James. I'm miles away.'

'Tuesday,' he says, thoughtfully. 'If memory serves, that's lasagne, isn't it?'

We've talked regularly about what Alex would cook up for me when I got home. The menu was set out for the week from the first day he was unemployed. I did it so we knew what we had to buy, what our food budget was. And as he was at home all day, there was no reason he couldn't cook from scratch. Plus I loved his lasagne. It was the first meal he cooked for me one night when his parents went out and left us home alone. I say he cooked it, a few years later, when he tried to recreate it the first night in our own flat – if you could call it a flat – he confessed his mum had actually made it and he'd just warmed it up, but by then I was smitten. And pregnant. He seemed to like the routine to begin with, he said it gave him focus. Did I say anything when he stopped cooking a few months ago? Did we talk about it? Or did I just do what I always do, come in, take over, sort it out and get food on the table whilst he sat in the same chair, the same TV programmes playing out for him to ignore?

I might have started suggesting he needed to get up off his arse and help. Or find a job. I was tired. I was feeling the pressure of holding it all together. I was losing patience.

It's no wonder he's gone away.

This is my fault. I've nagged. I can hear myself doing it, now I think back. Or maybe I've shown so many signs of just how well we're going to cope whilst he's out of work, that I've missed some telltale signs about a bigger problem. A different one to his lack of a job. And I've felt invisible for a long while now; he's not really been interested in me. He's rejected many of my cuddles and affection, given to make sure he knew it was all okay. That *we* were okay. That *I* was okay. I've put his resistance down to stress, not… not that he'd fallen out of love with me. Maybe it's this polyester jumper.

'Right, I'll be off then.' James moves slowly. He picks up an old paper, dropping it in the bin as he goes past.

'Hey, leave that, I'll clean up.'

'It's okay, I was just making myself useful. Consider it my bus fare.' He pauses, giving me another smile. But as he gets off the bus, he catches his leg on the step, flinching as he lands flat-footed on the pavement, muttering something undetectable under his breath.

'Oh, James, did you hurt yourself?' I jump out from the driver's seat as he stands up tall, stretching out his back.

'No. I'm fine, thank you.' He stands taller as if to prove it.

'Are you sure? Do you want me to take a look?'

'Ach, getaway. It's fine. Ah'm fine.' He turns to face me. 'We're all fine!' he declares, baring a toothy grin at me. I spy a split-second glance of devilment in his eye, a sniff of mischief. 'We're all fine, aren't we?' he says again, eyeing me carefully.

'Course we are,' I agree, gazing down at my shoes, at his, then back up to his inquisitive look. 'Yes.'

'You wanna tell ye face?' he says, wryly. 'It's looked pretty vacant most of the day. That smile you've been painting, it doesnae reach your eyes, and your chat's no' been so hot... if you don't mind ma saying?'

I thought I'd done a pretty good job of hiding it. 'I'm tired. Probably. An off day. Ignore me.' He stares. 'Hey! Don't challenge an almost middle-aged woman on her mood, I can categorically tell you it's a topic full of minefields. And hormones.' I bury my head in the takings bag, searching for something; it has that nasty money smell so I opt for a walk down the bus to check for rubbish instead.

'Get home, put your feet up. Enjoy your dinner and sleep. I'll see ya.' He starts to walk away, then slowly turns back, like a hobbling, slightly muckier-macked Columbo. 'Sometimes, we're waiting for the right moment. The right words. For someone else te make it easy for us, te say the right thing at the right time 'cause we don't know where te start. Ya know?'

I stare at him, is this code? Does he want me to say something for him? To him? I don't understand.

'Sometimes we have te feel the fear,' he says.

'My friend Vicky says that. Feel the fear and do it anyway.'

'Your friend Vicky sounds smart.'

I nod. 'She's a teacher.' As if that answers everything.

'Ah. Right. Well, so long,' he says, his back towards me as he wanders into the night.

'Yeah... bye.'

I go back to the money bag, keeping an eye on where he goes. He looks up and around him. He looks to the sky, the inky black of this crisp January night. The stars, the moonlit clouds, thin and shimmering. I look, too, until my phone dings out with a message and I dive into my bag to wrench it out, pulling my back in the process.

Have you seen our Alex?

I rub the offending muscle and sigh in frustration at the message from Rob, his brother. He's not there then. I flick my call history up and down, maybe I should try again. Maybe I shouldn't give up. I sit back in the driver's seat, steeling myself to call because I'm now not sure what to say. It's not been too long. And I've been pretty irritated by the sudden disappearance. But if he's not with his brother… where the hell is he? Should I be ringing round? Should I call the police? No. That's stupid. I try Alex again, wondering why I feel nervous. I mean, this is my husband. I can call him. I'm allowed.

But the number rings out and I sigh so deeply, it feels like it comes from my bones. *Pinky promise we'll always talk.* I drop my phone back in my bag, seeing the notebook instead. I take it out, the ribbon falls between my fingers as I flick through the pages again. I should probably hand it in to lost property. Somebody has to be missing it. And yet it feels like a secret. And I like the writing, the words, I like the feeling that there is more to this story and I want to know what it is. Is it bad that I'm keeping someone's notebook with such personal thoughts within? I mean, yes, is the short answer and yet… I close my eyes, letting the pages fall open where they choose.

Chapter Fourteen

My love,

Sometimes, I recognise things. Behaviours. Oddities. Things that set off alarm bells. I will never stop believing that things might have been different if someone had cared enough to put their hand on my shoulder and tell me they could help.

Except you have to be open to that. You have to hear what's being said. Would I have listened? Could I hear it now? What could we have done differently? And is it even worth sharing those thoughts with others? Why do we feel the need to? Just because I've lived what I think I see, doesn't make me any stronger to advise. Let's face it, I didn't think I needed help. I didn't think I needed anything, or anyone. Least of all you.

It wasn't true. I see that now. If only I could find a way to make you understand.

From,

The love you wished I could be.

Chapter Fifteen

It's a good question. Motivation. Why do any of us do anything? Why do I let James on the bus? Why do I get all tongue-tied when Martin looks at me? Why do I not get angry when Alex doesn't text, like Claire thinks I should? Why do I play the happy rescuer all day every day, when inside my mind is spinning with questions? Questions that make me feel a bit uncomfortable in my belly. Like maybe all those altruistic things I think I'm doing, aren't quite so altruistic after all. Do we all do things for others to make ourselves feel better, or is it just me? And does it make me a bad person. Am I a total fraud? I gaze off into the middle distance, thinking about exactly that when my phone rings and I all but jump out of my skin. Maybe I should put it on silent, just to save my nerves.

'I've got a job for him!' Claire is heavy breathing down the phone. She's probably juggling Clemmie, one of her older kids, and an order on the laptop; all whilst pouring coffee from her AeroPress. (It's better for the environment, don't you know.) 'Honestly, Helen! I don't know why I didn't think of it before.'

She tells me the details and I scrabble to make a note in my phone as she talks over the loudspeaker. 'It sounds great, it sounds amazing, Claire. Would you really do that for us?'

'Of course, I love you both. And I think he'd be great. Do you think he'd do it?'

'Christ knows. I don't think I can second-guess him at the moment. I mean, he should do, shouldn't he?'

'Have you heard from him?'

'Nope. Not yet.'

'Still no idea where he is?'

'Not a clue.' I can hear the tone in my voice.

'You not feeling quite so okay about it all today then?'

'Nope. Not really.' I pinch the top of my nose with forefinger and thumb, screwing my eyes up until I see inky black and stars, just like before. 'I've tried texting. I've called. Several times and again just now. There's nothing. Should I call the police? Log it with someone?'

'I don't know. I mean, he said he was going away, it's not like he's disappeared without giving you the heads-up.'

'No... he just didn't tell me where. Or for how long. Or who with.'

'What do you mean who with? Don't go making assumptions. This is Alex, he'll be fine. You'll both be fine. Don't let your mind run away with you.'

'I can't help it. I just... I don't know what to do. Or think.'

'Have you tried calling people? To see if he's with them? Put yourself in his shoes, where would he go?'

'I don't know what shoes he's wearing?' It's a lame joke, but that's about all I can muster right now.

'You know full well I meant it figuratively.'

'So did I. I think. I mean, I don't know what mood he's in, or the way he thinks any more. I don't understand any of it.'

'FINLAY, GET OFF THAT!' Claire tries to muffle her shouts but the volume seeps through what I assume is her hand, cupped over the speaker to muffle. 'Sorry, Hel. Fin's in a shitter of a mood today. Doing

my actual nut in. NEVER MIND MY SWEARING, YOUNG MAN.
PUT THE FISH BACK IN ITS BOWL BEFORE IT SUFFOCATES!'

I can't help but laugh. 'Is that the suicidal fish or the one that likes
to hump the plastic skull?' I ask, because Claire's fish seem to be much
more dynamic in personality than any fish I've ever come across.

'Christ knows, they both look alike to me!'

I head into the depot office, dropping the takings on Little Mary
from Accounts' desk, waving her an apology that I'm on the phone.
There's clattering in the background of our call. 'Look, Helen. I need to
get off. Text me his number and I'll text him about the job. Mention I
want to talk to him if you do speak to him though. He'd make a great
ops manager and I could rely on him to take over a bit, maybe he can
start to take on some of my supplier relationships too. I'd love to be
at home a bit more.'

'You work from home!' I point out, bipping my car unlocked.

'Okay, I'd like to be off the laptop a bit more. FINLAY! For the
fish's sake if not my own.' I hear her rustle and stomp across her heated
kitchen floor. There's the wail of a kid and the splash of water. 'I've got
to go. Before my child murders the aquatics. I'll let you know if I hear
from him. Love you, bye.'

She's hung up before I can answer. I drop into my car seat, text her
his number, dump my bag in the footwell and head off. It's a good
idea, calling round a few people. Someone might just know where
he is. I can eliminate Rob, his brother, who would have been my
first thought. Who else? And then my brain shifts into irrational and
for the second time in as many days, I remember Amanda Hobson.
We were what, twenty-two, twenty-three? Tom was a toddler, life
had suddenly got very hard, very grown up. We just lost our way
for a while. Alex went off, I thought it was work and it took several

days before he came back and confessed to the fact that he'd been sleeping at Amanda's.

She'd always had a bit of a thing for him, even back at school. I sometimes wonder if she hadn't let him stay to try and make something happen, but he swore nothing went on; that they were just talking, that he slept on the sofa. I believed him, he told me they talked and that he'd realised that's what he missed about us. That we'd stopped talking. That our lives revolved around Tom and he wanted that connection back. I took it hard. Mostly because Amanda hadn't had children. She was known for her peachy bum and pert boobs. Mine were never that pert, even as a teenager, and breastfeeding had not been kind to them. Plus, she had a reputation… that now I can see was a bit unfair because none of the boys she did anything with had the same reputation, but still, I didn't like her. I didn't trust her. I was frightened and tired and didn't know how to fix things. That was all different though, wasn't it? And he wouldn't go back there, would he?

No… no… he wouldn't do that. That's just stupid. Besides, Amanda's probably moved on by now, I've not seen her for years. I pull out of the side road and into a stream of teatime traffic out of Keighley, waiting for my hands-free kit to kick in. No, not Amanda. Who would he talk to now? In a crisis? Barrie? Yes! Barrie. I dial his number. They've not spoken in ages, apparently. Never answers his calls. Okay, Luke then. Luke's wife answers. Nope, they've not seen him since the summer when we all went to Blackpool for the day. Apparently he was pretty rude and they thought they'd leave him to it but he's not been in touch and they've not tried either. I do remember he was bad that day. I tried to make apologies for him. Bought everyone rock as a gift. It didn't really work.

Maybe Rob would have some ideas on places he'd go. Or people he'd see. His voicemail kicks in. I leave a message. 'Hey, Rob. It's me.

I got your text. I haven't seen Alex, no. He went away, yesterday. He texted me to say so but hasn't said where and I haven't been able to get hold of him. Let me know if you hear anything.'

I hang up. Annoyed. Frustrated even. I mean, what am I doing? Chasing around for my husband? This is ridiculous. I come up to the road I'd need to turn if I was going to swing by Amanda Hobson's old place. My hand reaches for the indicator before I hit the steering wheel instead. I am not going to do this. He'd never go there. It's stupid. I'm stupid. This whole bloody thing is stupid. And I'll bloody well tell him that when he finally gets back. If he ever does this to me again… I swear to God, I'll… well, I don't know what, but I'll think of something and make it very clear that's what I'll do just as soon as he comes home.

I want him home. I just want him home.

I pull up at a crossroads, home in ten minutes if I go right, or wind the back roads and reminisce if I go left. So I go left. The lights disappear and the roads narrow. The thing I always loved about living round here was how quickly you could be out in the sticks. I pull into a lay-by on the back road towards Skipton via East Morton. Alex and I used to love these roads, back when we first passed our driving tests. We passed within a week of each other and would take it in turns to borrow our parents' cars and head out to sit in the lay-by in the middle of nowhere. We'd hide for hours up here, enjoying music, and kissing. The kind of kissing you do when really you're desperate to have sex but you haven't quite got to that point yet because it would be the first time either of you had done it and you were both terrified. And a battered Ford Fiesta was not exactly the most romantic place to do it. He had an old tape, Enigma, 'Return to Innocence'. He played it practically on a loop.

Fuck! When did that go? That innocence, that love? How do we get it back? Tom's working, says he wants to move out. We're not even forty yet, this is the time we should be falling back in love, isn't it?

Maybe I should text him a link to Enigma on YouTube.

Chapter Sixteen

On Thursday teatime, Geoff stood peering into Connie's wardrobe. The big light wasn't giving off much brightness yet because the new-fangled energy saver bulbs took an age to heat up and light the way. He wished he'd bought normal bulbs but still, jobs to do.

'Right, love,' he said. 'What do you want to take? Clean nightdress?' Geoff picked out and folded two of her long cream cotton nightdresses. The touch of his hand released wash powder smells of lavender and iris, so he raised them to his nose to smell, whilst Connie sat watching from their bed. She was perched on the edge. They'd just had a lovely dinner together, they laughed about the time he scaled a wall to their honeymoon B&B because they'd arrived late and the landlord had locked the front door. They'd sat, hand on hand, just for a moment before she drifted off again and he found some mild relief in the fact, because then he could pack without her actively knowing the plan for her.

'It's just three nights,' he said, her eyes glazed as she gazed back at him. 'I'll pack both of these in any case though, you never know.' But he did know. 'Accidents', as they were referred to, were growing more and more frequent. His knees complained each time he knelt to clear them up. His back ached when bent low over the mop to wash their lino floors. Or both back and knees as he loaded the washing machine, again. And again. And again. Three days without Connie might mean three days' rest for his knees but he couldn't think like that, selfish thoughts of his own needs had no place.

He reached for the new pack of underwear Val had bought for Connie from the big Marks & Spencer in Leeds. He'd given her the money a week or so ago, no idea that suddenly they'd come in handy. He didn't mind buying clothes for his wife, mostly from charity shops in town, but he just didn't feel it appropriate to buy her smalls, some things were best kept private; a woman's business, she had such little privacy left.

'Where are we going?' Connie asked, as he folded socks, tucking them into gaps amongst the rolled-up clothes, rolled to prevent them creasing. 'Are we going back to Blackpool?' she asked, raising her shoulders and eyebrows in childlike excitement. 'We loved it there, didn't we?'

Blackpool. Seventy-odd years ago. Did she really remember the brief weekend granted to celebrate their matrimony? The weekend he feared might be his last with her because he already knew that he would soon head off as one of ten thousand men heading to Arnhem to try and secure bridges and towns that had fallen into German occupation. It was probably the last time he'd been entirely himself around her, the last time he could go to sleep at night without the memories of things he saw. It wasn't that he came back and pretended for the rest of their lives, but he changed. That much he had only recently begun to realise.

'I wish it *was* Blackpool,' he smiled, sadly. 'But no, this time you're having that little break we talked about this afternoon. Do you remember? Val showed you the rooms on her phone. It's the other part of St Stephen's Court, round Roslyn House.' He picked out an olive-green dress he'd bought last week. She'd hated it. 'Shall I pack this?' he asked, watching her reflection through the aged vanity mirror between their melamine his and hers wardrobes. 'Or this?'

She looked from the dress to a salmon-pink two-piece he'd picked up down the Cats Protection shop just before Christmas. She always bought things from the Cats Protection shop, said she liked to do her bit for charity so Geoff had always followed suit. She wasn't happy with the two-piece though, she wrinkled her nose. It was one of the few mannerisms he still recognised; for years she'd wrinkle her nose instead of saying what she actually felt.

'It looks like an old lady dress,' she said, shaking her head. Because these days she wrinkled her nose AND said what she thought. 'And you know I don't like it at St Stephen's Court. It's full of old ladies who wear dresses like that.'

'You've never said that before,' he lied. 'Have you?'

Connie looked instantly confused and Geoff felt bad for manipulating her like that. 'Are *you* coming?' she asked, watching him pack the dress anyway, along with some jumpers and an ancient angora cardigan that would undoubtedly moult. With any luck, she might leave that one at the home.

'Not this time, but that's fine because you'll be able to see some friends.' Geoff was keen not to get into a discussion about why he wasn't going. Because he couldn't say with honesty that he wanted her to go and yet, as Friday got closer, he could almost taste the space and freedom he'd have when she did.

Maybe after a day or so the guilt would subside? And she'd settle. Rosemary had assured him she would, as had the home when he called to check them out for himself. She needed to be in Roslyn House, they said. Her needs were more demanding than those of a day visitor, she'd be better catered for there. She was in the best possible hands. That's what Rosemary said too and Geoff pointed out that *his* hands were the best. The ones she'd signed up to stay with in sickness and in health.

'Maybe Audrey or Stanley will be there,' she daydreamed. 'We haven't seen them in years.'

Geoff had stopped reminding Connie that their old friends had long since passed on.

'Do you remember that cycle ride we went on with them? What should have been a couple of hours turned into seven and the chip shop was closed when we got there.' Geoff did remember that time. That *she* could sometimes remember such ancient history still came as a surprise. 'I was so cross that day.'

'Were you?' he asked, startled by her tone and clarity of mind.

'Yes. I was. There was no point saying anything, it wouldn't have helped and I think you felt bad.'

Geoff had felt bad but he'd never let on, he'd just pretended it didn't matter. That they'd get food elsewhere. Had he felt foolish? Was that the reason for covering it up? Had Connie sensed it? Did she always know how he felt... the times he was angry, sad, felt foolish... the idea made him pause for a moment.

'I don't know if they'll be there,' he answered eventually.

She made a noise and shrugged. 'What are you taking?' she asked. 'Where's your case?'

'I won't be...' He dug around for what to say this time, something that might keep it in her mind for a little while longer. 'Don't you remember, we thought it would be nice for you to have a little break from me?' he tried. Connie cocked her head to one side. 'You'll get some time to be with other people and...' His voice broke as his lie fizzled out. 'You remember,' he finished.

'Oh yes,' she said, uncertainly. 'I remember.'

His guilt piqued. Geoff had called them this week, told them this wasn't necessary. He told Rosemary to give Connie more time. Not to push them both into this irreversible situation and yet… the months of ignoring the woman that she had become grew increasingly tiresome. He'd begun to imagine what it *might* be like if she *were* away, just for a few days. The peace. The sleep. The not having to repeat himself: that Val wasn't their daughter, that Connie's parents had passed away, that they'd already eaten breakfast, dinner or tea. The not having to change bed sheets or clean floors late into the night.

Though Geoff hated to admit it, his feelings were shifting. It was just for a few days, he told himself. He could catch his breath. Let his frustrations fizzle out. He could sleep.

Maybe this was for the best.

Later that evening, as they waited for the carers to come put her to bed, Connie glanced over to the suitcase. 'What's that?' she asked.

'A suitcase, love,' he said. 'You remember…'

Chapter Seventeen

Eight o'clock has been and gone before I make it home. I drop my bag on the side then head through to the lounge to put the lamp on beside Alex's chair. I hear my phone ding out a text in the kitchen and, given that we're now three days gone since he went, I manage uncharacteristic athleticism, and leapfrog the sofa to get back to it.

Hi Mum, Going out for drinks with the lads, back late X

I guess that's one problem avoided for now. If Tom's not around, I don't have to come up with any more nonsense about where his dad actually is. Unless he's heard from him himself? Maybe I should text and ask… maybe that would look weird.

My tummy growls its discontent. I've not yet done a shop this week, the cupboards are pretty barren. There's a beef Pot Noodle that Tom brought back a few weeks ago. He had his first paycheck and wanted to get his own shelf in the cupboard for his own food, preparing for the big move out into a flat with his mates. He's scrawled his name on some masking tape and stuck it in full view, which means that each time I open the cupboard it feels like that bedsit place Alex and I shared back when we first moved in together and couldn't afford a whole house. God, that was grim. No amount of mood lighting could rescue it. All our mates were so envious of the independence we had and we never let on that in fact it was bloody miserable. And cold.

I open and close several more cupboards before going back to Tom's Pot Noodle. Could it be classed as comfort eating? Every time I think about them, I'm reminded of the Victoria Wood sketch where she told the dry cleaners it was snot up her sleeve because that was less embarrassing than admitting it was Pot Noodle. We've all been there, except mine was chow mein. Maybe I don't fancy one after all.

I sling it back in the cupboard and reach for a bottle of red and the last bag of Kettle Chips left over from Christmas instead. I pause by my handbag; the notebook is nestled in view, which makes me pick it up before heading back into the lounge to slump on my side of the sofa. Glugging back my first glass, the mix of grape and salty crisps comforts as I scroll through Netflix, picking out the latest episode of *Orange Is the New Black*. Unlike when there's anyone else in the house, pouring another glass and taking a large swig gives me no guilt. It's not long before I can feel wine in my legs, seeping, numbing, from the tip of my toes, up to my thighs. It numbs my heart. I'm working in the morning so mustn't have too much, no matter how appealing the entire bottle and its inevitable (albeit temporary) obliteration of life might look right now. I flick through the notebook, pausing to read a few lines before flicking on. I should really get this back to its owner. All these letters, they must be for someone, they must mean something. I check the front pages again, hoping I've missed a name or contact number. There's nothing, just the first letter:

My love,

These words are for you, but also for me. A chance for me to work through it all, to understand, to find answers. Maybe one day, I can give you those answers too, maybe one day we can make peace.

Make peace. I hear you, whoever wrote this. Wouldn't peace be nice? And to know, to understand, to find answers.

I think you tried everything, I was blind.

I know that feeling too. The sense that you're not heard or seen. Which makes me pause a second, the book in my hand. Such intimate words, such private thoughts. To read them is crass, yet I feel drawn, compelled. I feel like there's something in this, maybe I found it for a reason. Maybe it was left? On purpose? For me? Maybe, even if all that is a load of bollocks that just happens to fit the narrative I want, maybe I can learn something from it. I read the next, a letter about feeling lost, feeling as though all purpose has gone. Is this a woman writing to a man or a man to a woman? How old are they? What are their names? What is their story?

If only we could talk…

I glug back more wine, putting the notebook to one side so I don't get greasy crisp fingers all over it. And then I find myself with phone in hand and before I know it, I've texted Alex. *Where are you? When are you coming home?* And then I laugh at how ridiculous my easy-going messages have been these last few days. Would everyone be this casual? Claire wouldn't, I know that much for nothing. There's no way she'd be so calm about her husband walking out on her. Ignoring her calls and messages. If she hadn't sniffed him out, she'd have hired a private investigator by now, I swear. I should definitely call the police.

'For God's sake!' I shout out.

The lounge feels bigger today, in fact the whole house does. I feel swamped by it. Our dream home, three small cottages knocked in to one, practically built with our own fair hands, in between work and Tom and the very real threat of pneumonia due to numerous icy drafts and a total lack of heating. But we didn't care. It was ours. Alex built that kitchen. I sledgehammered out the fireplace. It's home, our home. He should be in it. I *miss* him in it.

I press call on his number, my heart in mouth. One last time before I call it in to 101 or whatever the non-emergency number is. I just really want to talk to him, whichever way I look at it, I want to hear his voice. If I can't look him in the eye and see we're okay, I can at least hear him. Then I'll know. He's my husband, I don't have to be—

'Hi, you're through to Alex, leave me a message.'

'Hey, Alex, it's me. How are you? Are you okay? I'm worried about you. I don't know where you are or when you're back and… well, I'm just worried. Let me know, if not where you are, when you'll be home. I just need to know…' I pause. Hang up? Have I said enough? 'Oh, and Claire has a job for you, by the way. She thought you'd be great. She said she'd text you. Or you could call her? I'll send you her number. Call me though, too… please. Let me know you're okay…'

I do hang up this time, then quickly text him Claire's number whilst I think of it. Another good glug of wine makes me feel a bit duller, and I try and work out what I'm going to say to the police as a text pings.

Thanks so much for today. You've made me feel things I've not felt in a long time. I know I said I wasn't sure about the setting, the formality, but yes, I think I would like to do it again. I can't fight this. Same time/place? Friday?

My mouth goes dry, my heart leaps to my throat. The telltale bubbles of him typing are there and another message comes through seconds later. *Shit, sorry, wrong person. Sorry. I'm fine, I'll be home soon, Promise. X*

What the fuck?

I re-read the first message then the follow-up. Should I be relieved there's a kiss at the end of the follow-up? Who the hell was the first one meant for? Who made him feel things? Who does he want to see again?

I dial his number straight away but his phone is switched off.

Bastard. Double bastard.

Chapter Eighteen

Connie looked down at the watch Geoff bought her for Christmas back in 1989. Three straps and many batteries later, the twisting of one of those fine angora hairs was in its mechanism and it had finally given up the ghost. Connie hadn't noticed.

'Is it time to get up already, love?' Geoff said, as if she'd told him the time. 'I wonder where the carers are this morning, they're later than normal.' He was secretly glad. She was going into the home today, and a few extra moments to themselves would be precious.

'It's nice to sit for a while,' she said, cradling her cup of tea. She took a final sip of her drink, offering him the cup back as the clock downstairs let out its quarter past chime.

'That clock,' she said.

'What's the matter with it?'

'It's noisy. Always noisy.'

Geoff stared for a moment, she'd never mentioned that she didn't like the clock. Had she always? He put the cup on the side to be rinsed out later. They sat side by side, him wondering about the clock, her just staring out of the window at the blue-grey sky above them. Eventually, he asked, 'Do you need the bathroom?' Connie nodded. She watched as he heaved himself out of bed. Wrapping himself up in a terry towelling dressing gown. He pulled the bed sheet from beneath her arms, bringing her up to stand. 'Come on, love.'

'Ooh, you're still strong.'

'For you, always.'

Taking her steadily from bedroom to bathroom, Geoff placed her hands on the council-fitted safety rails closing the door behind him to protect her modesty. Door closed, he leant against the wall. Had he ever seen himself caring for her? Most definitely not, if he was honest. She'd been the carer, it was in her bones. He'd begun to realise that she'd cared for him all his life. When he came home from work all tired and tetchy, she cared for him. When he felt the weight of responsibility, she cared for him. When Rosemary arrived, she still cared for him. When he wouldn't talk, when he hid his feelings, when life was dark but he was expected to perform... she still cared for him. The clock was probably another example, something he loved because it had cost him a small fortune and he'd always wanted one. A clock like the one in his grandparents' house when he was a child. A clock that kept good time. Was the clock the only thing she'd never said she disliked?

'Okay,' she said, a few minutes later, peering round the door.

He offered her an arm. 'Come on, let's get some breakfast.' She smiled and nodded and the look of love in her eyes was enough to give him the strength to focus on the task at hand. She gave his arm a squeeze and he kissed her papery cheek. They took slow steps across the landing, standing arm in arm as he pressed the button for her stairlift, letting her head rest against his chest as they waited. He drank in the moment to feel her, to breathe in her soul, to see her when she saw him. It was in these briefest of moments that he could forget their age, the aches in their bodies that marked the many years of their lives together. Instead, in these moments, they were just Geoff and Connie Steele. Married. Happy. In love.

He flicked up the footrests, taking her by each arm to gently lower her into the chair, ignoring the twinge in his lower back as he did so. Seated, she waved like the queen, then giggled. He bowed in mock service, pressing the button for her descent. And just as she reached the halfway point, there was a knock, then a rattle of keys and two care workers pushed open the door. And with that rush of new energy from their arrival came a bitter cold air, and a fog that stole Connie back.

'Geoffrey Steele,' said the main woman, her hands placed firmly on generous hip. 'What have we said to you about this? We're paid to come here and look after Connie, for your sake as well as hers. You really must let us do this – it's not good for you on your own.' The force of her words and her matronly size, not to mention her abundant efficiency, stopped Geoff in his tracks. As Connie reached the bottom step, the footrests were flipped up with a flick and Connie was deftly whipped out of the chair. She looked from the care worker to Geoff, seeing, it seemed to him, neither.

'I was just...' he began, but he stopped because it was pointless trying to finish. If the authorities had their way, Connie wouldn't just not be here in mind, but miles away in body too. Perhaps he had no choice but to embrace it. The break in their quiet connection had all but packed her away and each time that happened, he never knew if she'd come back again. The clock chimed half past the hour.

Chapter Nineteen

My shift starts in ten minutes. I'm sat in my car, my palms itching
because I know the notebook is in my glove box and since I woke up
this morning, Alex's text message still fresh in my mind, I couldn't help
but wonder if perhaps there lay some answers in those pages. I had
every intention of handing it into lost property but now I feel that I
can't. Or at least, that I don't want to. I tried to kid myself that I wanted
to protect it, to keep it from prying eyes, but in truth, it's because I
feel like it's a book containing letters about my life. If not explicitly,
then certainly in a way that a tarot reading can be interpreted to fit
what you want to hear. The eight of cups. You'll definitely find love.
The queen of swords. Your nemesis is going to get it. I could manage
another letter before I clock in.

My love,

*This morning when I woke, I kept my eyes closed. I wanted to
see your face as it was when we first met. The face I first fell in love
with. Eyes, soulful and caring. The smile that made my heart sing.
You were fresh and worry free then, perhaps we both were. Some
days it's hard to see, others it's as clear as the day we first met. And
as my eyes remained closed, there you came. Walking towards me,
the sun behind you, bleeding gold. Your hair bounced with the*

motion of your walk. I held my arms out to you, ready to feel your touch. And as we embraced, you disappeared. Disintegrated. Like sand through my fingers, you were no longer there and the part of my heart that hurts each time I remember why that is, fractured all over again.

So, I package you up. I push you as far to the back of my mind as I'm able; tightly sewn up and out of reach so I can live another day. Because although I write these letters, these notes especially for you, I can't bear to think too much about your face, your touch, your love. About how I've kept secrets from you, over the years.

Do you still feel the pain? Would you ever let me make things right? I believe I could, if not today, then one day.

From,

The love you wished I could be.

Chapter Twenty

Since opening the letter on Tuesday, Geoff had wished time would slow down. He wished the dreams would stop. He wished this day wouldn't arrive. His sleep had been fitful, his mind full of Connie's tear-stained face from the night before he left for the war, barely old enough to be there. Called up because they needed more men. It was the same face that haunted him on those cold nights in the Glasgow gymnasium as he lay amongst row upon row of men awaiting their deployment, a sense of anticipation hanging in the air. He had no idea that he'd spend so much time on British soil, working strategically to defend the borders, the threat to his life not fully realised until Arnhem. But Connie didn't know that when he left. And Geoff didn't know enough to appease her. And now, though miles and years were between himself and the war, he could still feel the cold gymnasium floor beneath him. He could still hear the sound of guns. He could still place himself in the remains of the houses along the Rhine River, unlikely sanctuary when the men around him had been shot and he'd sought out temporary safety. The images, the sounds and smells, they were never far away, he'd never been able to escape them; just like there's no escape here, now. Only this time it was Connie going away, not him. And though it was only for a few days, and she'd be cared for in her absence, they'd never been so far apart, for so long, not since the day he was released from the

German prison camp and finally made his way home, a different man to the one who went away.

Just as she hadn't wanted him to leave back then, he didn't want to be without her now.

Connie looked out of the window, perched on the nest of coffee tables so she could see down the road. She would sit there like that over the years, waiting for the grandchildren to arrive. Did she know she was going away? He didn't like to ask, he didn't want the same conversation, over again. The when? The where? The how long for? Geoff stood beside her, affectionately pulling her shoulder into his hip. She wasn't soft, like once upon a time. Nowadays, she was sharp, the edges of bones and life had taken away all her comfort. The care home bus turned the corner and she hardened further still. Was that recognition? Did she know what was coming?

'This is them,' Geoff said as cheerfully as he could. The driver pulled up at their gate and jogged down the drive. He knocked on their door with a wide grin like a man on the Wallace Arnold pick up, collecting Connie for a coach trip tour of the Devon coast or some such place. How Geoff wished he and Connie were heading off for a week in Devon; food, drink and day trips included.

'Your carriage awaits,' said the man, as Geoff opened the door. He leaned against their house like an old friend and some pebble-dash cracked off. Geoff picked up Connie's suitcase about to head through the front door, which made the man move out of his way and a bit more pebble-dash fell.

'Don't worry, I'll take that,' said the man, scooping up the bag before Geoff got a chance to object.

'I put the padlock on,' said Geoff, handing the man a tiny golden key. But as it was loaded on the bus, the man attached the key to the case then shoved her bag to the back where it would languish until next retrieved.

Geoff closed his eyes.

'Come on, love.' He held open her raincoat. She fed frail arms into the puffed purple sleeves, dutifully turning so Geoff could zip her up. Keep her warm. 'Have a lovely time, won't you?' he said, trying but failing to do up a few poppers, his fingers no longer as nimble as they once were. He laid her handbag across her body. 'I've put you some tissues in, and some Murray Mints,' he said. 'I know how you like a stash of Murray Mints.'

'Oh, I do. How did you guess?' she asked, smiling widely in gratitude.

'Just a hunch,' he answered.

'Lipstick?' she asked, lifting the flap to peer inside.

'Yes, yes,' said Geoff, patting the flap down again so she couldn't actually see that no, there was no lipstick. She no longer had a steady hand for putting lipstick on and he'd begun hiding them when he noticed how much her hands shook. How far off her lips the bright pink gloss would go. And he knew that was wrong, he knew that said more about him than her... but he couldn't help it. He disliked the idea that people would judge her for the way she heavy-handed her rouge, or forgot to remove her curlers. They'd assume she was not of sound mind and he knew she'd have hated that. 'And your phone book is in there, in case you want to call anybody,' he said, quickly changing the subject. He knew she wouldn't be calling anybody, but she patted his arm with an approving smile.

'Oh, you are good,' she said, squeezing his arm. Geoff welcomed the affection.

'Come on then,' said the bus driver, one arm reaching for hers, the other sweeping backwards to present the big green minibus that usually drove straight past them on a Friday. It was hardly the carriage his flourish suggested.

'See you later, love,' said Connie, her eyes sparkling just like they always had. 'Have a good day,' she said, lifting her face to place a kiss on his cheek.

'You too.'

'See you tonight?'

And Geoff nodded, because that was easier. And for the best.

The man walked her down the ramp. Geoff dutifully followed. The man buckled Connie into her seat and Geoff, dutifully, waited. And as the engine fired up and the minibus pulled away, Connie turned to wave through the window, grinning and blowing him kisses like the sweethearts they once were. Geoff waved back, desperate for her to travel out of sight so that he no longer had to keep a Yorkshireman's control of his emotions. And when he could no longer hear or see the minibus, he stepped back inside their house.

The firm click of the front door behind him was louder than normal. The chime of the clock, the clock that she suddenly disliked, shouted that it was half past the hour. The tap dripped in the kitchen and a car that passed by their house at reasonable speed, sounded like it fair raced up the road. There were voices from next door, people moving about, life continuing like nothing had changed because for them, he guessed, it hadn't. Which made it all the more noisy for Geoff who found that suddenly, the silence and the loneliness in their happy home was deafening. After he came back from the war he'd taken up the job with the council, his office just twenty minutes' steady drive away from the home they lived in at the time. A commute that meant he'd always be home for tea. Since 1946, there had just been no need for them to be apart for more than the working day and that was just how they had liked it.

And as it got to nine thirty-five, Geoff sat in her chair in the lounge. The familiar rumble of Helen's bus made its way up the hill, but this time, Geoff didn't move. He had to be okay, for Connie. He just wasn't sure quite how okay felt.

Chapter Twenty-One

'That's not like Geoff,' I say to James, who's sat on the bench seat to my left, reading.

'Hmmm?' he asked, looking up and around.

'Geoff, he's not waiting for us.' I pull up to the corner by his house. No sign. I put the handbrake on and wait a few seconds longer. Still nothing. 'It is Friday, right?'

'Yep. Friday.'

'Hmmm. That's what I thought.' In truth, the days of this week have morphed into one long wonder of *Where the bloody hell is my husband?* and *Who was that text message meant for?* So it's no wonder I need to double-check.

'Friday all day,' joked James. I'd probably have laughed, on any other day.

I look up through the rear-view mirror, aware of the other passengers, including Martin. Each time I catch sight of him through the mirror, he looks for longer than is entirely necessary, mischief in his eyes, before looking away as if I might not notice. I notice. As does my heart rate.

'Shall I go and knock?' I ask, checking my watch to see what time it is. It's one thing to make non bus-stop stops, but it's probably another to call at their homes.

'Maybe he's having a lie in. Or a day off. It's all right, isn't it?' James says, going back to his book. He's been odd today too – maybe there's something in the air.

'Mmmm.' I'm unconvinced but well aware of the lady in the fourth row who's giving me daggers whilst checking her watch. Just wait until she's old and I need to give her a bit of time to get to my door. Maybe I'll just drive on by.

'Dinnae worry, ah'm sure he's fine.'

'I guess so.' Slowly, I pull away. I catch sight of Martin again and try to ignore the heat that creeps up my neck. The same heat that I felt when I saw him at the bus stop this morning. The same heat I felt as he grinned, showing the machine his pass. I wanted to punch myself in the face for getting hot and fluttery.

I'm functioning this morning. That's pretty well as far as I'd go. Since the text from Alex, I've tried him a few more times and heard nothing. I considered sending him a sex text or telling him I was pregnant. Anything to get a response. The sex texts I came up with were a bit lukewarm though, and I couldn't get my cleavage to look sexy in my uniform, and he'd know I wasn't pregnant unless I am the new Mary, Mother of Jesus.

A few people have got back to me to say that they've not heard from him either. Most haven't seen him in ages. A few asked how he was, or how we were. The couple we met at baby group when Tom was born said we should get together over dinner because 'it's been too long'. I can see just how much he'd like that idea right now. And to be honest, I get it. The last time we went round they presented us with a raclette and I just couldn't get on with cooking my own steak. Was it rare? Was it raw? Was I going to come down with salmonella? Also, I'm out with the girls tonight which is the last thing I can be doing with.

I considered calling one of them this morning. Maybe Vicky, she's sensible. I'd tell her everything and get her unbiased, calm opinion but I was too busy reading the notebook, and I know what she'd say anyway; she'd say that nothing was obvious and we shouldn't assume. If I called Claire, she'd remind me that it's me and Alex. Alex and me. That we're together forever and to just give him whatever space he needs. She'd find some reason for the text, she'd make it not sound so bad and I'd probably begin to agree with her because she knows us both so well. And I don't want him to be having an affair or whatever other reason there could be for that sort of message. And then there's Zoe… well, Zoe would tell me to tell him to right royally fuck off.

The bell dings and I pull up at the next stop. 'See you, Mary, take care,' I chirrup. She gives me a wave over her shoulder as she potters up to her house. I travel on. Mind still full of questions. Like one that has been lingering: what would I do if he left me? If he was seeing someone else and decided to call it a day? Where would I go? Where would he go? Who would get the house? For some reason I also wonder who'd get the *Rocky* box set he hardly ever watches. I decide it would be me.

The thoughts, the whys and wherefores circle and seep around me, crawling inside my subconscious so much so I don't even realise I'm thinking them. They leak into my brain and that can be the one and only reason I went on to have an entirely inappropriate dream about Sylvester Stallone last night. Except that Sylvester turned into Martin and after a certain amount of heavy petting, I woke up with a start and the raging horn. I wonder if he could tell when he saw me this morning. And I wonder if he really does have a tattoo of Mighty Mick's Gym on his thigh?

Chapter Twenty-Two

By the end of the day, I've delivered the bus back to the depot. I've checked up and down the aisles for rubbish and items left behind. With the mundanity of such a task, the letters I've read come back to me: the words, the hope, the reflection. I can see so much of Alex and I in it that I begin to wonder if they could be his words, his thoughts, his reflection on our life together. And then I've wanted to kick myself for the spectacular levels of self-obsession, forgiving myself only because I've also found a weird sort of comfort from it. A calm that maybe Alex and I aren't alone. Our marriage is not unique in its challenges. And maybe, if I keep it and read it and learn, I can make things different for him and me. And each time I've taken a quick sneak of a read, I've found more to relate to. More that makes sense to me. I'm also now beyond desperate to work out who it belongs to. At one point I thought maybe Geoff. Then I considered James. Either Jenny or Bill could be an option to, though I'm not sure which one of them would have such poetry in their bones. The thing is, if I find out, I also have to give it back, so I probably need to have a little more patience. Or something. I don't know. I close my eyes and think about Alex, about our marriage, about how much I've tried to make things work whilst he's been stuck. I stick my finger in the pages and read.

My love,

There was a moment when I realised, when I felt what you'd been trying to say all that time. When I knew that you'd been right all along. I was watching something, a documentary about the closing of the mines down in Nottinghamshire. All these families talked about the dark days, the lack of opportunity, the poverty. The men talked about how it made them feel, the despair. The children – many now men and women themselves – talked about seeing their families fracture under the weight of sadness and that was when I realised.

How I wished then, as I do now, that I could call you and tell you that you were right all along. All the times when I never knew you knew. When you cared yet I didn't really notice because I needed to focus. To be in control. To be the person you expected, society expected. The person I was brought up to be.

But it was too late, and it will always be too late.

Apart, maybe, for me.

From,

The love you wished I could be.

I wonder how many wives nagged that the bin hadn't been taken out. Or the washing was still in the machine. Or that they were tired and needed a bit of help.

I wonder how many made it all about them.

Chapter Twenty-Three

By the time I've unravelled into my steering wheel with the realisation that I've been a shit wife these last few months, had a little cry then pulled myself back together again, I'm running pretty late to Vicky's birthday drinks. Before setting off, I'd tried calling another few people ticking them off a list of possibilities. I called Alex himself. Again. Needing to hear his voice, needing to tell him I'm sorry. He didn't answer. Insecurities peaked and finally on my way to meet the girls, I found myself driving past Amanda Hobson's house, straining to see inside it. I'd say she's definitely moved on, I never had her down for net curtains and a dreamcatcher in the window.

I flit between fear and guilt and anger and worry and thank God the pub lights are on low and the girls won't see the state of my actual face.

'So basically,' says Claire, as I walk up to their table, 'I said that until the non-surgical, anti-gravity breast was invented he was going to have to make do with searching for mine beneath my armpits!' The girls all shriek with knowing laughter, myself included – laughter that comes from my boots and brings a welcome relief. Claire mock hutches her boobs up with her forearms. 'I mean, none of us are getting any younger,' she goes on. 'He should have worked that one out for himself the other day, as he stood tweezing the grey hairs out of his chest for God's sake!' She clinks my glass as I sit down. 'We're talking sagging tits and chest hairs. Gary's chest hair, not mine... I had mine sugared.'

'Oh God, stop! Please.' Zoe wipes laughter tears away. I take a swig of wine, feeling the Shiraz warmth bleed into my bones. 'I now have visions of your husband that I really don't need!' she said.

'Ditto,' I join in. 'Maybe *he* should get them sugared if he's that bothered?'

'I like a man with chest hair,' pipes up Zoe. 'It's one of the first things I always ask on Tinder.'

'Jesus, you and Tinder,' says Claire, filling her glass up. 'Bless him, he tried to deny it but there he was, stark bollock naked, lit by the strip light that bounced off the porcelain.' She shook her head in mock pity of her husband, picking at the remains of what looks like cheesy chips, and my belly growls in hunger. 'It's not like any of us are kids any more, is it?'

'Damn right!' agrees Zoe. 'I found a grey one the other day. Down there.' Vicky and I recoil. 'I know, girls, right! Basically, my vagina's turning silver fox! Up here for Holly Willoughby, down there for Phillip Schofield.'

'I'd go down there for Phillip Schofield,' purrs Claire.

'Woah-okay, everybody!' Vicky stands quickly, clapping her hands like the primary school teacher that she is. 'Shall I get another bottle?'

'Hang on, you can't get 'em in, it's your birthday!' protests Zoe, trying to escape. She's wedged in between our table, the window, and a smooching couple next to us. With a roll of her eyes in their direction, she pushes a twenty towards Vicky. 'Here! At least take this, it's my turn anyway. My usual and a bottle of whatever you lot are on.'

I offer another note to Zoe. 'Get me some cheesy chips, Zo. I'm hank!'

'Will do. Then, when I get back, you can tell us what's going off with you.'

'What do you mean?'

'She means, your face, since you walked in tonight,' agrees Zoe. 'I've noticed it too.' Claire nods in agreement and I realise this is the problem with friends you've known for ever – even in the darkest of pubs, they can spot what you're trying to hide.

'I don't know if I want to talk about it. I don't even know what to say.'

'Well, it's that or me complaining about Clemmie, or Isaac's latest maths homework.'

'Ah, the impossible long division made its way home, has it?' I say, clutching at deflection. 'And what about Finn, has he stopped tormenting the fish?' I empty my glass looking over to Vicky who's still waiting to be served.

'They appear to be safe for now.'

'And Clemmie?' I ask, embracing the new subject matter.

'Well, far be it from me to hold her back, but she suddenly decided she no longer wants to breast feed. Hence the wine.' She lifts up her empty glass. 'I mean, don't get me wrong, I was beginning to get a little fed up of her hanging off my boobs whenever the whim should take her, but even still… I feel a bit rejected, to be honest.'

'Sounds like you've made a lucky escape, if you ask me,' says Zoe, grimacing. 'I mean, I love your little darlings, but Christ, the idea of having to carry one for that many months, then feed it for however long afterwards as well. When do you get your body back?'

'Judging by my stretch marks, some of us never do!' I say.

Vicky comes back to the table, putting Zoe's pint down and topping up the wine for the rest of us. 'Your chips are on their way,' she says to me.

'Thanks.'

There's the briefest of lulls in our conversation but I can feel what's coming. 'Out with it then,' says Claire. I sigh. Then groan. Claire reaches for my hand and from out of nowhere I have to bite hard on my lip. 'Come on, from the second I saw you, I knew there was something up.'

'And me,' agreed Vicky.

'Even I noticed, and we all know I'm oblivious to these things normally,' said Zoe.

I put my head in my hands. 'I don't know if I want to.'

'Why on earth not? Who else can you tell? Christ, if we're not talking any more, I'm finding new mates. I only keep seeing you so I can slag my husband off!' says Claire. Vicky makes a noise as if in agreement and Claire gives her a look. 'You can't agree on that! You'd never slag off Jules. In fact, has she ever got on your nerves?' We all look at Vicky, waiting for her response because Claire's right, in all the five years Vicky and Jules have been together, we have never heard her once bad mouth her. 'In fact, have you ever even fallen out?' Vicky crumples her nose to suggest that no, they haven't.

'Is that cos you're gay?' asks Zoe.

'What?' Vicky is unusually animated.

'I just wondered! Is being gay easier? Like, not in general, I'm not totally oblivious to the state of the world and the prejudice you guys live with. But still, living with another woman has got to be easier than a bloke, hasn't it? I bet you'd never catch her tweezing her chest hairs in your basin.'

'No, Jules tends to take a Bic razor to them instead.'

'Oooh, can you imagine? The nicks,' says Claire, clutching at her boobs.

'That's a no then?'

'No, Zoe! I don't think it's any easier with a woman than it is a man. And you can't just opt to be gay cause you think it might keep your house tidier, or whatever reason you think there is. You sort of have to fancy them too.'

'Yeah… I'd struggle with that bit, I reckon. I mean you're both lovely and all that, but I don't really want to have sex with you.'

'Likewise!' points out Vicky.

'Fair enough. So, anyway, Helen. Come on, tell us. What's going on?'

A bowl of cheesy chips is placed in the middle of the table and I draw it close, picking at the chips despite them being too hot and burning my fingers. Then my tongue. Shit, they're hot.

'Let them cool down whilst you talk,' says Claire, pointedly. 'Have you heard from him?'

'I don't know if I want to do this now, girls. I don't want to be a downer on Vic's birthday.'

'You wouldn't be,' says Vicky. 'We're friends, this is what we do. We talk to each other! And have you heard from who?'

'Alex. He texted her Monday to say he was going away for a few days and she's not heard from him since,' explains Claire.

'What!' Zoe knocks her pint back, picking up the new one and taking a sip.

'I have heard from him now. Twice.'

'And?' Zoe folds her arms, expectantly. I pick some cheese off a chip. 'Helen?'

I take a deep breath. Belt and braces for the offload. 'He texted. But… it wasn't meant for me.'

'What do you mean?' Vicky asks, nicking a chip from my bowl. 'Ow, they *are* hot!' She fans her mouth, then takes a slug of wine.

'It was weird, something about him being grateful for feeling stuff again, or thinking stuff? I don't know, hang on.' I dig my phone out and pass it to Vicky first. She reads, displaying a poker face. She passes it to Claire who raises her eyebrows and passes it to Zoe.

'Well, he can right royally fuck off!' she says. 'What even is that? "Shit, sorry wrong person."? I mean, what the actual fuck?'

Zoe passes the phone back to Claire who reads the messages again, then gives it back to me. I consider passing it around the pub since everyone's had a good neb.

'Well, he can kiss goodbye to his job offer, that's for certain.'

'Claire!' I say.

'What do you mean? Claire! He's just upped and gone, he's told you nothing about where to, or when he's back, or where the bloody chuffin' hell he is for that matter, and then sends a text like this? I can't even... no, I wanted to help, but not if he's shagging someone else.'

'We don't know that's what's happening,' chips in Vicky. 'There is nothing in this message to say he's having an affair, we need the facts before we can judge.'

'What's there to know? He should be talking to Helen. Helen should be making him feel stuff? Who even is this woman?' says Zoe.

'Oh God, why are men such a pain in the arse? I want to help him, I really do. I mean... it's Alex!' says Claire. 'He wouldn't do that to you, would he? Surely not.'

'No. I don't think he would. I mean... maybe he's just in a bad place.'

'What!' say Zoe. 'So you're making excuses for him, are you? Good to know.'

'I'm not making excuses, I just... I don't think he is having an affair,' I lie. Because now that Zoe's said it, I can't stop thinking about it.

'This is pretty damning!' says Zoe, also nicking a chip, and I realise I'm doing okay at this point because I want to tell her to keep her hands off my dinner.

'I know it is, but something doesn't add up. It feels… confused, you know? In here?' I touch my chest, which is rising and falling with heavy breath.

'Maybe you should go and shag that lad… what was his name… Martin,' says Claire, unsteadily topping up her wine.

She must be pissed, she'd never suggest such a thing otherwise. 'Maybe you should go careful on that wine, you've only just stopped breastfeeding. That's gonna go straight to your head and then you're gonna have to get up in the morning with a baby and a hangover,' I point out.

'How can you be so calm?' asks Zoe. 'And, more importantly, who is Martin?'

I fix Claire with a look that I hope she knows means *well, thanks for that.* 'He's nobody.'

'Nobody that bought you flowers.' Claire folds her arms. 'When was the last time Alex did that?' she says, still talking despite the look on my face.

'Maybe we should all chill out a bit,' says Vicky. 'Change the subject.'

'Change the subject? We've got half a story here! But you might have to pause it, I'm desperate for a piss.' Zoe forces her way out of the table regardless of the fact she's interrupting the smooching couple. 'Please God when I get back can we talk about this seriously. And also I want details on Martin please.' She wobbles off and I shove my face with all of the chips because this is exactly why I hadn't wanted to talk to the girls about it until I was ready. I'm not ready.

Chapter Twenty-Four

The clock turned 8 p.m., its chimes rang out in the darkness and Geoff suppressed an irritated twitch. The phone rang for what was probably the fourth time and Geoff still didn't move to pick it up. As the answer machine kicked in and Rosemary left another message, he shivered, sat in Connie's chair. The pins and needles had subsided, his breath was calmer, perhaps he could get up now?

'Dad? Are you there? Please pick up, Dad. I'm worried about you.' There was a pause. The muffle of hand over handset but Geoff could still hear her talking to Peter, her husband. She thought Geoff was in. She thought he was ignoring her calls. She wished she wasn't so far away to pop in and check up on him. Maybe they should get him one of those panic buttons he can wear around his neck. Or send Val over. 'Dad? I just need to know you're okay?'

There was another pause and Geoff's guilt spiked hard. He huffed himself out of the chair, taking unsteady steps in the dark, towards the hall where their phone had always been; hung on the wall, address book pinned beside it.

'Dad?'

'Sorry, love. I was…' He stopped himself, it was one thing not to answer the phone, it was another to lie to his daughter. 'Hello, love.'

'Are you okay, Dad?'

'I'm okay, love. Thank you. Yes.' Geoff stretched out his left arm and hand.

'It's just, I know this is your first time without Mum and... well, I've been worried about you.' Rosemary's words trailed off. 'I almost called Val to check up on you. I've been torn between leaving you to have some peace and worrying you'd had a fall or something.'

'No, no. I'm fine, love, thank you. I've just been sat for a while.' His shallow breaths were growing deeper now, steadier.

'Have you eaten?'

'Not yet.'

'Dad.'

'I will, I was just about to. We have plenty in. I'll have one of those meals they bring round. I've plenty in the freezer.' He leaned his weary bones against the door frame.

There was a pause in their conversation. Geoff felt tired.

'Shall I come over, Dad? I can't get there tonight now, Peter needs the car. But maybe tomorrow?'

'No, no. It's fine. I'm fine. Stop fussing, love. Please. I'm perfectly capable of coping without your mother. It's the very least I can do for her.'

'I know you *can* cope, Dad. I suppose I just think you don't *have* to cope. When's your next meeting? With Social Services? Are they going through the detail of the longer-term plan then?'

'I think so, yes.'

'Right. Well... Peter and I were talking, we thought that... well, maybe it would be better if I was there. I could make notes or whatever, just... help. Support. You know?'

'That's not necessary.' Geoff felt himself prickle at the suggestion. He knew Rosemary was just trying to help but it was a reminder of his age, of society's assumption that he wasn't capable. It reminded him that he was old. 'I can manage without your mother and I can manage those conversations.'

'I'm just saying you don't have to manage alone.'

'I know, I know…' He paused, frustration shifting to guilt, none of this was Rosemary's fault. 'I suppose I just wish people would stop assuming that because I'm old, I'm incapable.'

'Nobody thinks you're incapable, Dad.'

She might not think that, but she had agreed with the care team when they first suggested moving Connie to a home.

'I really feel… well, both Peter and I do, we really feel that this would be in both your best interests.'

Which was precisely why Geoff didn't want Rosemary there, she might notice something wasn't quite right, she might see he was not coping as well as he wanted to. He was weak and weary and relieved to have a few hours' peace. But he was also ashamed that he could not be the man Connie needed in her sickness. The kind that could put aside their own feelings, their own frustrations, their own exhaustion, to look after his wife in her time of need. And he really didn't want Rosemary to see that.

'Look, love, I'd like to call the home before I have tea. They'll be putting your mum to bed soon so I'll get off. Don't feel that you have to come up tomorrow, I really can cope.' He paused, something making him relent. 'The meeting is on Monday. Before your mother gets home. I understand if you decide you'd like to be there, but I am more than happy to speak to them on my own. I'll leave it up to you.'

'Thank you, Dad. Okay. I'll call you tomorrow. Maybe I can come up on Sunday, give you some time to rest before I do. We could go up to the pub for dinner. Save either of us cooking.'

'Okay, love,' he said. 'Talk tomorrow.'

Geoff hung up the phone. Should he have told Rosemary about how he was feeling? He looked towards the kitchen then up the stairs. He couldn't face food or eating alone so he climbed the stairs and went to bed.

Tucking himself in, swapping his own pillow for Connie's, he gave in to his tiredness on one condition. He would wake up tomorrow ready to take on the day, the weekend in fact. Connie needed him now more than ever and he was not going to let her down. Just as she had never let him down. In all the years they'd been together, in all the years he'd focused on work, on his photography, his archery, his time helping out at the church, he'd left Connie to run the home and the family because that's how their generation did things. She'd never complained, even when times were hard, and he knew she found it so, she never complained. She had coped, because that was her job. And now it was time for him to cope. That was his job. Perhaps it was time to learn from her lifetime of gentle patience.

Chapter Twenty-Five

'Okay, talk to us,' says Vicky. 'I mean, you know, if you want to.'

'Of course she wants to, this is us!' says Zoe, loudly, spilling her pint as she nudges herself back into position. The couple beside us get up and leave. 'She just doesn't realise she wants to talk to us yet.'

'I don't know if I do, girls. To be honest, I don't even know what's going on myself. I don't know what to say.'

'How long have we all been friends? You never want to talk because you never want to make it all about you, but this *is* all about you and we are here to help. So how about you start with when things went so bad that he went off with someone else,' says Zoe, her face hard. 'Again.'

'Zoe!' Interrupts Vicky. 'That's not okay.'

'What? What else is that text about?'

'It could be anything.'

'He's got form.'

'He hasn't got form,' interrupts Claire.

'And none of us are perfect.' Vicky says this firmly, with her eyes pinned on Zoe and we all know that's because Zoe actually does have 'form' as she so eloquently puts it, having split up with her last boyfriend because she started seeing some bloke from work.

'Okay, okay, sorry.' Zoe takes a gulp of her pint, carefully put back in her pram.

'We thought you were coping,' says Claire. 'I mean, we know it's been hard, but… like you said the other night, marriage can be hard sometimes. It's ups and downs, it's compromise. And he wouldn't do anything like that…' She pauses, her confidence in Alex stalling. 'I mean… I can't believe he would. I just… I don't understand the text but, well, have there been any signs? Any hints that things aren't right?'

'Any hints that things aren't right?' I say. 'If you make me think about it I could probably give you a list. He barely talks to me. He hasn't looked me in the eye for God knows how long. He rarely leaves the house – at least not whilst ever I'm there. Which I guess is something in his favour.'

'Never leaves the house?' asks Vicky.

'Hardly. Not that I know of. Maybe when I'm at work. From what I can see, he pretty much sits in his chair, watching the same programmes, day in, day out. He ignores the job papers I bring back for him, has done for months. He doesn't respond to emails I forward with possible job opportunities, they now all bounce back because his inbox is full. He gets so cold from the lack of moving around that he whacks the temperature up to scorching and then when I turn it down, because it's too hot and we can't really afford the bills, he tells me I'm making him feel bad for not working. He doesn't eat much, he probably drinks more than he should, he doesn't help around the house and he is not great company.' The girls are staring at me. Each one with mouths open and a look in their eyes that tells me things are much worse than I've been prepared to acknowledge. 'But that's just him struggling, isn't it? He's finding it hard, he's… it's a phase… it's…'

'You were going to say normal, weren't you,' offers Vicky and I nod sadly.

'That's not normal, Helen,' points out Claire. 'You must know that, you must see that, don't you?'

I screw my eyes up to blink back tears. 'I don't know, do I? I've been working, I've been taking extra shifts, I've been… too bloody busy to notice. Maybe that's half the problem. I just keep on keeping on until he rights himself. Maybe I've neglected him or made it all worse somehow.'

The girls reach out for my hands. We all four sit together, arms stretched across the table, and their unwavering support is a bit more than my emotions can cope with, so I take my hand out from the bottom, placing it on the top. Zoe follows, as does Claire and there's a few moments of us doing that silly hand layering thing that ends in a mini hand scuffle until I drop my hand back on the table and they all pull theirs back.

'I knew we were in a down phase, of course I did, but I put that down to him being out of work and me being knackered from all the extra work. I didn't put it down to him having an affair or anything. If anything, I thought this was our time. Tom says he's moving out now he's got a job. He's getting a flat up Skipton with a mate. I thought, after the challenges of the last few months, Alex and I might fall in love all over again. We're still young, we've a whole life ahead of us.' I press the heel of my hand into my eyes to stop myself from losing control. Stars rush into the blackness. I drop my head on the table and one of them strokes my hair. 'Look, thanks, girls. For being here for me. For caring. For listening. But really, I think I just want to go home. Be there in case he calls, be there if Tom comes in. Hide a bit, you know?'

'You can't hide for too long,' says Claire.

'She's right, you'll get as bad as him if you do,' says Zoe.

'Just be kind to yourself, yes?' says Vicky.

'I won't hide. I won't get as bad as him and yes, I will be kind. I love you girls, sorry to piss on your birthday bonfire.'

Vicky gets up to give me a hug. 'It's fine. Don't worry.'

Claire grabs both my hands. 'I'm at yours at the drop of a hat, okay? Just call.' I smile at her, knowing that she would absolutely be there at the drop of a hat. They all would. Thank God for them.

Zoe walks over to the bar, following me as I leave. 'Hey, Hel. Sorry for making you share. I didn't realise things were as tough as this.'

'It's fine, don't worry. Thanks.'

'Whoever that Martin bloke is, maybe you should fill your boots and call it evens?' She makes me laugh. I think she's just joking.

I work out how much I've had to drink in the short time I've been in the pub, opting to leave the car to be on the safe side. I hail a taxi and hide in the back seat with a fuzzy head and my problems out in the open. It's hard to know if sharing them has helped. They're supposed to be halved when shared, aren't they? But that's not quite how it feels. What would the notebook say? The notebook, which I left in my car and now can't refer to. The notebook that feels like it's become a crutch, something I need to breathe. To survive what life is throwing at me. That's probably not terribly healthy.

Staring out of the window, the streetlights whizz by and the taxi dips in and out of traffic, down back streets and out onto the main road home. And that's when I think I see him. Walking hand in hand, down the main road. The woman is huddled up in a coat and scarf, long hair trailing down her back, making its escape from a beanie hat. Is it him? If it is, could the woman be the person he meant to send the message to? Then the man who looks like Alex and she seem to share a joke, and each fall about laughing before he pulls her into an embrace, and as we pass them, his face is obscured by hers as they kiss beneath the lamp post. And I think I'm going to be sick.

Chapter Twenty-Six

Geoff stared at the ceiling, the Teasmade whirred into action, just as it had every morning for years and years, hot tea pouring into two cups.

It had been their first night apart. Did Connie miss him as he did her? Did she have the lucidity to imagine him sat in bed right now, to picture him eating his breakfast or drinking tea? Did he even enter her mind?

She hadn't left his. Every moment he wondered what she was doing, how she was feeling, was she being cared for, was she frightened? Did she remember him? He wondered if she was up yet? Was she dressed? Did she opt for the olive dress or salmon-pink two-piece? The memory of her distaste of both raised a gentle smile. Had they dressed her and taken her to the breakfast room? What was she eating? She liked porridge, cooked to the right temperature. Sometimes she liked a few of those frozen berries to defrost on the top. Other times it was golden syrup all the way, her sweet tooth winning out. Her sweet tooth, the thing he'd been most able to satisfy over the years. Thorntons, that was her favourite. The Viennese truffles, all whipped up and coated in a fine dusting of sugar. Did she smile? Did she wonder where she was? Does the radio play? She liked the radio. BBC Radio Leeds usually. Unless it was a Sunday afternoon and then she liked the show tunes on Radio 2. She'd sing along, once upon a time. Just her and the kitchen radio as she cooked dinner or did washing. He loved to hear her, as he pottered about upstairs in his little office. The walls covered in photos he'd taken. They were together, in the same space, but doing their own thing and, for him, that was one of the things he loved most, just knowing she was there.

The Teasmade stopped. Steaming tea waited for him to put creamer in. But exhaustion took over and Geoff slid back down into their bed. Empty. He missed her.

Chapter Twenty-Seven

Saturdays used to be my favourite day. Tom would play, either in the house or the garden. Alex would potter doing jobs, getting Tom to help, or me to hold a spirit level or do the cutting in on a paint job; I was better at the cutting in. Normally, Friday nights would be spent with a takeaway, usually Indian because I was unable to go a week without a really good dhal. Then we'd watch a film, or something on TV that we'd recorded. We'd slope off up to bed and snuggle until we dropped off, then Tom would come in in the morning, bouncing on the bed with a book, a toy, or later on, as he got bigger, a request that he could go downstairs and make his own breakfast. Today, there's nobody beside me and nobody to bounce on my bed. I'm tired from a sleepless night trying to work out every reason why that couldn't have been Alex I saw last night. He's away. He told me. He wouldn't walk the streets in plain view. He wouldn't be affectionate like that. Except he would, he was, with me, back in the day. He was laughing, something he's not done in months. Once upon a time, he'd belly laugh. He'd make jokes. He'd spend our weekends purposefully larking about to entertain me and Tom. He is capable of laughing. Each rationale I came up with I could counteract straight away.

When Tom came back last night, he found me staring at the walls. He didn't ask what was up, just made us a mug of hot chocolate each.

We sat on the sofa, chatting about work and his mates. We watched *Gogglebox*; us watching them watching telly. It was wallpaper and I didn't pay attention. I stuffed my feet beneath the crook of his knee and appreciated the fact he didn't complain. When he got up to go to bed, he leant down to kiss the top of my head and I wondered when he got so big? So grown up? So mature? When did he start looking so much like his dad did, back when we were newly married? Except Tom's gentler, somehow, maybe more comfortable in his own skin. Or more aware of other people's feelings, empathetic.

He asked about his dad. I didn't know what to say. I still don't. I've been up since six, trying to work something out. I think because my brain is consumed, rather than because I really need to justify things with Tom. He seems to sense something's not right and isn't pushing any of our conversations. Getting up early has its benefits, mind you. The need for distraction is all good. It means that so far this morning, I've put a wash on, emptied the dishwasher and re-loaded it with my cereal bowl and mug. I've emptied every kitchen cupboard for the first time in… probably years… and am now sat with steaming hot, bleached water, cleaning out the cupboards. The strength of chemicals makes my eyes stream and the heat is seeping through my Marigolds but I don't care. Instead, I just scrub away at the marks and the stains. Gradually getting further and further inside the cupboard, reaching right to the back and rubbing until every mark has gone away. I curse at the stubborn ones and wonder why I don't do this more often… or perhaps why I started it in the first place.

'Jesus, Mum, what are you doing?'

I look up sharply at the sound his voice, narrowly avoiding cracking my head on the cupboard carcass because I'm not living in a farce. 'I'm cleaning! I know it's a novelty, but someone has to do it. And anyway, never mind what I'm doing, what are you doing? You do realise it's before midday on a Saturday. Who are you? What have you done with my son?'

'You're not funny.'

'I'm a little bit funny.' I wink.

'Whatever you need to tell yourself.' He fills the kettle up, yawning, looking in his cupboard before looking through the boxes on the worktop to find the cereal he wants.

'Thought you were buying your own food,' I tease and, quite rightly, he just ignores me.

Back in the cupboard, the most stubborn of stains has relinquished to my power, so I sit up, wringing out the cloth before shuffling along to the next, horrified by the filth ingrained. Do all cupboards look like this? I'm gonna check out one of the girls', next time I'm round theirs. Tom stands with his hand on the kettle, waiting for it to boil. 'Come on then, why are you up so early on a Saturday? How come you were on hot chocolate last night?'

'Driving lessons,' he announces, grinning broadly. 'First one at half nine.'

'What? You didn't say! That's brilliant.'

'Yeah, well, I figured it'd be easier when I move out if I can actually drive. Won't be able to afford the lessons when paying rent so gonna do it now. Got a two-hour lesson booked in then I'm getting dropped off in town. Stopping at Smith's tonight so I won't be back. You're all right though, eh?'

'Of course!' I say, more quickly than I probably need to.

'Mum…' I'm giving a stain some proper elbow grease. I can see how this would be odd for him. I'm not a natural house cleaner. 'Are you sure you're okay?'

I hide my head in the cupboard for a second before fixing a grin then looking up at him. 'I'm fine. Go enjoy your lesson. Text me when you've finished, let me know how it goes. I shall be here cleaning because these jobs do not do themselves, you will learn this when you've got your own place.'

'Yeah, you won't find me cleaning cupboards.'

'Nah… it's not much fun.'

And off he goes with his cereal and tea, back up to his room to get dressed and prepare for doing his own thing. Leaving me here, alone in the house with my bleach water and filthy cupboards. And the picture in my mind of Alex and that woman. It's going to be a long weekend.

Chapter Twenty-Eight

Normally on a Sunday, Geoff would go up to the chapel in the village. He'd sing with the rest of the congregation, he'd bow his head in prayer. He'd laugh and joke with the men and women he'd known for many years, then he'd walk home and sit with Connie until it was time to make them some lunch. There was something familiar about the routine, something secure about the knowledge that she waited for him at home. Something about the look on her face when he got home that filled him with love, because she was still there, over seventy years and she was still there. Familiarity didn't breed contempt, it bred a deeper love than he could ever have imagined.

This Sunday morning was different though. This morning he'd stayed in bed again. No inclination to pray or eat. All Geoff wanted to do was pore over photo albums. Reminisce. If she wasn't there to fill his heart with love, the photos would be her replacement. Each book, each photo triggered memories of all the good times they'd had. The canal walks with grandchildren, taking them up to the woods with home-made bow and arrows to find targets. The dinner dances he and Connie would go to at the Lodge. The weddings of friends and then, years later, friends' children. The mother and father of the bride stood side by side at Rosemary's wedding, each dressed in all their finery. Then later, a vow renewals party for a friend, dressed in

70s flares and stack-heeled shoes, all dancing in a circle during the disco. He paused on that photo for a while, studying Connie's face, her head thrown back in joy. Her dress, something she'd searched and searched for to find the right one. He remembered their life back then. He was at work, Connie volunteered down the local amateur theatre. Box office duty, making costumes, fundraising and coffee mornings. Rosemary had moved out around then he seemed to remember. She was twenty-three, twenty-four. He and Connie were in the process of readjusting to life as a couple again, parenting duties effectively redundant on a day-to-day basis. It had been strange, difficult in some ways, just as it had been difficult when he returned from the war, then again when they had Rosemary, because they'd adjusted to their lives as they were and change brought about challenge. But they made it, they were still here, all these years on. Was this their new challenge? The new normal to adapt to?

Before Geoff knew it, the morning had all but disappeared and the clock chimed eleven. Rosemary had said she'd be there by 11.30 and Rosemary was never late.

True to form, bang on 11.30, just as Geoff finished buttoning up his shirt, Rosemary pulled up outside the house. As he opened the door, she waved then reverse parked up as close to the side fence as was humanly possible, just as Geoff had always instructed. When she got out of the car – perhaps for the first time, and for what reason Geoff wasn't sure – he resisted pointing out that she could park a bit closer if she went back a little further with left hand down a bit.

'Is that okay, Dad?' she huffed, looking at her parking from back to the front of her car.

Geoff twitched. 'That's fine, love. Thank you. It's just so Mrs Hibberthwaite's son can get his BMW on her drive.'

Rosemary got her bag out of the boot. A bag that looked as though it contained more than just enough for one night. Did she have plans to stay longer? Connie was home tomorrow and he wanted to get back to just the two of them as soon as she did.

'Hi, Dad,' she breezed, giving him a kiss on his cheek, dropping her bag down.

'How was your journey?'

'Oh, it was fine. Steady. You know. Cuppa?' she asked, but Rosemary didn't wait for his answer.

She was organised, Rosemary. In control, on top of things. Someone to rely on. Perhaps more like him than either would like to admit. Whenever she arrived, she'd somehow take over, at least that was how it felt. She'd turn the telly down because she couldn't quite hear them both, she'd turn the heating down because she was going through the change, she'd put the kettle on whether it was time for tea or not. She'd pack plates away, clattering in the kitchen. She'd clean the bathroom and the downstairs toilet, jobs Geoff purposefully left for Val. She'd sort the post out. Even those with Private and Confidential on the envelope. Her efficiency, the energy it brought, it changed the room, somehow. It changed the home. Geoff knew it was her trying to help, he appreciated her not just sitting around and waiting for an instruction, but at the same time, her efficiency felt disruptive. She probably couldn't get it right whichever way she did things. He knew that much of himself. And it wasn't her fault that he actually wanted to stay in the emotional place he'd found whilst looking at the photos. The place where love and longevity was in his heart. Where his and Connie's future stretched out before them, unknown.

'Have you heard from the home at all, Dad?' she said. 'Is Mum still okay? What time is she due back tomorrow? Is it before or after the meeting? When's that? 1.30?' She didn't leave Geoff time to answer any of the questions, which on this occasion he was grateful for. 'I was thinking I'd take you to do a food shop in the morning, then we can make sure you're back in time for the woman from Social Services. Is it Mrs Barnes again? I liked her, she seemed efficient. Then, hopefully, we'll be done with her before Mum gets back. I've agreed with Peter that I'll stay on a few days, just to make sure you're both okay.'

As she talked, she'd wiped down the sides, restacked the bowls in a cupboard, sniffed and then poured away some milk from the fridge.

'You don't need to do all of this, Rosemary,' he said eventually, tired.

'I know that, Dad. I'm just helping. You're allowed to accept help, you know.'

'That's why Val comes around. To help. I pay her and she does what I ask. She doesn't…' They looked at each other. It felt like seconds, days at the most, since he sat with Rosemary on his lap, singing nursery rhymes to make her laugh. He stopped himself from saying that Val didn't take over. That Val didn't do jobs unless he asked. He stopped himself because Rosemary looked tired too. Perhaps he wasn't the only one who was struggling.

Chapter Twenty-Nine

Having spent last afternoon and evening in Rosemary's company, Geoff had really wanted to get the bus to Bingley that morning. He'd wanted Helen to wait for him like usual, they'd exchange pleasantries and he'd feel like a human being. He'd do his shopping then go to sit in the calm of the church. He'd prepare himself for this afternoon's meeting.

But Rosemary wasn't having any of it. Rosemary made him breakfast. Rosemary cleaned up and put some washing on. Rosemary bundled him into the car so they could go to pick up some essentials. Except Rosemary took him to the big Morrisons supermarket and it was all too much, which meant she took over and that sort of made things worse. Geoff knew she meant well, he knew she was trying to take care of him, roles reversed, but the more she 'helped' the less capable he felt. The older he felt.

Helen had pulled up at the drive that morning and Rosemary said a quick hello, asked about Tom, waved to James, then let Helen drive on because she was going to take him into town and 'she wasn't sure when Dad'll next be on the bus'. Geoff listened as hard as he could to that conversation, desperate that she would not let on just how hard things were, because he didn't want Helen to know. He didn't want her to change how she was with him. He couldn't bear it if she became another person to make him feel his age. Solemnly, she had nodded at

Rosemary, given him a wave and driven on. Did she have pity in her eyes? Geoff couldn't quite tell.

Then they got home from the big Morrisons, Rosemary unpacked the car. She put the shopping away and she made lunch: tomato soup and a cheese, onion and salad cream sandwich. Geoff should have enjoyed it, but the bread stuck in the back of his throat and the soup wasn't quite the right temperature and he just wanted to go back to normal where he was in charge of his own time. His own soup.

The clock chimed one o'clock and Geoff remembered once again that Connie didn't like it. Perhaps he should take the batteries out. Perhaps he should pack it away. Rosemary moved to sit on top of the nest of tables, taking up Connie's place as lookout for Mrs Barnes' arrival. Mrs Barnes' little red Micra pulled up to the driveway, parking where Helen normally stopped the bus to collect him. Geoff was going to ask her to move down the lane, but Rosemary jumped up before he could.

'You stay there, Dad. I'll get the door.' Which is exactly what she did, telling Mrs Barnes that her car was, 'perfectly fine'. Which it probably was, until Helen next came past. 'Come on in, can I get you a tea? Coffee?'

'No, thank you. I've just had a drink.' Mrs Barnes came in, her arms laden with bags full of files, her handbag, car keys and mobile phone. She asked where to sit down and when Geoff pointed to the chair by the window, she shuffled over, her thighs rubbing together causing her tights to make a static noise as she dropped into the chair. 'Feel free to have one yourselves though.' She shuffled her papers and picked out files whilst Rosemary disappeared to make herself and Geoff a drink.

'Right, Mr Steele. How are you? How has your last few days' peace been? I'm sure it must have felt strange not having her around, but lovely at the same time? To have a bit of a rest, I mean. It really does take it out of you having to look after someone with Connie's condition, we do understand.'

Geoff wondered if they really did understand because if they did, they might not wander in here with such banalities about having a rest, and Connie's 'condition'. Geoff wondered if this Mrs Barnes' had any idea what it was like whatsoever.

'In fact, since Connie's been in Roslyn House, we've been able to see for ourselves just how difficult it must be for you, Geoff.'

Geoff wanted to tell her it was nothing he couldn't cope with. That Connie was his wife and he would do anything for her. Geoff wanted to tell her that they were fine as they were, but Rosemary came back in with two drinks, placing his down on the side. It interrupted his train of thought.

Mrs Barnes handed an envelope to Rosemary who paused as if going to open it before passing it on to Geoff. He placed it on the coffee table beside him. 'Good news, Mr Steele, I know you got the letter about the plan for increasing Connie's respite, but late on Friday, a residential place came up in the home. Much sooner than we were expecting.' Geoff stared, his heart slowing. 'She can take that up as soon as you'd like.' Mrs Barnes smiled, her hands clasped to her knee. She had a look of someone very pleased with herself.

There was a pause. The room fell silent until Rosemary broke it. 'Wow! That's… well, that's amazing news, isn't it, Dad?' Geoff turned to Rosemary, stunned. 'Well, I mean, for Mum. It's the best for Mum, isn't it?'

Geoff didn't know what to say. He'd known this day might come, the letter made it clear what they thought and all the conversations leading up to this point had suggested it was pending, but now it was here. They were offering her a place. The efficient removal of his beloved wife from their marital home was imminent. Geoff was lost for words.

'Isn't it good news, Dad?'

He blew across the scalding coffee in his second favourite mug. It was a little too milky for his liking, but you can't take milk out so he'd just have to drink it and none of that really mattered because if they had their way Connie was going to leave him for longer than just a few days.

'Dad?'

'I'm not sure what, about this, you think is good?' Geoff eventually said, quietly.

'Well…' Rosemary looked from Geoff to Mrs Barnes and back to Geoff again. 'People wait ages to get a place for their loved ones, of course it's good news. I mean, Mum gets the support and care that she needs, you no longer have to look after her all day everyday and, whilst this might sound a little selfish, that's a huge relief to me, to be honest. I'm so far away and I'm not getting any younger myself, Dad. And I worry about you both.'

Geoff briefly wondered whether something being 'a relief' to Rosemary should be a considered factor in his wife's future. After all, wasn't this about him and Connie? Didn't the rest of them have a duty of care to support them in the lives they wanted to lead, until their final days, not project on them what was easier all round. He had no way of knowing what things might be like for Rosemary. Connie's parents died when she was young, his own parents passed away peacefully; there was no need for intervention, no need for professionals to get involved. He had nothing to compare it to.

'It's often very stressful for everyone in the immediate family, Mr Steele.'

Geoff nodded. 'I can appreciate that, I can, Mrs Barnes. But, Rosemary… your mother is my wife and I want her with me, at home. As we've always been. And surely, for a place to suddenly come available means that somebody, somewhere has lost a loved one. A mother, a father. A husband or wife. I don't like the idea of their sadness creating an opportunity for us.'

Rosemary's face fell. Mrs Barnes fidgeted in her seat.

'We do understand, Mr Steele. Of course this would be a big change. For you both.'

Rosemary cleared her throat as if coughing out what she really wanted to say so she might replace it with the next batch of, slightly better chosen, words. 'I know none of this is nice, Dad. It's awful, of course it is. And I can't bear to think of a family having lost someone they love… but… well, you must be so tired looking after her all of the time. And…' she paused, as if daring herself to finish the sentence before she said, 'it's not going to get any easier.'

Geoff put his tea down. He wanted no distractions. 'I want my wife with me, Rosemary. Mrs Barnes. That's what I want. That's what I really want. We didn't marry to walk away at the first sign of difficulty.'

Mrs Barnes' shuffled in her seat again.

'Dad, you've been married forever. I don't imagine this is the first sign of difficulty. It's not…' She stopped herself, fixing him with the kind of look he used to give her when she was young and he needed to remind her who was the boss. 'It's not that we don't understand that this is difficult for you. It's that we care about you both and want what's best. And if that means Mum going into a home, then so be it.'

'It's that easy, is it?'

'Well, maybe easy is the wrong word. But what's best.'

'What's best for me is having my wife by my side.'

'And is that what's best for Mum?' Rosemary snapped. Mrs Barnes opened and closed her mouth again. She'd surely been in situations like this before but Geoff noticed she didn't appear to know what to say.

Geoff stood slowly, tired. He took a step towards Mrs Barnes. 'I don't believe my wife wants to go into a home and that in itself tells me that it's not in her best interests. *I* don't want my wife to go into a home, which further tells me that this is not in either of our best interests.' Rosemary went to speak, but Geoff raised his hand to stop her. 'I do not wish to seem ungrateful, I appreciate your offer of a place and I appreciate your concerns, Rosemary, but I don't think we're so desperate that there are no alternatives to this very final decision, yet. Please do ensure it goes to somebody who needs it more. For whom there *is* no alternative. Now, if you'll both excuse me, I'd like to take a rest before my wife gets home. She's been away quite long enough.' And with that, Geoff retired to his bedroom, clutching another book of photos.

Chapter Thirty

'What did his daughter say to you this morning?' asks James as we drive back past Geoff's house.

'Pardon?'

'Geoff's daughter. Did she say he was okay? I was just thinking he's no' been on the bus Friday or today. It's no' like him.' I make a noise but James is still pondering. 'And whose car is that parked outside?' he asks, straining back to look.

'His daughter's. Rosemary.'

'No, not that one. The Micra.' I glance back in the rear-view mirror as the house dips out of view. 'I dunno,' I mumble, wondering if Alex has read my latest text that asked him when he might be home as I'm doing a food shop on my way home and want to make sure I get Alpen in if he's going to be home to eat it. It wasn't the most exciting text I've ever sent, but it was all I could think of and I'm just getting desperate now. Apparently, he and Tom exchanged a few messages over the weekend, but nothing of any substance and he still didn't say where he was. Or who he was with.

'D'ye think he's okay?'

'Who?' I pull in further up the road to let on a young mum and her baby who I've not seen before.

'Geoff! D'ye think Geoff is okay?'

'Oh, I don't know. I'm sure he's fine. Rosemary didn't say there was a problem. We saw Geoff, he looked fine.' James narrowed his eyes at me, so I fixed my own up ahead to avoid his scrutiny. 'She just said that he might not be on the bus for a while. He doesn't need to come with us if she's there, does he? She can drive him where he needs to go.'

I focus my eyes forward, not really in the mood for our usual chat. I don't have the headspace for analysing Geoff's situation. Rosemary was there, she had it all in order. My head was full of the letters in the book and how so much of it resonated with my own feelings. The letters that talked of new things the writer had learnt. Things they wished they'd shared with their love. Things that might have made life easier and that made me wonder what might make our life easier, mine and Alex's.

Maybe we should sell up, buy a smaller place and realise the money that's in the building. Maybe he could do something different for work. Take a risk, try something new. The person writing the letters has talked about wishing they knew what they wanted in life, wishing they hadn't been caught up in a career that they ultimately walked away from, maybe this is a blessing for Alex. He didn't love his job. He could do anything, this is an opportunity, this is his moment. And the part of my heart that filled with excitement about this realisation was quickly deflated with the part of my heart that reminded me I can't talk to him about the great chance he has to make a change if he's not around to listen.

Chapter Thirty-One

Mrs Barnes left, leaving the relevant paperwork for Geoff to look over. Since he heard her driving off, he'd been sat on the bed, photo album on his lap, staring at the threadbare carpet before him.

'Dad...' said Rosemary, gently tapping at the door. He reached into his top pocket to pull out a freshly laundered handkerchief, dabbing at his eyes. The door creaked open and Rosemary's face peered round. 'Dad, are you okay?'

Geoff didn't say anything. Rosemary stepped inside the room, something she'd rarely done. She'd never lived in this house and so never had the need to come into their room in a morning, like when she was a child, creeping in to wake Connie. She was alien in his haven, large and noisy in her presence, leaning against the wall beside a picture of her when she was fifteen or so. She hadn't changed much, not really. She always did stand and wait until he was ready to talk, even when she went on to disagree. Connie had always nurtured that strength of character in their daughter. Rosemary had his voice and Connie's patience. His grit and Connie's heart. He laid his hand on her side of the bed. He thought about the strength his wife gave him, the sense of purpose, he didn't honestly know if he'd have survived this far without her.

'I was eleven years old when my mum told me I was the man of the house, Rosemary. Eleven. Can you imagine?' Rosemary looked to the floor. 'You were riding a bike around the lanes at eleven years old. Calling for your friends.'

'Making sausage sandwiches for the bobby in the woods so he wouldn't tell us off for having a barbeque, I seem to remember.'

Geoff allowed himself a wry smile. He remembered hearing about it from his friend up the pub, his friend being the local policeman, or 'bobby' as they all called them back then, filling Geoff in on what Rosemary was getting up to when he wasn't about to see. 'You were being a child. Just as it should be.' Rosemary nodded. 'In fact, if memory serves, the hardest thing you had to deal with was the eleven-plus exams, which you just seemed to take in your stride. It was different, in my day; life was harder. We were poor. My father was too ill to work. Mum needed a man in the house and I was the eldest. By virtue of birth, the responsibility became mine. It's what was expected so I did what I ought. I took care of my brothers. I helped your grandma around the house. I got a job as soon as I could because we needed the money for bills. I got a scholarship to the grammar school but I didn't take it because it would have been more schooling and there was no time for that, I had to work.'

'Dad, I know that being in charge of everything is important to you.'

'What do you mean it's important to me?' Geoff looked up at Rosemary.

'I just mean, well… you've always had that responsibility on your shoulders. It's who you are, it's in your blood.' Geoff stared at her. 'It's part of you.'

'It's what your mother fell in love with. Somebody who could take care of her. Of the home. Someone to be the man of the house.'

'That's not the reason she married you, Dad. She married you because she loved you. Because you loved her.'

'Yes, and I still do. That's why I want her here with me.'

'I know, I… it's just…' Rosemary clasped her fingers together, her knuckles turning white. 'I understand if you are frightened, Dad.' Geoff shifted on the bed. 'Frightened of being alone. Of not having Mum. I understand, I really do, but her going into a home doesn't stop you being the man that you are, Dad. Mum being unwell doesn't mean you have to pretend. You're allowed to be…' Rosemary searched for the right word and Geoff hoped she wouldn't find it because he feared what it might be. 'You're allowed to be vulnerable.'

Geoff stood up, placing the photos on his bedside table, reaching for the door. 'Your mother is staying with me and that is final,' he said. 'Now, if you've nothing more to add, I'd like to prepare our home for her return. Perhaps it would be better if you weren't here when she got back. I don't want her to wonder who you are, and it cause her any stress.'

Stunned, Rosemary waited a moment, before going into the back bedroom, shutting the door behind her. Part of Geoff wanted to tell her he was sorry, that she could stay. But as he heard her unzip her suitcase and move around the room, he realised he didn't know how to take things back. That had always been Connie's job.

Chapter Thirty-Two

My back is wrecked, my head bangs and my mood is dark. Beyond dark. It's grown darker with every minute of every hour of this long and lonely day. It's dark like we're-out-of-gin-and-crisps-and-I'm-on-my-period dark. Yet none of those things are actually true. I'm not on my period for another ten days and I've a multipack of Walkers and a full bottle of Bombay at my disposal.

I've been so distracted today that James kept having to remind me of the route and one of the old ladies from East Morton had to walk much further than normal because I forgot to drop her off by her driveway. I can't wait to get home, put my pyjamas on, put some crap on the telly and try to work out a plan of action. I can't stay in limbo forever. He's been away for a week. I know he's alive because of the text message the other day, so the police aren't going to launch a manhunt. Besides, I have to be honest with myself, things haven't been good for ages. If he went off with somebody else, maybe it'd be the best thing for both of us. I didn't see it coming. It isn't what I want but if he can meet somebody else, maybe our marriage isn't all that. Fuck it, maybe Zoe's right, maybe I should call up Martin and get my own back. She texted the same advice as I was letting a load of people, including Martin, off the bus this morning and, Christ, did I turn puce. Which is an attractive look for an almost middle-aged woman… not that it matters. Obviously.

I head off the main road, down the unlit hill and around the corner to our house.

And there is Alex's car.

My heart simultaneously lifts, then drops to my knees as I realise that behind that front door, my whole life could be about to change. Their embrace the other night, that could have been him telling her he was going to leave me. I feel dizzy, and a bit sick. Actually, a lot sick. When we first moved in together, I'd be giddy each time one of us came home to the other. Even in that shitty old flat, I'd leap on him, wrapping my legs around his waist. I don't think he'd want that now… and I don't think he could carry me any more. God, I've let myself go. That must be the problem, too. That girl the other night, she looked all skinny and gorgeous and young. I look in the rear-view mirror. My mascara has panda'd my eyes and my face is visible-from-the-moon shiny. As is my hair, which I should probably have washed at the weekend. Shit. Why couldn't I still look like the girl he fell in love with? Yes, we were young. Yes, people judged, but to all the naysayers we'd held our heads high and flipped the bird.

Maybe they were right? Maybe we were too young. And now he's fallen out of love and lust and I don't want to go in. I want to stay in the car. I want to reverse off the drive. I want to go to Claire's and let her pour gin down my neck. But Vicky's words rattle round my head instead. We don't know anything. We shouldn't assume. It's all conjecture… I'm not all that certain what that means either, but I think I can guess.

I'm going in.

The sick feeling rises from belly to throat as I push the front door open, automatically reaching down to pick up the post that nobody else will have collected. I turn the thermostat down from high to our usual 20 degrees, wondering how long he's been home, to have turned it up so much that it's this warm already. It was always the first thing I'd bang on about when I got in each night. I had definitely started nagging. Or demanding, expecting certain things to be done because he was at home all day. Was I right to expect them? Or had I lost any compassion for his situation? Except I didn't see it as his situation, I saw it as ours. Teamwork. Like always.

Couldn't he have told me he was coming back? Maybe he wants me on the back foot.

'Hey,' I call out, trying to keep my strangled voice light but suddenly desperate to hear his. If I hear him, I'll be able to tell what's coming. I know him better than anyone. 'You're home!' I dump the post on the side, doing my usual routine in the kitchen so as not to crowd him. 'Tea?' But I'm not really expecting an answer to that one because he'd stopped answering it months ago. My hands rattle the lid of the kettle, nerves splitting, sending electricity to my fingers. I hold up one hand, it shakes.

Take a breath, Helen.

This is your husband. The man you've loved since you were a kid.

There is nothing to be nervous about.

The lounge lights are off, there's just the flicker from the TV. I resist turning them on. 'I didn't realise you were coming back... have you had a good time?' He's in his chair, on his phone, chuckling at the funny people inside it. It's like he never went away, it's like Groundhog Day and I want to rip it from his hand and throw it across the room and ask him who the fuck that woman was the other night. I clear my throat instead. 'Hey,' I try again.

'Hey,' he says, like all this is perfectly normal.

'You're home.'

'You noticed.'

I move round to see him properly, lit by TV screen and mobile phone. I reach for the lamp to add a bit more warmth to the situation before sitting down just as he gets up and heads into the kitchen. He doesn't even look at me. My eyes sting but I won't cry. He won't treat me this way and see me weaken. If he wants to play games, I can play them, too.

'Everything been all right here?' he asks, shouting through from the kitchen.

As if summing up my reality, a dead head drops off one of the carnations and I'm struck by the fact it would be funny if it wasn't so bloody desperate. 'Uhm, yes, fine.'

'Good.' He's back in the lounge, empty-handed. I want to ask what he was doing but I don't feel I can. 'So…' I look around to begin with but then realise, one of us has to be the grown-up. One of us has to take control. Take charge. It's been me for the last few months, so it may as well still be me. 'How was your trip?'

There's a deep sigh, a rise of his brow. What was once clean-shaven is now peppered with a short beard. Did the guy the other night have a beard? I can't remember… maybe it wasn't him. Maybe I should just ask.

'It was… fine.' He doesn't even look at me. He goes away for a week. He sends a text message meant for somebody else and when he gets back, unannounced, he can't even look me in the eye. Is he ignoring the elephant in the room, the one stamping all over my heart, or is he playing with me? I don't know him any more… I don't know.

'Look,' I begin. 'I tried calling… I texted. I've been worried about you. I've been…' I can't find the words. My heart is bursting out of my mouth. Alex just stares at his phone. 'Alex, please!' I jump up out of the sofa, I go to the window because a bit of distance is better than me going closer to him. I'd either reach out and face rejection or push him for a response. Neither the most constructive of approaches... and yet. 'Jesus, Alex! What the fuck is going on? How have we got to a place in our life where you go away for a week without telling me where or for how long? How do you get to do that, and not even talk to me when you do get home?' I pause, taking a breath because I want to scream at him. He clicks his phone off, placing it on the chair beside him. 'And then...' His jaw muscles flex and he stares dead ahead, as if he sees right through me. 'I don't know what to say! I don't know what to think! I just... please, Alex, please...'

Alex stands, he faces the mirror on the mantelpiece, scattered with photos of us and Tom, our lives together. Twenty years. 'Look, Helen...' He takes a deep breath before looking me in the eye for the first time in I don't know how long. 'We need to talk.'

Chapter Thirty-Three

My love,

The hardest thing, I realise now, is looking at all the moments when I could have changed the outcome. The way that I am. The things that I've done. When I could see what was happening to me, to us, but I didn't have the right words. When you needed my touch, but I couldn't give it. When I couldn't love myself and, in turn, had no love for anybody else, just the performance and the persona. The mask of a person in charge of their destiny. What would it have taken to reach out and hold your hand or look you in the eye when you needed it most. When I needed it most. How hard could it have been to simply say, I'm sorry, or... I don't know... or... help me.

Help me.

I wished I'd learnt the power of those words before it was too late...

From,

The love you wished I could be.

Chapter Thirty-Four

'Dad! You're back!' shouts Tom, energetic excitement rushing full force into the lounge, along with our son, and I want to shout, *Not now, Tom! Not now!*

'Tom!' Alex flips round, pulling his son into a bear hug, slapping his back affectionately and their embrace makes me feel jealous. Jealous that I didn't get that response when I came home. Jealous that he couldn't be bothered to put his phone down, never mind get up and greet me. Jealous that he smiles at Tom like he used to smile at me and it hurts so badly, as does the guilt, for thinking any of those thoughts in the first place. To be jealous of my own son, that's just ugly.

'Ahhh, you two…' I say, covering up my true feelings, all the while wondering what it was Alex was about to say. What do we need to talk about?

'Guess what?' says Tom, standing proudly between us. 'Work have only gone and moved me into the design studio for three days of the week.'

'Oh, Tom! That's brilliant!' I say, because I know how much he has wanted that.

'I know, they want to train me up on the design side as well as down in the print shop. They're going to take on another apprentice to do the other half of my print shop work and see how it goes. They've talked about some training courses too, a diploma at college.'

'Love, that's fantastic! How did it happen? Tell me everything!'

'They saw my portfolio and decided I could really make a go of design. They think I've got something, Mum, Dad. They really believe in me.'

I pull him into my arms. 'That's amazing, Tom!' We hug, super-tight. 'You're amazing,' I say into my teenage son's neck. He's so tall now, so grown up. Taking his face into my hands, I look at my boy. Our boy. God he's amazing! 'You must be so proud of yourself, baby! We're proud of you!' Alex still stands by the fire but his expression is blank, his eyes are dark and hollow. He looks torn. 'Aren't we, Alex?'

'Of course we are. So proud.' He pulls Tom in for another hug, staring at me over his shoulder.

'I brought some beers to celebrate, do you want one, Dad?' He offers up a clinking carrier bag.

Alex pauses, falters somehow. He nods and shakes his head, almost at the same time. He looks around the room, then back to Tom. 'I'm… agh, Tom, mate. I'm…' he stretches his arms out, yawning.

'Dad's had a long journey, love. He's probably shattered. Maybe you could let me have one of those beers and let Dad get to bed. Talk to him tomorrow when he's not fading.'

Alex says nothing.

'Ah, of course. No problem, you do look knackered actually. Where did you end up? We've been wondering this whole week!' He opens a bottle of beer with the little jewelled pharaoh bottle opener we bought back from a family holiday to Egypt, years ago. I remember the fun we had back then. Tom was seven, or just eight… Alex and I celebrated our wedding anniversary out there. It was lovely. 'Look, don't worry. Talk to me tomorrow. Go get some rest.'

'Cheers, buddy.' Alex forces a smile but now doesn't look at me.

'Mum?' Tom passes me the bottle.

'Thanks, love.' I take it from him as Alex disappears up the stairs and I want to shout after him, *What do we need to talk about?*

Chapter Thirty-Five

Geoff waited for the care workers to pin tuck Connie into their pale-yellow eiderdown, forcing her into the mattress like a swaddled baby. She hated it like that and Geoff always had to wait until they'd gone, before going back upstairs to untuck her. To begin with, she'd say thank you. She'd pull the cover up to her chin and give him a bright smile with sparkling eyes. Tonight, he wasn't sure what he'd get when he got upstairs. She'd barely spoken to him since she got home. She'd had an 'accident' just as they arrived so they cleared that up before cleaning her up and putting her to bed. His heart swelled with love for her, and sorrow for what she'd become, as they huffed and puffed with their hands covered in rubber gloves and their uniforms protected with thin blue, plastic aprons. They had pulled them from around their necks when done, which just seemed so clinical, so unlike what Geoff wanted for Connie. He couldn't see how it would be any better in the home, plastic aprons and protection gloves were standard uniform. Who would hold her hand each day? Who would make contact with her? How often could he visit? How long would he be able to stay? Questions he didn't have the answers to because he wasn't going to ask.

He climbed the stairs, fearful yet desperate to lie in their bed beside her. He took a breath before pushing open their door, she turned to face him and her face broke into a smile. She reached out her hand for him, which he took up, holding it to his chest as he perched on her side of the bed. He focused on her eyes, the part of her that hadn't changed, the part of her that looked exactly as they always had when they first met as teenagers, when they stood before the vicar on their wedding day, when he returned home after the war, when she handed over their newborn daughter, when she handed him lunch on his first day of retirement. She blinked, slowly, her eyelids dropping as he held her hand and she fell asleep. And as she let out a quiet breath, peaceful back in their bed, he knew without a shadow of a doubt that she was back where she needed to be. Perhaps this was no longer about what Geoff wanted for Geoff, but what Geoff wanted for the woman who loved him into the man he became. The man he was today, sat beside her, on their bed, loving her just as he always had.

Chapter Thirty-Six

'Is Dad all right?' Tom asks, swigging his beer, then flopping down into the sofa.

'Course he is. He's just had a long drive, that's all.' I drop in beside him.

'Right… so where did he go then?' Tom takes another swig, reading the back of the bottle as my eyes widen because I can't answer the question and I don't know what to say and I can't lie and—

'Shit!' he says, suddenly.

'What? And also language.'

'I just realised how insensitive that was, wasn't it? It's no wonder he's gone upstairs,' Tom stage whispers, shifting to sit closer to me. 'That was such a dick move. Coming in being all mouthy and self-congratulatory about my new job.'

'Don't be silly, love. He's thrilled for you. This is the start of your career, you deserve all the opportunities and you're allowed to be excited about them. Your dad is thrilled for you, I can see it in his eyes, I promise.' Tom looks up, uncertain. 'I'd know,' I say, wishing I knew anything any more. 'Look, don't worry about it. Of course he's happy for you. He's just tired, like I said. That wasn't a "dick move", as you so eloquently put it. You're allowed to be excited.' I clink his bottle. 'Cheers, bloody well done.' Tom half smiles, looking back up the stairs. 'It's fine, love. Now, come on, tell me everything about it.'

By the time Tom eventually goes to bed, he's told me every last detail about the job, as well as some gossip on a mate, and some passing comment about a girl he's just met that he apparently totally doesn't fancy, but *she is really cool, Mum.* Gone midnight, he wobbles upstairs, with a kiss on my cheek and I sink back down into the sofa, pulling a throw across me to snuggle into. I wonder if Tom was more accurate than I let him believe. Was Alex hurting with the news of Tom's job? Is that why he disappeared upstairs? Or was it because he'd been interrupted from saying something he's obviously been working up to, and when will he start that conversation again? And what is it he wants to say? Does it have anything to do with fixing how lost he looks? How broken he seems? How can I get him back to the man I knew? The man whose face I could once picture vividly in my mind, each line, each detail. The colour of his eyes, the fullness of his lips with their down-turned edges until he'd break into a wide grin which reached every corner of his face. The strength in his arms as once upon a time he held me. Actually, I still can see him vividly, it's just that he doesn't look like that any more. Which, despite his absence this week, and the text messages, and his need to tell me something, makes my arms ache to hold him. I want to reach out and pull him in close to me to see if I can fix him like once upon a time. Because this is us, me and him. We're together forever, we need each other. Whatever he was going to say, it's not going to be anything we can't get over because… this is us.

By the time I've been in the bathroom, changed into my pyjamas and cleaned my face clear of the night's fears, I've gone over and over and convinced myself that it's a good idea to get into bed and give him a hug. We're married, after all. Surely it's okay.

'Helen,' he says, as I gently slip my arms around him.

'I just want you to feel loved,' I whisper, reaching to clasp my hands across his chest like I always did, kissing the base of his neck, like I'd stopped doing recently because it didn't feel right, because nothing did. But maybe we'd got ourselves into a pattern. Maybe we just need to reboot. Switch us off and back on again. Maybe all he needs is to feel wanted. I know I could do with that right now, too. 'It's okay, love. I know it must have been hard, that's all. With Tom, earlier. He didn't mean to make you feel bad. He's just excited.'

Alex unclasps my hands and sits up in bed. The room falls cold.

'If it's hard, Helen, it's only because I'm not man enough to put his happiness over my own misery. If it's hard, it's only because it's a reminder that I don't have a job. That I can't get a job. That the world expects us all to have a job and if we don't, we're abject failures.'

Stung, I move backwards slightly, pulling the covers around me. 'Nobody thinks that about you, Alex.'

'No?'

'Of course not!'

'So why did you automatically assume that I'd be upset over Tom getting this job? Hmmm? Why was *that* your first thought rather than the fact that I'd just told you we needed to talk and Tom came in and interrupted us after I'd finally worked out what I wanted to say.'

'Alex, I didn't mean to… I was just… I…' He blurs before me as my eyes fill up, which is really bloody irritating because I do not want to bloody well cry. 'I don't know what to do or say, Alex. I'm trying but I just don't know what to do.' I draw my knees to my chest and hold myself in tight. He puts his head in his hands and I notice flecks of grey I've not seen before.

'What did you want to say, Alex?' The sick feeling in my stomach returns tenfold but I'm determined to be a grown-up. To tackle this head on. He stares at me, the muscles in his jaw flexing again, as if he grits his teeth. I used to love seeing his jaw flex like that, I think he used to do it on purpose, because he knew I found it insufferably sexy. Enigma in his car sexy. 'I just keep thinking about that message you sent, Alex. And the other night... I think I saw you...' But I can't finish the sentence because my determination to be a grown-up is faltering at the prospect of hearing a truth that I don't think I want to hear. 'Alex, are we okay?'

He drops his gaze, taking too long to answer. 'Of course we are,' he says eventually, his voice no more than a whisper.

'It's just that...' I start, but I don't know how to finish and he's taken hold of my hands in any case. He gives them a gentle squeeze, though no love is felt.

'We're okay,' he says, simply. Then he turns over, his back facing towards me, and I've never felt so alone, or not okay, as I do right now.

Chapter Thirty-Seven

My breath is held as I lean against the bannister, straining to listen to Alex's hushed voice downstairs.

'The problem is, I love her. I don't want to hurt her but… I just… I've never felt like this before… I don't know what to do… I have to tell her something, I'm just not sure either of us are ready. I don't know what the truth will do to her, to us.'

I want to run downstairs and rip the phone from his hands. I want to crawl inside and see who it is he's talking to. Find out what he's talking about. Work out who he can open up to about this stuff? Is it her? The woman from the other night? And is she the truth that might break us? I want to put a face to the hair I saw, the head back laughter with a glossy mane that he ran his fingers through. Well, I didn't see him exactly running his fingers through it, and I know I didn't really see his face, but there my confidence that it wasn't him has disintegrated and therefore if it was him, I bet he bloody well did run his fingers through her hair because that's exactly what he used to do to me; before my hair got all thin and matted and dry and not remotely something he'd want to run his fingers through.

'I just know it won't be easy,' he says.

I shift my weight from left to right and the landing floorboard creaks right in the place I always hop over because I know it creaks and why didn't I pay more attention? If it's possible to hold my breath even more than I already was, that is what I do.

'Hang on,' he says so I lean back out of sight, letting my breath go as carefully and quietly as I possibly can before I pass out. He seems to wait, before hushed tones start again, this time I can barely make out a word but I daren't move again and give my game away.

What the hell am I doing? I'm ice cold with a too small towel barely wrapped around me. My hair's in a turban and I'm straining to hear, to get an inkling of what's going on instead of just going and outright asking him. Asking why his side of the bed was cold when I got up, what time did he get up? He never gets up before me normally. I thought about going downstairs to find him and try and have it out, but I'm due in work and if Tom gets in the shower before me, there'll be no hot water left. When I got out of the shower, I could hear Alex talking so I stood in the bathroom, straining to listen, wishing the fan wasn't so loud, wondering if Tom was down there with him. When it was clear he was alone, I turned into one of those wives who checks mobile phones and stalks their husbands, just in case. And now I have even more questions for him. His voice grows louder again so I lean a little further over the bannister in an attempt to pick out more words. 'I just don't know how to, I don't know what to say.' *About what?* I want to scream.

'Mum, have you finished in the bathroom?' Tom pads sleepily out of his bedroom.

'I've got to go,' Alex whispers.

'Erm, yes, love. I'm done. Morning.'

Tom looks at me weirdly, like it's not normal for me to be leaning over the bannister of a morning. Listening in to his dad's phone calls. He didn't know that's what I was doing, which I guess makes the sight even more perplexing. Shit. Does Alex suspect I've heard? What's he going to say? Tom's here, we can't have this conversation whilst Tom's here, can we? We've always tried not to row in front of him, apart from that one time we fell out about an unnecessarily high phone bill back when we were skint and I screamed at him all the way around town because I was so bloody angry. I like to think Tom doesn't remember, though that's probably wishful thinking.

'I was just…'

I twist round to open the airing cupboard, pretending the sudden movement doesn't hurt my ankle. I rifle through towels and sheets as Alex comes up the stairs. 'Nope. Not in there. Sorry, what were you saying?' Alex opens then closes his mouth. 'Tom's in the shower,' I say, meaning it to sound like I'm just letting him know so he doesn't try and use it, as opposed to, don't start talking to me about this whilst our son is in the house. Either way, Alex doesn't respond. He just looks at me, saying nothing. 'I've got to get ready for work.'

He follows me into our bedroom and starts getting dressed himself. Another unusual sight. Through the reflection in my mirror I can see him. His face may be older, and his body softer, but I still love it. I still love him. I still want him, even if it *has* been months. I mean, not in a rip his clothes off kind of way, just in a we still love each other after all these years, kind of way. Which I appreciate is perhaps not as passionate or exciting as the kind of sex he could probably get off the flicky-haired woman, but it still counts, doesn't it?

'Alex…' I say, towel drying my hair, pulling my uniform out of the cupboard. He grunts, which I think is supposed to be a response. 'Where did you go?' I ask, quietly. He stops dressing with a sigh, his jumper just pulled over his stomach. 'I just want to know where you went?'

'Does it matter?' He stuffs his hands in his pockets, unable to hold my eye.

'Of course it matters!' Just like that time when I screamed at him about the phone bill, I can feel frustration seeping in. That sort of acid build up in your bones where everything hurts and you want to lash out. Tom sings loudly in the shower and though he's tone deaf, it's a useful reminder to keep a hold of myself. 'It matters to me,' I say, my voice low. 'You just went, you never said where or for how long. You've been so… distant these last few months, I didn't know if you were okay even. You could have done anything, gone anywhere, how would I have known how to help?'

'I didn't want your help.'

'I rang round after you, nobody seemed to know. Most people said they'd not heard from you in months, Alex. What's going on?'

'You checked up on me?' For the first time since he got back, he looks me dead in the eye without breaking contact.

'I was worried. I still am worried!'

'You needn't have been.' He drops down on the bed to put his socks on, pausing as if he's going to say something before carrying on.

'You just upped and went.'

'You don't trust me.' It wasn't a question.

'Can you blame me?' He twitches so I lower my voice again. 'Christ, Alex. You sent me a message that was meant for someone else! Something about feeling stuff you've not felt in years, I mean, what even was that? Then you came home and said we need to talk. I tried to be affectionate and you outright rejected me. What the hell am I supposed to think other than something bad? Something's up and I need to know, I have every right to know. I'm your wife, Alex. I'm…'

'I went to see an old mate. Up in Scotland. He runs a pub in Dunblane.'

'Which mate? Which pub!'

He sighs, standing. 'It was Wigsy. Okay? Remember him? Richard Wiggins. I went to see Richard Wiggins.'

'Wigsy?' I remember him, he moved away years ago. We were just kids. 'I didn't know you were still in touch?'

'Yeah, well. Twitter.'

I let out a hollow laugh.

'What?'

'Nothing.'

Fucking Twitter. His entire life has revolved around hashtags and @mentions for months. Maybe I've been getting this all wrong, maybe I should have just tweeted him. *Hey Alex, is our marriage on the rocks? #divorce#sad #yourebeingapainintheass.*

I ruffle my hair as dry as the towel will get it, no longer caring about the need to take more time and care, ramming it into a wet, messy bun instead… which is promptly pulled loose when I pull my work jumper over it. Nor could I give a shit.

'I'm going out,' he said, walking out of our room.

'Well, there's a novelty,' I say, under my breath, because I'm not actually feeling as brave as my flippancy suggests. I ram my legs into my trousers, so cross that I could cry, but actually I could cry because I'm not just cross but frustrated and frightened and what the hell is happening to us? I drop down onto the bed, reaching for a tissue to bury my face into as I go but as I sit down, I sit on something sharp in my handbag which hurts my bum and that makes me cry even more out of sheer frustration. I lift up just enough to set it free and see the edge of the notebook, which is now slightly squished, was the offending item. Accident or karma? I open it up and find a page to read as if giving two fingers to the universe.

Chapter Thirty-Eight

My love,

We were never meant to be apart. It hurt the first time and it hurts just as much now. Together, I always felt stronger. Like I could take on the world, like we'd win no matter what because it was me and you. And yet, here we are. Miles apart; emotionally, physically, psychologically.

We were always a team. We could always work through even the hardest of times, at least, that's what I always believed. If we couldn't talk, or listen, if the subject matter was too big for us to discuss, we could at the very least hold one another and our hearts would know.

I don't remember when that changed. When you were too far out of reach. And sometimes, things said can never be unsaid and that is the worst part of it all.

If I could, I'd reach out now. I'd hold you as you've held me and you'd know. And that, my love, would be enough.

From,

The love you wished I could be.

Chapter Thirty-Nine

The bus came up the hill. Geoff heard it before he saw it. He stood at the back of the lounge, every part of him wanting to get on it and run away and every sense of him making him stay. If anything were to happen, Connie would definitely be taken from him. She hated that home, he could tell. She'd been a ghost, since waking this morning. She'd barely spoken to him. She held herself tightly together, sitting primly at the breakfast table. Whatever had been left of her last night, appeared not to remain this morning. Geoff held on to every hope that she'd reappear. But each day her moments of lucidity grew shorter, and further and further between, and he knew at some point they'd go altogether. Hands clasped before his cereal bowl, he had prayed that today wasn't that day. So even though it was Tuesday, and no matter how much he needed to go to church, to sit in his pew and take in the room, the spirit, the atmosphere, no matter how much he felt he needed to top up his spiritual battery, he knew he had to stay at home more, just to make sure that he didn't miss it if she did come back. He'd never forgive himself if he missed it. She had to know he was still there and so he would be. For every moment she needed him.

The bus pulled up. Geoff sat down.

The engine ticked over and he could imagine Helen looking, waiting. James might be too. Gazing out of the window in expectation that Geoff would appear. There'd been times she'd had to wait before, and she had, without question. The bus rumbled. It kept rumbling. The latch on their gate creaked and within seconds there was a knock at the door. The bus engine still hummed. There was a second knock. Geoff didn't answer.

'Geoff? It's me, Helen, is everything okay?' She must have her face pressed up against the door, trying to get her voice through the crack. She knocked again.

'There's someone at the door,' said Connie.

'It's fine,' said Geoff. 'It's fine.' He closed his eyes. He waited for the bus to pull away. Except the next sound he heard was the front door opening then he felt the rush of cold air. 'Connie!' he said, pulling himself up.

'Geoff, you're there. I'm sorry to…' Helen peered into the house. Her face was flushed, she took a step onto the threshold, holding the door open as Connie wandered off back to her seat. 'Morning, Connie,' Helen chirped. Connie just sat back down.

'Is she okay?' she asked, and Geoff waved her back onto the top step.

'She's fine. She's just… I'm not getting the bus today. Sorry to have kept you. You've no need to call for me.'

'Sorry, Geoff. We were just worried about you. It's not like you to miss so many days and I just wanted to make sure that you were okay, that you didn't need anything. James was concerned, too.' Geoff felt a bit bad because Helen's bottom lip had seemed to wobble at his rejection of her concern but he wasn't able to change that now. 'I can pop to the shops if you like, pick up a few things? I could drop them off later, on my way home. You've only to ask.'

'I'm fine. We're fine.' He motioned to Connie who sat with her back to them both. 'We don't need anything, thank you. Maybe I'll see you tomorrow. Or Friday, perhaps. Bye for now.'

Helen nodded, looking over to Connie, her face etched with concern. Geoff smiled but closed the door on her, locking it shut and hiding the key from Connie's view. This was their home, their sanctuary. Nobody would come in unless he wanted them here. And today, he wanted nobody except the one person who seemed impossible to reach.

When did he lose the fight? The will to face things head on instead of hiding at home? The fight that saw him survive as a prisoner of war. The fight that brought him home with heart and soul intact, if a little dark. When did he become a man that locked his wife in their home and lost battles with the authorities? With his daughter? The man whose wife was being taken away and the man who, if everyone else had their way, would soon become nobody?

The letter said she'd have everything she needed. But it didn't answer what he'd have. Perhaps nobody had thought to even ask the question. Who was he, if Connie wasn't there? What was his purpose, if not to care for her? She had taught him how to be a husband, a father. He owed her everything. He would not let her down, no matter what anybody else thought.

Chapter Forty

I run back on to the bus. 'Sorry, sorry. Sorry to keep you everyone, I just wanted to make sure Geoff was okay.' I look back up to his house, then through the rear-view mirror. A few people nod as I pull away. One woman looks at her watch, lips thin, disapproving. I bite my tongue.

'Is he all right?' asks James, unsteadily moving to the front of the bus.

'I don't know.' I buckle back up and pull away. 'Connie opened the door, didn't say anything, just went back to sit down. It's so unlike her, she was always so thrilled to see me when I've been round before. Would invite me in. Would pull me in for a hug. There was nothing, it was like she didn't know who I was. And Geoff... well, he just seemed... flustered.'

'Hmmm...' James links his arm through the pole beside me. 'Something's no' right there.'

'I guess not, but what?'

James is deep in thought, watching behind us through the wing mirror. 'I don't know. Flustered, you said? It's no' a mood I'd associate wi' Geoff. He's no' as chatty these days, either. Don't you think? I mean, he chats. But... it's different somehow. There's a guard up, a sort of invisible shield. I don't feel like he's at ease.'

'Maybe he's just not in the mood, James.' Right now, I know how he feels. Giving James a free ride is something I've never questioned before now and though I feel bad about it, I have to admit that his chat is irritating me this morning. Too harsh? Probably. Irritating isn't the right word. It's not him, it's definitely me. Maybe that's how Geoff feels. About chatting to James, and me rocking up on his doorstep just now. It was well intentioned, I just had that overwhelming panic that if I didn't make sure he was okay he'd be lying on the floor of the lounge, or at the bottom of the stairs, or they'd both be ill or... I don't know. It was all probably a thinly veiled attempt to make myself feel better by doing something good for someone else, and that he didn't need it nearly made me cry and says more about my emotional state than it does his needs... or lack thereof.

'Go on, sit yourself down. There's a sign,' I point. 'Don't interrupt the driver.' I wink at him and he eyes me suspiciously. 'What? Go on, let me concentrate.'

He does as I suggest slipping into one of the seats up the back for a change. I swallow, as I have been all morning, trying to dislodge the paracetamol I took when I got downstairs this morning. It feels like it's stuck in the back of my throat and I keep trying to work it down my chest with the heel of my hand. Which, actually, is pretty much how life feels this morning. From forcing wet legs into my trousers to stalling the car twice at the lights and some bloke looking at me like, oh, typical woman. Yeah, well. I flipped him the bird and I think that's all he needed to know on that front.

'Morning, Janet, how are you?' At least I can fake chirpy bus driver.

'Yes, good thanks. You?'

'Yeah, not bad. Off to look after the grandson?'

'Yeah.'

'Lovely.' I paint on the smile and I don't think Janet notices. And nobody can see that everything in my body aches, despite stuck paracetamols, from a long night perched on the edge of a mattress because it hurt each time mine and Alex's bodies touched and he flinched. Despite hanging around for as long as I could, to the point where I actually started opening and closing cupboards for no reason, it seemed Tom was in no hurry to go to work and I couldn't hang around and wait for Alex to get back from wherever he went off to. And I'm on a split shift today, so I'll be home late. By which time I'll be too tired to talk and he'll no doubt be asleep if recent months are anything to go by.

James keeps looking at me with suspicion, so I smile super wide and bright, which after a while gives me aching cheeks; I suspect I may be trying too hard. I even smiled super wide when James pointed out the fact that as we passed the stop Martin usually gets on, he was, in fact, climbing into an old Ford with some young woman who was, in James' words, very pretty indeed. I caught sight of him through the rear-view mirror, sadly she'd already got in the car, and smiled widely through the butterflies that leapt to attention on spotting him. Apparently she was blonde. In her early twenties. Good. Excellent. Much more his age. Quite right too.

I pull up to the terminus; pretty much everyone gets off, with the obvious exception of James. I roll the destination sign to Out of Service for a moment and reach into my bag for my phone. Alex and I need to talk. I've read about this sort of thing, meeting on neutral territory is advised. I can't wait until this evening and besides, Zoe says there's a new chef at The Potting Shed and the chilli is on point. Alex loves a chilli.

Are you free for lunch? If so, meet me at The Potting Shed, 1.30. X

For the first time in months, Alex texts back straight away. *See you there.* I try to ignore the fact there's no kiss, it's swings and roundabouts at the end of the day. So, lunchtime it is then. Just three and a half hours to go. I roll the destination sign back round and ping open the doors to a waiting queue of passengers. 'On you get. In you come. Bitter out there, isn't it? Mind yourself. Do you want a hand with the pram?' Faking it till I make it.

Chapter Forty-One

My love,

For years, I suspect it was all about me. All about my life and my choices. I think you slipped in alongside, going about our lives quietly, methodically, letting me be me. Accepting. Encouraging. Were you happy? Or did you dutifully comply? That's what I sometimes wonder. Did I notice if you needed me? I can't remember, which perhaps gives me your answer. Were there times when you hurt? When you cried? Were there times when you wished I'd notice something you did or said? I fear there must have been. In those early days, I blame youth for my lack of awareness. Nowadays, I don't blame anything because blame changes nothing. Forgiveness, that's what changes things. Finding a way to forgive myself because I knew no better. Because my behaviour was learnt, was a product of circumstance. I take responsibility, I do, but if you can't change an outcome, if too much has happened, then the only route you can take is forgiveness.

I was a product of the man before me and the man before that. I was the outcome of upholding tradition and stiff upper lips. I was, and perhaps on some level still am, shaped by the world in which we live. A society that expects us to behave in certain ways, to be certain kinds of people. Some manage it without a problem, as if they've never questioned the role they need to play. None of it ever felt right to me and yet I had no idea how to speak up, how to make a change. So I didn't. I didn't communicate at all. I showed no flexibility. I walked the line that was expected and I'm certain that's what ruined us.

If you said it now, I'd hear. So I'm listening.

From,

The love you wished I could be.

Chapter Forty-Two

Well, I'm not sure I've ever experienced three hours that dragged more than the last three. When I jump out of the bus and hand the keys to Denny, I run to the customer toilets at the shopping centre. The looming doom feeling in my chest makes me wonder if this is a bad idea, but it's too late to turn back and we need to talk so I've just got to hope that neutral territory is the right way to go. But what if we sit down and talk and he tells me he has met someone else and does want a divorce and I have to get back on the bus in two hours' and pretend like life hasn't just pulled the rug from under me? I told James to wait for me later so I have to go back to work.

I try and stare at my face in the mirror but it's one of those plastic mirrors, which are basically useless and no amount of wiping it with the sleeve of my jumper makes it better. I try wiping my face in any case and even though the mirror's rubbish I can still see the bags under my eyes. Bags that are definitely not wipe-off-able. I dig around in my ancient make-up bag for some colour to add to my cheeks. I try to unclog the mascara wand and wonder if I can remember when I last bought a new one. With a bit of pumping and wiping, and a few choice words, I manage to get enough on the brush to cover my lashes a little. No such luck with my powder, which has been knocked about so many times, it's now a collection of tiny porcelain pellets that drop down the sink.

I bet she wears make-up.

I pull the hairbrush through split ends and flick it about a bit but it's limp and lifeless. Aren't we all, I want to say, but shove it in a ponytail instead.

Right, it's half past one. I jog out of the shopping centre and over the road. I don't want to keep him waiting. I stick my head inside The Potting Shed doors in case he's gone in already. Maybe he's picked out a table by the window because he knows that's where I like to sit. But there's no sign, indoors or out. Huddling my coat around me, I lean against the wall outside and wait.

And wait.

And wait.

1.50 p.m. and there's still no sign. Maybe I should call him. Perhaps he's got stuck in traffic, it is pretty bad at the moment and he doesn't have the luxury of a bus lane. His phone rings out, no answer. I check inside again, maybe he'd gone to the loo when I looked before. Or was hidden by something or someone. But I think I know in my heart that he's not coming. I try his phone again, leaving a message this time.

'It's me. Are we still meeting for lunch? I'm here… I'm waiting.'

I send a text message. I drop my phone into my pocket then pull it back out again.

2.15. I've watched people come and go. I've been looked at, pityingly, presumably because it looks like I've been stood up. Which I suppose I have been, but he said he was coming. He agreed. He texted within seconds of me texting him. Is he taking the piss? Or was that text not meant for me either?

My phone rings and my heart leaps until I see it's Vicky. 'Hey, love, sorry to bother you but I was just talking to one of the other teachers and we thought about taking the kids over to Salts Mill and wondered if you guys still did the private bus hire? And, if so, can we put you in as our designated driver?'

'Vicky, hi, erm… I think we are, but I don't think I could drive for you. I tend to stick to the timetable driving these days.'

'Oh, shame. Still, no worries. I'm sure the other drivers are as lovely as you.'

'Yeah.'

'Wait, what? No come back about you being the loveliest of them all? What's up?'

A couple huddle together, giggling, as they wander into the pub and I feel that pang of jealousy that I used to get as a kid, before I found true love. Or the nudge of hope when I'd see Connie and Geoff in their garden, pottering around with their own tasks, coming together every now and then to talk about something, to show one another something, to sit in the sun on the bench they had that was two seats connected by a small table, a pot of tea for two in the middle. When a love like theirs was all I ever wanted. 'I'm fine,' I tell Vicky. 'Just distracted, that's all. I'm on a splitty and I've loads of jobs to do before I pick the bus up again. You need to call the office, let me text you the number.'

'Sorry, love. Don't worry, I can google it. Are you sure you're okay? Just distracted, not… having a bad day?' she asks, gently. 'Have you heard from Alex?'

'He's… back.'

'Oh, well that's something.'

'Yeah, it's all fine. Great, look I need to go. Give the office a call, any problems, let me know, okay?'

'Okay, bye love.'

I hang up, checking there's been no message or call whilst I was on the phone, then groan at the fact that I spend so much time waiting for a message. For him to talk. For him to show any sign that our marriage can survive whatever the hell is going on right now. My life revolves around my husband's. A husband who can't be arsed to come and meet me for lunch despite telling me he would. A husband who— 'Martin!'

'Helen.'

'Hi.' That familiar puce shade creeps up my neck again so I pull my coat up to my chin.

'Hi.'

His face spreads into a cheeky grin. It's boyish and makes my belly do a weird flippy thing and then I realise it's Alex he reminds me of. When we were young and he used to give me a cheeky look across a room, a wink and a promise of something clandestine when we were alone. It always made my belly flip.

'We missed you on the bus,' I say, searching and failing to come up with something casual.

'You missed me, eh?'

'Well, I say missed… I mean, we… I noticed you weren't on it.'

'No. I got a lift.'

'Right, yes, the pretty blonde.' He gives me a weird look, which is probably fair enough as it does sound as though I was stalking him. 'That's how James described her.'

'It was my brother's girlfriend.'

'Oh, right? I didn't see. Nice.'

'She's all right.'

'Lovely.'

He's waiting for me to say something else and I'm waiting for him to leave. Neither of us moves though. 'I was just waiting for my husband,' I say, motioning to the pub. 'We were going to go for lunch.'

'Okay.'

'Well… it would have been if I hadn't been stood here for almost an hour, waiting.'

'Not okay.'

'Yes.' And before I can stop myself, I say. 'Drink?'

And before I can change my mind, he says, 'I'd love to.'

And before I know what I'm really thinking or doing, I've walked into The Potting Shed with Martin and feel a flush of excitement about the fact. Followed by a shade of, this isn't a good idea, which is quickly replaced by, fuck it – if Alex can, why can't I?

Chapter Forty-Three

My love,

It wasn't temptation as such, so much as distraction. It was something different. Something to avoid the reality. Something to make me feel like a man. And as we talked, I had that voice in my head that said I shouldn't do it. That this was the lowest common denominator. That I shouldn't be such a cliché and yet, when I made her laugh, it felt good. I hadn't heard you laugh for a long time. Not with me, at least. I don't suppose there was much to laugh about and yet I couldn't bear to admit that I had a role to play in that sadness, in you tiptoeing around me. I would hear myself being short with you and I'd wonder why I couldn't just pause, breathe, start again.

I always thought I'd be the first to share the things that worried me. It seems, that's not the case. Because what you see, and what you think you see, are never one and the same. And it's this tiny detail that can drive people apart. I guess we know that better than anybody.

From,

The love you wished I could be.

Chapter Forty-Four

'I'm not going to get through this afternoon's shift without food by the way. So, er…' Martin smiles and nods, browsing the menu, whilst the girl taking our order patiently waits. 'One of my best mates says the chilli con carne is really good. Do you like chilli? I love chilli. I think their burgers are pretty good too though and, oh look, mac'n'cheese.'

Martin's smile has evolved to an amused grin as he stares at me fawning over what is a lovely but fairly standard menu. There's a pause as he waits to see if I've finished before eventually saying, 'Yes. I like chilli. And burgers. I'm less keen on mac'n'cheese after my mum force fed me the tinned stuff when I was a kid.'

'Force fed you!'

'Not literally.' He laughs. 'It just seemed to be at every meal I ever ate and now, like when you've been sick from drinking whisky or something.'

'Bacardi, in my case.'

'Right, so I'm like that with mac'n'cheese.'

'I see.' He's staring at me and still has an amused grin and I wonder if it's too late to get up and leave because I'm clearly out of my depth, but the girl is still waiting for my order and now I don't want to seem rude. And unlike most people who go off food in a crisis, my hunger escalates. 'A chilli and an elderflower pressé, please.'

The girl nods, turning her attention to Martin. 'A chilli and a Coke. Cheers.' He's giving her his order but looking directly at me. Eyes fixed. Burning a hole in my confidence. 'And I shall blame your friend if it's crap.'

The waitress takes our menus having committed our order to memory, which I've always hated. 'Why can't they just write it down?' I say, picking at the serviette that's in front of me. Fiddling with the condiments, putting them in an orderly line. 'It's lunch, not a memory competition!'

'Wow, you're quite the control freak.' He grins, hovering a hand over the ketchup before moving it slightly. 'Does this unsettle you?'

'What? No! It's just lunch and a drink, why would that unsettle me?'

'I meant my moving the ketchup.'

'I was joking.' I cringe. 'And no, it's fine. No problem at all. I'm absolutely not a control freak.' Alex preferred to call me Lady OCD when he opened a cupboard to find all labels on cans pointing outwards. Or found I'd moved the toilet paper so it unravelled the right way (over the top of the roll). I won't mention that. 'One man's control freak is another man's efficient.'

His eyes glint and I wonder again, what the hell I'm doing here. Less than two minutes in and I'm embarrassed... and a teensy bit irritated by the condiments. I cross my arms to stop me moving anything back in line. I should never have suggested this. I should ask him to leave. He's looking at me with an intensity I can barely stand. 'What?'

'What do you mean, what?'

'You're looking at me.'

'We're sat opposite each other. We're having lunch together. And I like looking at you.'

'Are you taking the mick?'

'One man's mick-taking is another man's flirting,' he says and I'm relieved the girl comes back with our drinks.

'You should be flirting with people your own age. I must be old enough to be your mother.' Why did I say that? What am I doing? Why does it feel a teensy bit exciting? Who am I?

'I'm sure you're not old enough to be my mother. What are you? Thirty?'

'Now you ARE taking the piss!' I laugh, in spite of myself. 'Smooth. Very smooth.'

'What?' He sips at his drink, not taking his eyes off me. 'Go on then. How old are you?'

I stare right back, surprising myself with a brazenness that Zoe would be proud of. I wonder if he's on Tinder? 'I'm thirty-eight.'

'Well, as I told you before I'm twenty-eight so unless you were a really early starter, I'd say you're very definitely not old enough to be my mother.'

'Well, okay, no. It seems not.'

'So that's that worry solved.'

'Worry? It was never a worry.'

'Not to me.'

Oh God. The brazenness is subsiding. 'Look, Martin. This isn't… this was a bad idea. I mean, it's flattering – really, it is. It's nice to feel… well, anyway, the thing is, it isn't going to go anywhere. I'm married.'

'I know, you said that. But in my defence, you don't wear a ring so I had no idea. I was hook, line and sinkered before you dealt that bitter blow.'

I rub at my ring finger; the indentation has almost gone. 'I lost it. Months ago. I mean, it must be in the house somewhere I just…' I trail off because there's a sudden sad feeling in my belly. 'Anyway, as far as I'm aware the ring is merely a symbol and not something that annuls the paperwork the second I take it off.'

He flexes the muscles in his jaw like Alex used to and I find something interesting in the serviette again. 'True, but – and forgive me asking – but if you're married, why are we here?' He stares at me. His deep green eyes penetrate my bravado and it makes me feel desperately uncomfortable. And a little bit silly. And a teensy bit hot. Serviette for a fan? 'I mean, I'm not being funny, but if you really weren't interested at all, why are we having lunch? Because, from where I'm sat, this is nice. And you seem to be enjoying it, which – for the record – so am I.'

'You're enjoying having lunch and banter? Banter with a married woman.'

'A married woman whose husband, I think you said, stood her up.'

Our food is placed down before us. 'Here are your chillies, can I get you both any sauce with that? Mayo? Ketchup? Any more drinks?' The girl, all smiles, is particularly taken with Martin, who is still looking at me and still flexing his jaw muscle.

'No, no, thank you. I think we're fine. Aren't we? Yes. We're fine.' The girl nods and walks away. 'This was a bad idea,' I say, prodding my food with my fork.

'Looks like pretty good chilli to me,' he says. 'Your mate was right.'

'No, I mean, this. You and me having lunch. You're right, I was stood up. And you're right, there are aspects of this that are quite nice.' He cocks his head to one side so I take a bite of my food. 'Like the chilli, the chilli is, as you say, pretty good.' I stick a massive forkful of food in my mouth, which makes him laugh. I swallow it back, preparing another forkful. 'Look, we're here now. It would be wasteful to leave the food. It's just lunch. That's it, lunch. Don't overthink it.' And neither will I.

'Just lunch.'

We start eating. I can't work out if it's an awkward silence that descends or if he is one of those people who is happy to be quiet when in the company of an almost stranger. And I can't work out what the hell he sees in me, or why I thought it was okay to do this. Or why he is still flirting when he knows I'm married, or why I am enjoying it even though he clearly has no morals and I don't approve of that kind of thing. Which means I don't approve of myself or what I'm doing either. 'Shit!' I throw my fork down.

'What?'

'This is ridiculous.'

'What is?'

'This. Me. It's all ridiculous.' He puts his fork down, leaning on the table. His arms remind me of Alex's when we were kids, before things got softer. Before he stopped putting them around me. 'Christ, I was so bloody cross with my husband for not being here when he told me he would be that when I saw you, I thought I'd get back at him because—' I stop myself.

'Because?'

'Because I think he's having an affair.' Martin raises his eyebrows. 'Because I think our marriage might be over and I don't know what to do about it, and I'm sorry, Martin, this is massively inappropriate and you really don't deserve to be played with like that.'

He leans forward, moving his hand so it brushes against mine. 'Maybe I don't mind being played with,' he says, his voice low and, irritatingly, unnervingly sexy. 'I mean… maybe it would be good for you.'

Jesus I'm out of my depth here. 'Martin, please…' He pulls his hand back but is still watching me and, fuck, it's hot in here. 'I should pay for these, then leave.'

He narrows his eyes a little, flexes his jaw, then reaches for his coat. 'Look, I'm teasing. And clearly this is not okay. I'll go, if you feel that bad. Please, don't leave on my account, eat your lunch.' He pushes his food away makes to leave then leans closer to me, searching out eye contact, which is making my stomach flip, hard. I brace my hands on the table before me. 'If you aren't sat here thinking *what if, maybe, just possibly…* then I'll go. If you aren't remotely attracted to me, I'll go. If you haven't once thought about what it might be like to…' He chooses not to finish his sentence, just moves his hands back, slipping his fingers between mine. 'Then I'll go.' I swallow hard. 'I like you, Helen. A lot. I think you're sexy, like, really fucking sexy. You have no idea how hot you make me feel. You sit there, biting your lip, your cheeks flushed. And I can't help imagine what it might be like to—'

'Stop! Jesus Christ, Martin. You've got to stop.'

'Because?'

'I'm married. And you're… God… okay. I admit it, you do make me feel all sorts of things I thought might have been dead. I've been married forever, it happens. And yes, I am attracted to you, you're a good-looking bloke… and I don't know why you are attracted to me, but that's… well, it's nice. More than nice. It's… but I shouldn't have… I'm probably hormonal. You see… you don't need that. You need one of those young girls in that group over there, the ones that have been looking at you since you walked in.'

'They're not as hot as you.'

'Shit!' I pull at my jumper, pushing my food away, now – and possibly for the first time in my life – not remotely hungry. 'I shouldn't have led you on, however much I might like to… Well… my friend says I absolutely should have sex with you just to brighten my day…' And as I say those words, that last sentence, I realise Alex is stood in the doorway. 'Oh no! No!' I'm hot under the collar, clammy and cold and a little bit sick in my stomach. I. jump up but before I can go after him, Alex has spun on his heel and gone. 'Sorry, Martin, I'm sorry… oh shit.' I get up, grabbing my bag and coat and chase out the door after my husband.

Out in the fresh air, winter sun suddenly low and bright in my eyes, I squint up and down the street, straining to see through the rays. 'Alex!' I shout. But I can't see him. And when I dial his number, his phone is switched off. Shit. What have I done?

Chapter Forty-Five

Val pottered around the lounge, tickling the duster over ornaments, making small talk with Connie. Connie had no idea who she was or what she was doing there and watching her fake it made Geoff desperately sad. He needed fresh air, he needed respite. He hated the fact that she'd only been back five minutes and he was already struggling.

'I think I might just pop up to the post office,' he said, standing, stiffly. 'I wanted to send some money over to our Rosemary's account for some bits of shopping she's been doing over the last few visits.'

Connie looked up and smiled.

'Are you here for a bit longer, Val?' he asked. 'Would you mind stopping with Connie 'til I get back?'

'Of course, that's fine. I was going to sit down and have a cuppa with her anyway, wasn't I, Con?'

Connie looked up and smiled again. 'Rosemary said she'd have a tea with me,' she said.

'Val,' he corrected.

'Pardon?' asked Connie.

'That's Val. It's Val who said she'd have a tea with you.'

'That's what I said.'

Geoff nodded, Val mimed to him that it didn't matter. Connie continued smiling. 'Okay, love. I'll be back in a bit.'

'Take your time, Geoff. No rush. It's a nice day for a walk, that winter sunshine is beautiful.'

'Thank you, Val,' he said, checking his pocket for wallet and change. 'I won't be long.'

Stepping out the front door, Geoff felt the fresh air nip at his fingers. He reached into his coat pockets for his tan leather driving gloves and adjusted his corduroy flat cap. It took him fifteen minutes to make the steady walk up the hill to the post office. There, he joined the queue, patiently waiting his turn. It was no problem to wait, in fact, the longer the better. More time to think about how he was going to defeat the people who wanted to put Connie in a home, yet survive the daily challenge of taking care of her.

Ruby, the postmistress, caught Geoff's eye at the back of the queue and smiled brightly at the sight of him and he smiled back. She stamped people's books, handed over their cash, chatted about the weather with those in the line before him. It reminded him of the days Connie used to work here, making small talk with the regulars, checking up on people's parents, children or grandchildren. He smiled at the memory of her empathetically patting a hand or offering to bring a spot of dinner round for the woman whose husband had left for another; or agreeing to pop in on the aunt of a woman who was going off to work away, just so she wasn't alone. He'd always thought the post office sat alongside the pub for defining local community. Connie had been the epitome of a postmistress, once upon a time.

'Morning, Geoff,' said Ruby through the glass, when his turn finally came.

He handed over his bank book. 'Good morning, can I transfer some money from my account into the one there, our Rosemary's. Fifty pounds, please.'

'Of course.' She stamped and made notes, then she tapped a polished fingernail on the touchscreen. 'You're looking well,' she chirruped.

'Thank you. A bit of a walk and some fresh air, it does us all the power of good.' Geoff reflected Ruby's tone and mood and felt how it lifted him. This was what he needed more of.

'How's our Connie?' Ruby asked, head cocked to one side with a look of sympathy he didn't want to see. He wanted to keep the image of her working happily behind the counter. He wanted to hold on to the positivity a bit longer. 'She's very well, thank you,' he said, picturing her at home reading a book, or pottering about in the garden. 'She sends her best.'

'What is she getting up to these days? What's keeping her away from us?' asked Ruby, tapping away. 'We haven't seen her for an age. I said that to Beryl the other day, didn't I, Beryl?'

Beryl looks up from pricing a tray of baked beans. 'Eh?'

'I was just telling Geoff how I'd only said to you the other day that we haven't seen Connie for an age, didn't I?'

'Oh yes, you did, Rubes, yeah,' she agreed, going straight back to her pricing. 'Bring her up to the pub, Geoff. It'd be lovely to have a natter over a ploughman's. We don't half miss her.'

They'd no more want to see the shell, the husk of a woman she'd become, than Connie would want them to see it. 'I'll mention it to her, she's enjoying a bit of a quieter time these days. We're getting on a bit, Ruby!'

'Away with you, you two won't ever get old. It's not in your make-up. Forever young, I've always thought that about you two, forever young.'

'Wouldn't that be nice,' he said.

'Give her our love, won't you?'

'Of course. Lovely to see you, Ruby. And you, Beryl.' Geoff took his bank book. He stepped back, bolt upright, a salute short of attention, nodding to both the women with a renewed sense of importance.

Outside, the sun still shone. Geoff looked at his watch. 1.30 p.m. He wasn't ready to go home. He wasn't ready to let go of his sense of identity, the normality. He wasn't ready to spend the afternoon watching old films with a stranger.

Over the road, Bill, the landlord at the East Morton Inn, wiped down the specials board. Noticing Geoff stood over the road, he threw him a wave. 'Afternoon.'

Geoff waved back, then crossed the road. Maybe he could make this last a little longer.

Chapter Forty-Six

Frantic, I look up and down the road, up and down again. There's no sign of Alex in any direction. What have I done? What was I playing at? Who do I think I am? This isn't me, this isn't how I behave. He looked so hurt.

Martin is settling the bill when I get back to the table. 'Please, let me,' I say, shoving my hand in my purse to pull out notes to cover the price of lunch. Change spills on the table and I scratch to pick them up, hands shaking.

'It's all paid for,' says Martin.

'Please, take this.' I offer a ten-pound note but he pushes my hand away.

'Look, keep it. Don't worry about it.'

'No, I can't. That's not fair. I'm sorry…'

'If you're that bothered, you can buy the next lunch.'

'What? No! There won't be a next lunch.'

'Shame. Though, I understand of course. Despite the fact that your husband seems a bit of a dick.'

'He's not a dick. He just walked in on me having lunch with another man whilst discussing the prospect of having sex with him?'

'Maybe he should ask himself why you feel the need to have lunch with another man. Never mind discuss the prospect of anything else.'

He fixes me with one of his looks again but the sensation of hot under the collar from before has completely iced over. This was so stupid. I am so stupid. 'I should probably get back to work,' he says.

'Yeah, me too.'

He puts his coat on, then pauses. 'Hey, I hope things get sorted between you two.' He pops his collar then turns to the door before offering a parting shot. 'And you know, I'm around if it doesn't…'

'It'll be fine.'

'Cool.'

Staring at the ground is easier than watching Martin leave. I go to sit back down, but the waitress comes to clear the half-eaten plates and I've lost my appetite anyway. My head is light and my stomach churns. What do I do now? I try Claire. She'll know what to do. But her phone just rings out. As does Vicky's. And Zoe's is switched off – she's probably high powering it in a meeting which means she'll come out all pumped up and ready to fix everybody's problem with expletive-laden platitudes, or she'll tell me I should have skipped the lunch bit and gone straight to dessert. I won't leave a message.

Why didn't I do what I normally do on a split shift and just hide at home for a couple of hours with a copy of *Glamour* and a Weight Watchers tomato soup? Tom would have been out, Alex and I could have talked. I could have asked all the questions I have, maybe I'd have had a chance to get through to him, to get to the bottom of what's going on, instead of making it worse. Why did I suggest lunch? Why did he agree only not to turn up? Or turn up late, anyway. Did I give him the wrong time? Maybe I said 2.30. Oh no, is this my fault? Again? I check my phone but I wasn't wrong. We definitely said 1.30 p.m.

And that sums everything up, really. I say one thing, he does, or doesn't do the next. Everything is up in the air, it's all questions. I'm guessing the answers because nobody's talking to me. I'm questioning Alex, I'm questioning me. And I'm so tired of it all. I'm tired of all the eggshell walking, the questioning. Maybe I'm tired of me and him. Maybe that's why he went away, because he felt the same. Maybe I should go too. Except that if I go, who brings in the money? Who pays the bills? And there I am, back on the hamster wheel. A hamster wheel that is making me want to cry again. I don't want to cry… I must not cry…

But I can't not.

Outside, a large cloud passes overhead, sucking up the weak winter sun. Glancing up the street this time, I can see everything. I can see the people, the life. The drivers in their cars. The shop workers. The birds up above. The Yorkshire stone beneath my feet. And I can feel everything too. The pain, the hurt, the unknowing, the knowing, the feeling of utter despair. I shiver inside my coat.

'You reckon it might snow?' says a voice from behind me and I wipe my eyes and face clear of the last hour and a half.

'Hey, James. How are you? It's getting cold.'

'Ah'm fine, built with Scottish grit. Girders. We don't feel the cold. I was going to take a little sit for a while, in the market square. The coffee truck's parked up, do ye want to come people-watch with me?'

'Oh… I don't know…'

'Come on, it's good fun. We can give people names and jobs and backstories. I just saw this woman, let's call her Helen-a,' he says, pointedly. 'She had this sad face and too much on her mind an' I cannae help but wonder about her backstory.' The last hour and a half creeps back on my face, tipping salty water out of my eyes. 'Come on, how about hot chocolate?' he asks, nudging me gently. 'A sugar rush can help.'

'No, it's fine. You go on, have you money? Shall I?' I reach into my bag for my purse but James touches my arm to stop me.

'Let me. A return for all those bus journeys.'

I feign a smile but I can feel its weakness. Not only does it not reach my eyes, it barely reaches the corner of my mouth and the salty water is now definitely tears and they're following the age creases down my face. 'James... what have I done?'

He puts my arm through his and leads me down to the market square. 'Sit there, love. I'll get the drinks in.' I drop onto one of the benches, exhausted. When he comes back, James passes me a cup complete with squirty cream and marshmallows delicately balanced on top. 'Here.'

'Thanks.' I sniff, picking a marshmallow off.

We sit quietly for a moment, each of us clasping our hands around the cups. A woman wanders past. She's trying not to look at James, but I can see her do so out of the corner of her eye.

'You sure you don't mind being seen with a vagabond like me?' he asks, licking at his cream, which inevitably takes up residence in his beard.

I shake my head. 'Vagabonds are cool,' I say, stirring the cream into my drink. 'They're gypsies and travellers. They're the knights of the road. They're the unexpected protagonists in books and films. Let's vagabond together,' I say. 'In fact, after the last few weeks I've had, I could do with skipping off into the sunset and just enjoying some anonymity for a few days. Weeks.'

'Well, I know it looks like I lead the life o'Riley, but believe it or no', it's really no' all that.'

He makes me laugh, which turns into one of those deep, heavy sighs that come up from your boots. 'Shitting hell, James.'

'What?'

'Adulting. It's hard.'

'Tell me about it. Ah've been faking it forever. Badly.'

He sips his hot chocolate and I do the same, allowing, if not enjoying, a moment of silence. A toddler breaks free from the old market square stocks where her mum was taking a photo. She wobbles past us, staring at James then me. Her mum hurries to catch her up, shielding her with her arm. It makes me wonder what she's shielding her from, what threat does she think James poses? Or maybe it's me. I give her a very British stare which I think makes her know that I've seen her judging and I do not approve. And then I remind myself I'm in no position for moral superiority.

'So, how are things with you?' I ask, desperate for diversion. 'Are you managing?'

'Aye, course I am. I always manage.' He grins. 'It's the rest of ye who don't.' His Glaswegian accent accentuates the O. I've always loved an accent.

'When did you move down here?'

'Ten years ago or so, my wife—'

'You were married?' I say, looking up sharply. Then wishing I hadn't because it's clear I'm surprised by the fact and I might as well go and stand with the toddler's mum in the judgy pants corner.

'Aye, fe twenty years. 'Til a few years ago, in fact. Let's just say that I didnae do it very well…' The paper cup looks tiny in his large hands as he too nurtures the warmth. The sky's hue of blue-grey has cast a darker shadow. Snow now definitely in the air. 'She was a nurse. We moved down so she could work at St James, with the Cardiac Team.'

'Wow, that's amazing.'

'She was.'

The shine in his eyes, the life, it briefly dissolves, leaving them black, empty like.

'I'm sorry,' I say. 'That must have been…' but I trail off because I realise I've no idea what happened or how it must have felt.

'I wish I knew then what I know now.'

'Hindsight, eh.'

'Aye.'

I gaze down at my cup, swilling it round to mix the remaining cream and hot chocolate with melted marshmallow, searching for what to say like I might find something profound in the tiny chocolate whirlpool I create. I want to ask him what happened. I want to know how he ended up here, travelling the bus for warmth, no wife to speak of.

'But ye didnae sit down here to talk about my life, did ye?'

I look up sharply. 'I didn't sit down here to talk to you about anything.' Then I sigh again. More heavily than before, like a really rubbish, noisy, sighing poker player.

James adjusts his position, leaning against the arm of the bench. 'I'm listening.'

Chapter Forty-Seven

'Busy lunch?' asked Geoff, watching as Bill wiped clean the blackboard that stood beside the entrance.

'Yeah. Really busy. New chef seems to be quite the hit though, so I've not much left if you wanted to eat?'

'Excellent news for you. Maybe I could trouble him for just a teacake?'

'I'm sure we can manage that, come on in.'

Although the pub hadn't allowed smoking for years, the faint smell of one form of tobacco or another lingered still. Or maybe Geoff was just confused with the thick, hoppy beer smells from the microbrewery out the back. A few lunchtime stragglers sat at cluttered tables of empty plates and glasses. Geraldine, the pub landlady, busied about collecting plates and chatting to the punters whilst expertly balancing plates and bowls up her arm.

Though the lights were on, small windows and a sort of orangey glow to the lamps made the pub feel dark. An atmosphere Geoff had always liked. It felt safe. Womb-like. It also cast a shadow over his face meaning he didn't have to work so hard to pretend he was okay.

'You're looking well. How's Connie?' asked Bill.

'Yes, she's good, thank you. You know, taking it steady, but she's fine.' Geoff scratched at a mark on his trouser leg, preferring not to make eye contact whilst telling his tales. 'Life pretty much happens around us these days, Bill.'

'Sounds quite nice.' Bill rubbed at the small of his back, sticking the clichéd landlord paunch out as he did so. 'Two years,' he said, straining almost as much as the buttons on his shirt. 'Two years, then I can hang up my beer barrels and sit in front of the telly. And it can't come too soon. Coffee with your teacake?'

'Lovely. Thank you.'

Bill rang it through the till and Geoff thought back to when he retired, was it really twenty-five years ago? More, even. What has he done with his time since then? What have he and Connie done together? He didn't really want to retire when the time finally came. Unlike Bill, Geoff hadn't counted the years and then days down. It had always felt rather like the beginning of who he was being stripped back. His identifiers being peeled, layer upon layer, until now there was little left. He'd replaced his career with helping out at the church. To Connie's frustration, he started taking over jobs at home too.

'Will Geraldine finish then too?' Geoff asked, wondering if Bill would get under her feet as he had Connie's.

'I expect so. She makes out she doesn't want to hand over the reins, but the new chef is a giveaway.' He put a coffee down in front of Geoff along with two creamers and two sugars. Geoff didn't take sugar and had said this to Bill many times before. *Only on a gooseberry*, he used to say, but as it never sunk in, he stopped bothering and just left the sugar on the side, handing over his money instead.

'Hope she's not giving up the roast dinners though yet?' said Geoff.

'Oh no, no. She'll keep doing that.' He leaned over the bar, conspiratorially. 'She'll just complain about it.'

'Who'll complain about what?' asked Geraldine, giving Bill a stern look as she dropped plates on the bar. She took out a cloth from the pocket of her faded blue tabard, watching and waiting for his answer.

'Oh nothing, love, just saying how nice it'll be for us to retire and spend some quality time together, like Geoff and Connie.'

'I'll bet that's just what you were saying.' She turned to look at Geoff. 'I am no fool and I've met my husband before. He will have been complaining about something I do or don't do the way he thinks I should or shouldn't do it. Bet you never complained about Connie like that, did you?'

Geoff remembered all the times he would complain. When he first retired and realised she wasn't washing the clothes on the right temperature, or following the instructions properly on their tea. He remembered how quietly cross she'd get that he was trying to correct her and how she'd hold back a huff or a puff as she walked into a room to find him there, during the daytime, when she was so used to him being at work and her having the house to herself. And as he now saw how much she might have censored herself over the years, the dementia ripping apart any notion of self-censorship, there was a tiny part of him that wished she still would. Or that, at the very least, her occasional outbursts of frustration would be because she had finally decided to say what was on her mind, instead of her mind forcing her to say it.

'Are you eating?' Geraldine asked.

'Teacake,' Bill said, handing her a chit with scribbled notes that she could perfectly read.

'You're going to have to write more clearly,' she chided.

'You can read that!'

'I know I can, but the kitchen staff won't be able to. I've told you, I'm not hanging around there just to translate your scribbles.' Geoff sipped at his coffee, enjoying the normality of their bickering. 'Oh, and can you call the bakers, Bill? I'm waiting on them baps for Dennis Robert's wake. We've got fifty open egg mayo to prep. Teacake coming up, Geoff.' And with that, she turned on a Clarks' wide-fit heel.

Bill gave Geoff a look, before heading off to do as he was told. Geoff nodded to a couple in the corner, took a sip of his coffee. He pulled a newspaper to him, flipping through the pages and, for this briefest of moments, it was like nothing had ever changed.

Chapter Forty-Eight

'You're listening? That's brave. Christ, I wouldn't know where to start.' I avoid James' gaze. My feet are like ice. The tip of my nose the same. 'It's fine. I'm fine. I…' My words trail off and we sit in silence.

James adjusts his position again, stretching his legs out before him. Eventually, he says, 'I don't have many regrets. I think they're a waste of time. They eat away at ye energy, they make ye look back when we should all be living now, being thankful, being open to what the future has in store.'

I bite down hard on my bottom lip because I have so very many regrets… and not just about all the years I willingly wore Crocs.

'But if I could change one thing,' he continues, 'it would be talking. I'd talk more. Which, believe it or not, is pretty ironic all things considered, but I guess it's easy when it's no' you.' My throat is raw and sore. The more he talks, the more I feel it unpicks me. 'But talking, definitely, that would be what I'd do different.'

'I don't like to put on people,' I say, quietly.

'Hmmm. We do that, human beings. We assume our woes will infect others. We assume it will make us weak. You know, when I felt I had nowhere to turn, when it all seemed so useless and pointless and without hope, I realise now that that is exactly the time I should have found the way to talk. To anyone, really.' I sniff. 'I dinnae blame past me, I just wish *now* me could go back and tell *past* me that to talk was no'a weakness.'

I nod. He nods back. Then he waits. I wipe my nose on my sleeve. I can feel the last few days, months maybe, bubbling in my belly. The fears and the frustrations. The lack of direction, the need to take over. The focus and the distraction. The need to search out answers from anything that isn't an actual human being who can give me their opinion. The notebook. The love they wished they could be...

'Alex lost his job. Ages ago. I guess that's maybe when things took a turn. When things got hard. I started doing extra hours, partly to bring in the money that would hold us together until he found work. Partly, maybe, to get out of the house because then I could ignore the fact that things weren't right.'

James sits patiently waiting. Listening. He doesn't look at me and I'm grateful for that.

'He stopped caring. It didn't take long, two months maybe. Two months of rejections and that was enough. He stopped caring and he stopped trying. He stopped looking at the job sites and applying for anything and everything like he did back in the first few weeks. He went into himself, we'd barely talk. I kept trying to encourage him. I wanted him to know I believed in him. That things would be fine. That the right thing would come up. But it's been hard, on me, all the extra hours. I've been tired, I'd get frustrated with him for not making more effort. And now I can see that he's not happy. I can feel it. He's even said we need to talk but we still haven't. We were supposed to today but...' Shame creeps over me. 'Well... it didn't work out. Because I was stupid and put the need to feel good about myself over the need to have patience and work out if there is anything I can do to sort things out. And I just want to know what's going on. I want to understand him. I want to save us because I don't want it to end. I don't want us to walk away then wish we hadn't tried harder, you know? When it's too late. When time has passed and we've learnt but we can't go back because life has moved on. You know?'

'I know,' says James, quietly.

'He won't let me in, James,' I continue, because I realise the floodgates have opened and I don't think I can stop talking now. 'He's shut down and I don't know what to do. And then he just walked in on me talking to someone about having sex with them.' James looks up. 'I mean, I wasn't actually going to and it's probably too much information, but it happened, and he heard it all wrong and I'm scared I've made things worse.'

'It's no' easy, when you've shut down. It takes more than anyone could know to pull yourself back from that.'

'I understand that, but I don't want us to split up, James. I don't want that. I keep reading these letters in this notebook I found, I keep reading it and it's like a snapshot into what might be. Into a future where I don't have Alex, or he doesn't have me and we're trying to put things right, but we can't because we've done too much damage. We're too far gone. It's the worst thing because whoever wrote it knows they've become the person the other one wanted, or that they're on their way at least, but there's nothing they can do, it's too late, and I don't want to be that couple, James. I don't want it.'

'No,' he says, sadly. 'I shouldnae think ye do.'

'It's so bleak. Reading all this hope that's wrapped up in sadness because for that person, it's too late. For that couple. They loved each other. It's clear to see that in the letters. They loved each other, and I don't think they made it and that makes me wonder how the hell Alex and I can make it because I don't even feel like he loves me any more. There's nothing to hang on to. There's nothing to work with. And that…' The pain in my heart overwhelms. 'That makes me feel devastated. Confused. Worried. It makes me feel unloved and unlovable because I've contributed to where we are at. And it makes me feel frustrated. And angry! God, I'm so angry.' I picture the look on Alex's face when he saw me in the restaurant with Martin. He's never looked at me like that. 'He's numb, James. And that is the worst state of all.'

'So what else do these letters in this notebook say?' James asks, sitting up, arms folded.

'All sorts. There was one in particular, about hindsight. God, it was so perfect.'

Chapter Forty-Nine

My love,

What gift is hindsight? It comes too late to be of service. It comes with insight that offers us little for the past and a bitter taste for a future we're too late to influence. And yet there it is, the obvious staring us down. You have to learn to live with it. Eventually, the stare, the taunts grow quieter. They're occasional thoughts, passing through. They become words of wisdom that may or may not be heard.

Whilst I live in the now, sometimes I'm reminded how much I would give for hindsight before the fact. What might have come of us had it been so? Could we have avoided the place we ended up?

That I will never know is the thing that I can't let break me, for me, for you, for the life we led and the life that's now on pause.

From,

The love you wished I could be.

Chapter Fifty

'And what do you think the hindsight might be?' asks James.

'I don't know. I don't know. And I can't keep reading because it hurts too much and I feel guilty and can you imagine, James? Can you imagine what the person who wrote these things might think if they knew I'd spent so much time with their secrets?'

'Maybe they're no' secrets.'

'Maybe.'

'Maybe there are answers within that you've just no' read yet.'

'Maybe.'

'Or Alex. Maybe Alex needs to read them.'

'Unless it's on Twitter, he reads nothing.'

'How did he cope with being out of work?'

I think back to the morning he called me to tell me what had happened. I had the day off and was wallowing in the bath with a book. It was something off the Booker Prize list because I thought I should expand my mind away from the kind of books I normally read, but I was getting really annoyed at the lack of speech marks and wished I'd just picked up a Marian Keyes, the kind of book I really wanted to read.

'He was devastated. He didn't know what to do. He kept saying he was sorry, that he'd find something, he'd be providing again before I knew it. I told him it was all going to be fine because I really believed it was.' I search in my bag for a tissue, the notebook at the bottom. I pause for a moment, my hands over it. 'I think, what I hadn't expected, was that it really knocked his confidence. I wasn't sure why at the time, it wasn't his fault. The company went into liquidation but he seemed to blame himself.'

'Some people get their identity from their work. To lose their job is to lose everything they believe they know about who they are.'

'But that's nonsense, we don't get ourselves from work.'

'Don't we?'

'Well, of course not! Our work is such a tiny part of who we are. I'm a bloody bus driver, for goodness' sake, there has to be more to me than that! He was then and is now, just the same as he ever was. The man I loved. Him being without a job doesn't change him, in fact, it shouldn't change anything.'

'Well, it changes something.'

'It changes money, I get that. It changes what he brings into the house, his contribution, but it's not like that defines him. It's not like he is who he is because of…' But I stop talking, because suddenly things are dropping into place. 'I mean, I don't care about any of that,' I say, feeling uncomfortable in my skin.

'*You* dinnae care?'

'No… I mean, who cares… we're a team. We get through the tough times. I've told him that. I've told him I don't care.'

'*You* dinnae care?' he says, again, more pointedly.

'No!'

'Perhaps this isn't about how *you* feel?' he says, gently, and I stare at him. 'I mean, of course, it impacts on you, but, and forgive my being so bold, I'm hearing you talk about how *you* feel. About how it doesnae matter te *you*.'

'Because it doesn't!' My determination to make this point is beginning to waver and I sound less and less convinced each time I open my mouth.

'Which is great. I mean, great that you're supportive in that way, but perhaps it matters te him. And perhaps, telling him it doesn't matter compounds how he feels.' James' voice is calm, thoughtful even. But his words pinprick my emotions. They make me feel uncomfortable. They make me feel defensive. He is saying everything I'd completely ignored and can now see with 20:20 vision. 'Do you talk?' he asks.

I sit up to face him. 'Of course we do! We've been together forever. I listen. I help. I offer solutions. I try my best, like we all do. I'm just not the sort of person to sit back and watch it all fall apart, you know? If he's having a rough time, I pick up the pieces, that's how teams work. When one is down, the other steps up. He'd do the same for me.' My voice verges on shrill. There's something in the pit of my belly that tells me I'm getting it wrong. Something in my heart makes me question the choices I've been making, even the ones before I'd got to lunch with Martin. The words I've been using, the way I've swooped in to solve it all.

'Living with a fixer,' he says, looking at me with dark eyes, all joy gone. 'Maybe…' He swills the last of his hot chocolate. He clears his throat. 'Maybe that's no' what he needs right now.'

Chapter Fifty-One

Geoff made the downhill walk from pub to home. The clouds looked ominous, the air was bitter. He'd stayed longer than he intended though not as long as he would have liked, especially considering Bill put the fire and the snooker on and there were very few reasons for Geoff to go home. But go home he knew he must.

The crows were cawing in the churchyard and he was reminded of his granddaughter's story about crows and graveyards, back when they'd walk hand in hand to the shop for a quarter pound of sherbet pips and a comic. *Don't let her eat them all at once*, Connie would say. And like any good grandpa should, he never passed on that message.

But the walk was harder today than it was back then. Each step was tougher, more breath-taking. A chilly breeze whipped up to suffocate his breath. Geoff paused at the pylon to capture a lungful of air, but his chest was tight and restricting. He'd just had two hours of pretending life was fine, of ignoring the worries, and feeling better for it. Joking with Bill, chatting with Geraldine. Exchanging pleasantries with Ruby and imagining those days when Connie was at the post office helm. It had all gone towards making life better for just a moment. It had lifted his heavy load and reminded him that there were still things in life for which he could smile. Yet as he made his way home, each step brought the stress back to his weary bones. The stress of not knowing. The stress of change. He'd never been good with uncertainty. He liked plans, formulas. He liked to know what was to come. And better still, he liked to be in charge of it.

By the time he got home, he could barely utter a hello to Val who had been looking out of the window, perhaps waiting for his long overdue return. 'Shall I put the kettle on before I go?' she shouted through to him, collecting her handbag and coat from the kitchen.

'Yes, please.' He coughed. Great big hefty coughs to re-line his lungs with breath.

'Oooh, Geoff, that sounds bad. Two sugars?' she checked, but this time, Geoff could only grunt. 'Shall I make one for Connie?' But Geoff had closed his eyes to concentrate. 'Ooh, Geoff, love. What's the matter?' she said, as she stood before him with worry etched across her face. 'You look a little peaky, love. Are you okay?'

Connie leant forward to see past Val. She smiled at Geoff. Geoff smiled back, then nodded. 'I'm fine, I'm just...' He whipped out a pressed handkerchief to wipe his brow. 'Something went down the wrong hole or something, fresh air, maybe... it can...' He paused to cough again. 'It can take your breath away, can't it?'

Val eyed him suspiciously. 'I suppose so, yes. Let me make that cuppa,' she said, not taking her eyes off him until she was through the kitchen door. He could hear the squeak of her slippers on the newly mopped lino. A few moments later, when she came back in, she popped the tea and biscuit barrel on the lampstand shelf beside him. 'Here, a bit of sugar might help,' she instructed, pointing towards the biscuits.

He reached for a digestive, dunking it in his tea before scooping it into his mouth. The salty, malty, sugary sogginess definitely helped. 'Thank you,' he said, breath slowly returning. Chest easing up.

'You need to take care, Geoff, if you don't mind my saying.' He looked at her. 'For Connie,' she said, quietly, motioning at Connie behind her. 'I don't wish to pry, but… well… maybe now would be a good time to get some extra help for you both. Or… maybe…'

'They already help me.'

'I mean properly, like I think they've suggested. I mean… they wouldn't offer her a place at the home if she didn't need it, love. They don't have that kind of money to throw around any more.'

'What do you know of what they've offered?'

'Well… only what Rosemary has said. And they obviously think it's the best and perhaps it's the best for you too?' She added that second sentence quickly so he wouldn't cut her off before she'd said her bit. Geoff and Connie had known Val for years. She was younger than them both, moved in across the road with her children just as their grandchildren started to come and stay. It was a long time ago. And neighbours become friends over time like that. But even still.

'I don't wish to discuss the matter, thank you.'

'I'm sorry, Geoff, I'm not meaning to pry. I know this is private, and I do respect that it's just that… Rosemary is worried. And we're none of us getting younger. And Rosemary would feel so much more comfortable if—'

'I didn't realise you and Rosemary kept in touch that way?'

Connie got up to fetch a newspaper then sat back down, putting the paper on the floor at her feet as if she'd finished reading.

Val lowered her voice. 'Well… she calls, from time to time. She worries. She's a long way from home and just wants to know you're okay.'

'We are fine. Now, thank you for your time, your money is on the side. This is my business. Mine and Connie's.'

'We care about you, Rosemary cares.'

'Goodbye.'

Val gave a shallow, and somewhat embarrassed, nod, before getting her coat from the kitchen, and placing her slippers back under the sideboard until her next visit. She paused at the front door. 'I didn't mean to overstep the mark,' she said. 'I apologise.'

Geoff reached for the remote control and the paper by Connie's feet. Val closed the door firmly behind her.

Chapter Fifty-Two

'You rang?' It's Claire. 'Sorry I couldn't answer. Clemmie was screaming because apparently, she's the only baby in the world to have ever had to wait for her formula to warm up in the microwave. Don't try that at home kids. Hot spots. I wouldn't mind, but if she hadn't rejected my tits, they'd be right there for her the second she decided she was about to die from hunger! Honestly, Hel, I'm in a puddle of hormones here. How the hell am I going to cope for the next eighteen years? She is NOTHING like the boys!'

'Oh, love!' I sniff, motioning to James that I need to talk to her. 'You're gonna be fine, you've been here before. You know this passes. It's all going to be okay!'

'It is, you're right, and I told myself that whilst eating my body weight in Caramac. I just can't believe how different she is. I mean, I don't want to stereotype, for all the obvious reasons, but I genuinely think girls might be higher maintenance than boys.'

'Ha! I'll remind you of that the next time you hashtag everyday sexism!'

'You're probably right. Anyway, enough of my whining. Why did you call? Are you okay?' I groan down the phone. 'Oh. As good as that?'

'I don't even know where to begin.' James taps me on the shoulder to mouth that he's heading off. 'Thank you!' I shout after him to a hand wave and a shuffle. 'I'm making a mess of things, Claire.'

'Come over and we can chat if you like?'

'I can't, I'm back on the bus in twenty.'

'Okay, tonight? We can meet in the pub again?'

'I think I need to get home.'

'Is Alex okay?'

'No. Not really. Or if he was before, he definitely isn't now.' I start walking back towards the bus stops, via the toilets in the shopping centre. 'Fuck, I'm such an idiot, Claire.'

'Why?'

'I've just spent the last few months making Alex feel even worse than he already did. Basically.'

'Says who?'

'James.'

'Freeriding James? Since when do you go to him for advice?'

'Since I went to lunch with Carnation Martin, and Alex walked in.'

'Oooh... ouch.'

'Yeah. Ouch.' I head into the public toilets, leaning up against the sink to talk to Claire but I see the state of my face in the mirror and turn my back.

'How did that even... I mean, you said you weren't interested.'

'I'm not, I just...' Somebody comes into the toilets so I lower my voice. 'I wanted to get my own back. It's stupid. A long story. I just... I wasn't thinking straight and then Alex walked in just as I was beginning to think straight but he heard me talking about having sex with Martin.'

'Oh no!'

'I was just explaining what Zoe had said, that was all, but he heard none of that, just the sex bit and so he turned and left and now I can't get hold of him.'

'Again. Who is he? The Scarlet Pimpernel?'

'Eh?'

'Never mind. So he's disappeared again.'

'Claire, you've got to give him a break. I think he's taking this whole work thing way harder than I realised.'

'Of course I'll give him a break, this is Alex we're talking about. I love him. I love you, I just think he perhaps doesn't realise that this hasn't been a bed of roses for you either, my love. So where did he go before? Any news on that?'

'No.'

She groans. 'God, he makes defending him hard sometimes. What is his deal? Why is he not being open with you?'

'Maybe I've pushed him away. Maybe I've made it worse. Maybe he just needs that job offer you made.'

'I don't know if I want to give it to him any more.'

'Please, Claire. Can't you try? Just in case it helps.' I can hear her move around the house. 'Look, I need to get back on the bus. Just see if he'll listen to you. He likes you.'

'Am I his favourite of all your friends?'

'Of course you are. And probably even more so if you offer him a job.'

'I do need someone,' she says, only slightly begrudgingly.

'I think I've made mistakes too, Claire. I think maybe I've not handled this whole thing very well. He needs a break, we need a break. He needs a job.'

'Okay. Leave it with me.'

'I love you. You're the best.'

The beginning of a child's whine ramps up in the background. 'Tell that to Clemmie!' says Claire, raising her voice over the sound.

'She'll work it out!' I shout back.

'God, I hope so. And, Hel…'

'What?'

'This is not your fault!' she shouts then hangs up.

It might not be my fault as such, but I have definitely made things worse. Maybe James is right, maybe I need to take responsibility for my part in all of this. I type out a message to Alex. *I love you. I think I've been getting this all wrong, I'm sorry. What you saw/heard today, it was nothing. Let's talk, but only when you're ready. X*

Chapter Fifty-Three

Half past six. The front room lit up briefly, the carers' car headlights reflected off the mirror before bouncing back outside onto the garden then disappearing down the hill. And then, all lights switched off the moment they left the house, Geoff sat in the near dark, save for a gentle orange glow from the street lamp outside.

Connie might be safely tucked up upstairs, back in her home, safe with him, but he felt lonelier than he ever had before. Sometimes, in the early days of the carers putting her to bed, he would join her, lying awake for hours because the carers came at seven and it was well before he was ready to retire. There, he'd walk through life's memories. The letters he'd written whilst he was away, never sure they'd get to Connie. Rosemary, years later, as a toddler, escaping through the little garden gate that he'd categorically told her not to go through. The flat on the Bridlington Beach, their lounge crowded with neighbours taking advantage of the only TV set in the building, cooing over the Queen's Coronation. The grand house they lived in when they first moved to Keighley, a Hall granted by the council when he worked for them as a rent collector. The happy times, the sad times, the challenges, the laughter. The love.

Other times, he would just sit in the lounge with the telly on but the volume right down. He'd listen instead to the tick of the clock passing seconds that turned into minutes then hours before it was his turn to climb the stairs.

Today, Geoff can't quite get the energy to collect the remote control and turn it on. Today, he can't quite find the energy to move to put even the little lamp on. Today, he can barely move his left arm as an ache needles its way down to his fingers, across his chest, inside his heart. But he will be okay, because Connie is upstairs and he can't be anything other. And he'll be okay, because he's told the carers that he will not pack his wife off to a home when he is perfectly capable of caring for her.

And he'll be okay because today, just before the carers came to put her to bed, she saw him. She recognised him. She knew exactly who he was and for a few, beautiful, lucid moments, they exchanged love. They hugged. She squeezed him as hard as her frail arms would let her. She looked up to him, inviting him to kiss her. She told him she loved him and he kissed her again. So, he will be okay because she still needs him. He will be okay because he was just going to sit in the chair and breathe carefully, until the pain would subside. Until the stress would deplete. Until his strength returned and he could head into the kitchen to fetch painkillers and a large glass of water.

Geoff reached across to his left arm, massaging the pain. He used the heel of his hand to rub at his chest. He took more deep breaths to try and control the suffocation that began to overwhelm. He took in a deep breath as a sharpness daggered into his heart and neck and down his arm and he couldn't breathe and he couldn't breathe and... he couldn't do this to her, and he couldn't breathe, and he must fight this because she needed him and he couldn't breathe and...

Geoff slumped in his chair. In pain. In the dark. Alone.

Chapter Fifty-Four

I cut the engine. The heater, on full blast to keep my takeaway warm, stopped short, plunging the car into silence. Snow had started to fall as I left the depot. Nothing too heavy, more a dusting, like icing sugar. But with even the finest of snow, comes that silence. The one you only get when it snows. Like the flakes absorb all sound and the earth falls still.

I'm not sure I've ever bought curry for one before. I'm not sure it was the right thing to do but I keep thinking about what James said and wondering if Alex just needs space, and, if so, I should give it to him. When he's ready, we can talk. On his terms. If he needs headspace, maybe I need a bit of self-care. A bit of time to be me, to look after me. A bit of time to work out who I am and what I want in life, too. Which right now is a chicken tikka masala and my feet up in front of the fire. I want to avoid all of my feelings for everything that's going on at the moment because I am confused and conflicted and knackered.

I juggle food and handbag, fumbling to get in. I sling my keys in the bowl by the door, I flick lights on with my nose and attempt to turn the thermostat down too. 'I'm back,' I call out, not expecting a response. Not sure actually if I even want one. I grab a plate and fork, tipping curry onto it, stuffing the chapatti on the edge, licking my finger clean of the tiny bit that escaped and dripped. I break another bit of poppadum off and leave the rest in the kitchen.

'I didn't get you any,' I say, seeing Alex sat in his chair. 'Sorry. I didn't know if you'd be here. Or be hungry.' I pause, feeling bad I didn't at least get two plates, or try to call and see if he wanted anything. I guess his silence is a lack of interest, so take up my usual spot on the sofa, tucking my feet beneath me and huddling up into the arm to rest my plate on a cushion. 'Tom texted, he's stopping at his mates. Did he mention it? I think maybe he's got a girlfriend.'

'Yeah, he texted me too.'

'Great.' I pause, not sure what to say or do next until my belly growls and I dunk the chapatti and take a large bite.

'Is that it?' Alex says, eventually. He's not looking at me; he focuses on the fire, flames dancing.

'Is what it?' I ask, but the atmosphere in the room tells me we're on the edge of a precipice. It suggests that whilst I may have got to a point where I want to give him space and maybe take some for myself, it's possible he's not there yet. And I suddenly wish that the mood is caused by me not offering him any curry, because at least I can do something about that.

'You just come home and pretend like nothing happened?'

This time he does look at me. I reach for the side lamp, lighting his face as I switch it on. He looks angry, disappointed, sort of disdainful too, which after first making me feel guilty, flicks a switch that hints at cross. And I can feel my inner argument, that whatever he might have seen today, or thought he saw, I am not the bad guy here. At least, I'm not the only bad guy. We're in this together. We're failing each other, together.

'I suppose I could tell you it wasn't what it looked like, but I don't expect you'd believe me.' He stares. I bite my lip. 'Maybe we should both explain ourselves, maybe that's the place to start.'

'You invited me to lunch, then I walk in to find you sat there with someone else. Not just that, but talking about sleeping with them! But sure, we've both got stuff to explain.'

My energy, such as it is, evaporates. 'Fuck, Alex! What…? What can I say…? Yes! I was sat there talking about having sex, but the sentence prior to it was that Zoe thinks I should be going out to get some to get my own back on you. And believe it or not, I disagree with her. And yes, I do think I am owed an explanation. Yes, I do think I deserve to know what the hell is going on in your head. You know what? I deserve to know who that text message was for, who the whispered phone call was with the other morning. The one in which you talked about the fact that you loved someone. The one in which you said you didn't know what to do. The text that said she'd made you talk or feel stuff you hadn't in ages. Yes! I do want an explanation, but it's been quite clear that you don't think I need one so, there we are. I'm getting on with it. You want space? Have it. Have it in fucking spades. I'm cool. I'm just getting on with my life! And today – sex conversation aside – today was about me being stood up for an hour, wondering if you were ever going to arrive and based on recent behaviour, assuming you probably wouldn't. Today was about standing in town, desperate to save my marriage and my heart sinking each time I looked at my watch and you still weren't there. Each time someone came and went, my heart broke that little bit more because we were supposed to be having lunch, we were supposed to be talking, and you cared so little for my feelings…' I pause and take a break refusing to lose focus. 'You cared so little for my feelings that you just didn't bother turning up!'

'I did turn up,' he whispers.

'Yes! Alex. You did. But maybe it was too late.'

We fall silent. I tickle my plate with a fork, pushing the chicken around.

'Who is he?' Alex eventually asks.

I put my plate down. 'He's a passenger. I've known him for years. He asked me out the other day. I turned him down and then today, he walked past whilst I was waiting for you and I thought chuff it. Why not? This guy is flirting with me. This guy wants to take me to lunch and make me feel good and why the bloody hell shouldn't I feel that because my husband doesn't make me feel that way right now. And those flowers?' He looks down at the hearth where I'm pointing. 'They were from him.' I sigh. 'When was the last time you bought me flowers, Alex?'

He's still staring at the flowers and now I feel bad because this is exactly not the way I wanted to handle this situation. With every fact I deliver, there's a hint of spite. A spit of in-your-face. 'I was wrong, Alex. It was stupid. I don't know what came over me except that… I'm tired. And I'm confused. And I'm angry, then I'm sad. But most of all, I don't know what the hell to do.' My breath is heavy, Alex is staring. I shift the plate out of sight because not only am I not hungry, but the sight of the food now makes me feel sick. Maybe it's not the food. 'Today, earlier, I thought that maybe I can be patient, give you space. I thought maybe I've been getting it wrong, maybe I need to try being a supportive wife in some other shape or form, but I can't. Alex… I can only be the person I am and if that's not what you need or want, then… well, then I don't know where we go. Because…' – all breath leaves my body – '…I am trying my hardest and it's obviously not what you need.' He nods, slowly. 'I can't go on like this, Alex.'

'*You* can't go on like this!' he says, his voice low. 'You can't go on like this?' He repeats it but runs out of energy.

We sit in silence until he eventually moves to the fireplace, his whole body sinking into himself. He looks small, he looks vulnerable. He doesn't look like the man I saw the other night with that woman.

'I feel like that's the problem here, Helen. I feel like it's all about you. About how *you* are coping, how *you* are feeling. I hear you talk to your friends about it, I hear you say what you're doing to keep us going, to keep the bills paid and I want to speak up but I've nothing to say.'

'Exactly! You've nothing to say. You won't talk. You won't open up about how you feel. And I talk to people because people ask, because people care and I don't know what else to say other than, we're fine. We're coping. And I want to include you in those conversations, but I don't know how to because you've completely shut down and I am lost, Alex. I am totally lost with how to deal with this. I don't know what to do!'

'Why don't you fix it like you fix everything else?' He doesn't sneer but his words still hurt. 'Surely that's the solution? You've always got the solution, you tell me that often enough. You tell everyone.' He lifts the photo of us on the narrowboat we hired a few years ago. Tom was at school and we'd wanted a day together, just the two of us. Quality time. We, a pair of narrowboat rookies, successfully navigated Five Rise Locks on our own, as we got through the fifth and final, the sun shining, both sweating and knackered, we took that selfie as proof of what we'd done. He'd pulled me into a cuddle and taken the shot. Teamwork, that's how it looked. Teamwork and determination and communication.

Communication. Not getting angry with each other. Patience. Time.

Why do I keep getting this so wrong? Why do I get the hindsight and change nothing?

'I know…' I begin, quietly. 'I know I have a habit of jumping into fix everything. I can't help it, half the time I don't even realise I do it.

But I want to get this right, Alex. I want to sort this out. I want to help you. To help us.'

Alex braces himself against the fireplace. I wait. I give him time. I don't know how long it takes, probably not as long as it feels, but after a while, I hear it. The sound of him crying. It's gentle at first. Perhaps easy to miss. But soon the sound grows louder. It takes over his whole being, he pushes against the mantelpiece, bracing himself in the room. And I want to go to him, with every fibre of my being I want to rush up and take him in my arms but I don't. I've never seen it before but this time, hindsight tells me I can't fix this. I can't fix him.

So I wait.

Chapter Fifty-Five

My love,

I liked to think that you never heard me cry. I would hide the tears in the same way I hid the fear, the hurt, the anger, the despair. Nobody saw the despair. Might things have been different had I realised and found the words to express how I felt?

Sometimes it feels like such a simple solution and our lives could have been different. But it wasn't the done thing. It was frowned upon. It wasn't believed. If it existed, it was the perverse privilege of new mothers and their hormones. It certainly wasn't for the likes of me.

To admit such weakness would expose me.

And yet, weak is the very last thing that I was. I know that now. I was surviving in spite of the challenge. I was a warrior. A fighter. I was someone who was walking the walk, despite every single part of my being fighting against me.

We should have talked.

From,

The love you wished I could be.

Chapter Fifty-Six

'I don't know where to start,' Alex says, eventually.

'Start wherever, however, just… start.' I put my plate on the table beside me and sit on my hands, desperate to go up to him but resisting every single instinct.

'I just feel… I'm so… it's like…' He stops, he shakes his head, he seems to travel further away somehow. 'Everything's black. Everything's bleak.' He pushes himself off the mantelpiece, dropping back into his chair. His face is pale, his eyes dark and lifeless. 'It's like I'm deep under water, looking up at the surface but no matter how much I swim, I can't reach it. I can't touch it. I can't break through the suffocating seal. I can see what's up above me but I'm sinking lower, darker, deeper.'

I bite my bottom lip, I must not respond until he's finished. And yet, I want to tell him this is brilliant, this is perfect. This is what we've been waiting for. This is a breakthrough, we can talk, if he's honest and we communicate like we used to, we can make everything okay.

He runs his hands through his hair, resting them on the back of his head, eyes to the ceiling. I follow his gaze towards the beams, heavy, sturdy, holding the fabric of our house together. 'Some days I can't get out of bed. Some days I can't move. Some days you come home and want to know why the heating is up and the fire is on but the lights are off. It's because I turn it up when I come downstairs and then I don't move. The light fades and I don't care. The night draws in and the house is empty and all I want to do is wallow in the black. I want to wrap myself up in the dark. I want to… I want to hide.'

My heart aches with each word, with each eloquent description he gives of what he is feeling, of how this is. He starts to cry again and I can't help but move to him this time, I kneel before him, I lift his head up. I hold his face in my hands. 'It's going to be okay,' I say. 'It's going to be okay. We can sort this, we can.' But his eyes harden.

'*WE* can't do anything,' he says. 'That is exactly my point.'

'Of course we can, we can get you help. We can find someone for you to talk to.' He shakes his head. Half laughing, half in disbelief. 'What? We can? I can find someone if you don't have the strength, we can do this.'

He takes hold of my wrists, moving them from his face. It's the most contact we've had in months. He gets back up to stand by the fire, leaving me on my heels where he had been sat.

'We're not scaling the locks now, Helen. This isn't a bit of water and some grit and determination.'

'I know but—'

'I feel like you're not hearing me. Like you're not listening.'

'I am listening.'

He shakes his head. 'No, no you aren't. You don't or can't and that's why this won't work. You don't hear what I'm saying.' He pauses.

I lift myself up to sit on the edge of his chair.

'I've found someone to talk to,' he says, his back facing me. 'I've found someone who can hear.' I think about the woman with the hair and the laugh and the romance captured beneath the lamplight. 'I've found someone who I can open up to, who I can talk it all through with. That's who the text message was for.' Bile rises. 'That's who I was talking to.'

I feel sick. 'I see. And that's who you were with, when I saw you. When you went away.' I've watched this happen. I've let go and watched him pull back further and further and I've let it happen. This is my fault. 'I knew it.' My stomach plunges to my feet and I feel faint. 'So it was you. The other night.'

'What was me?'

'When you went away, when you disappeared. When you were supposed to be with Wigsy. Nice cover story by the way, throw in a name from the past and I'd never question it. But I saw you! Or someone who looked just like you. With a woman, walking down the street. Kissing!'

Alex looks at me, his eyes wide.

'What, you're not even going to deny it?'

'Is there any point? You've made it quite clear what you think! Why deny what you clearly already know!'

'How could you?' I shake my head, I want to scream, I want to lash out. I pull myself up, reaching for the photo of us. I can't believe we're the same people, they look like strangers to me. And it makes me angry and sad and frustrated all at the same time and I can't see how we ended up here and how could he do this to me? 'Maybe Zoe was right, maybe I should have started something with Martin, see how it feels to be wanted because it's obviously working so well for you, you…' The anger pushes through all other emotions and makes a noise as I throw the photo in the fireplace, dropping to my knees.

Alex thrusts his hand into the fire glove, pulling the blackened frame out of the fire. 'What are you doing?' he shouts, rubbing at the photo to reveal our faces, making sure it hasn't caught fire. He turns to face me, his eyes glassy, his breath hot in my face. 'I don't know who or what you saw, but I can assure you it wasn't me… I wouldn't do that, I wouldn't.' He sits back, his legs crossed. We used to sit like this, before a little heater in our first flat, desperate to keep warm and I would give everything to be back there, to have those times again.

Eventually he says, 'If you think I could do something like that, then maybe I've been wrong all along. Maybe the problem isn't me.'

'What do you mean?'

'Maybe the problem is us.'

I want to tell him he's wrong, but I can't find my voice.

'I was at Wigsy's, Helen. Just like I said. You can call him if you like. He lives in Scotland, Dunblane. He owns a pub. I sat at the bar and watched the football. I ate the food. I chatted to him. I chatted to his wife. They have two kids. They have this normal life. This steady, capable life. And when I burned all bridges with everybody down here, he, it turns out, was someone I could turn to.'

'For what?'

'He's my friend, Helen. And his wife… his wife is my counsellor.'

Chapter Fifty-Seven

My love,

I remember the night it all changed. It was supposed to be a cry for help, a way to get you to see me as something other than your husband, the man of the house. I wanted you to see me, the human being, the person who was losing the fight, but I got it all wrong. I couldn't hear myself, I couldn't feel what pain I was causing because my own was too strong. I couldn't hear you because the voices in my own head were too loud, the ones that told me I was a failure, that I'd let you down, that I should be ashamed of myself. I heard nothing, apart from when you cried that night. I heard that and then I cried myself because I couldn't see how to fix it. I couldn't see how to make you know this wasn't your fault. I didn't know then that it wasn't mine either. I didn't appreciate that my thoughts, my behaviour, my inability to pull myself out of the deepest pit of despair and everything I said was action and reaction creating a wake. A tidal surge that would wash us away. And it wasn't my fault.

Sometimes, I wish I could save people from their own tidal surge.
From,
The love you wished I could be.

Chapter Fifty-Eight

His words hang in the air, in the space between us. I stare at him. My husband. The man I loved. The man I love. The man I don't recognise.

'I don't know how to function, Helen. Wigsy and I were talking on Facebook.'

'You said you met up on Twitter.'

He sighs. 'Yes, we did. Then we moved to Facebook. And he suggested it might be good for me to talk to someone and I had nobody—'

'What about me?'

He looks at me then back down to the floor. 'He suggested I went to stay with him and see if his wife could help me.'

'But… why couldn't you say where you'd gone? Not even that? Why wouldn't you tell me about Wigsy? All of this, it's like I don't even know you any more.'

Alex sighs again. He looks at me, and for a moment it's almost tender and I'd like to press pause, to look into his eyes and have us share the moment because it feels so desperately needed. 'Maybe I couldn't,' he begins, exhausted. 'Maybe I didn't know where to start. I didn't know how to explain it. I didn't know what to say, fuck, maybe I'm a stranger to myself!' he says. 'Maybe that's another part of the problem. You don't know who I am any more? *I* don't fucking know who I am. Or what the point of me is. Christ, Tom came home the other night all excited about his new job and what did I do? Made it all about me! I turned the situation into another reason to mope around all day.'

'And I could see that, that's why I came to you. That's why I put my arms around you because I needed you to know that I understand, that I get how hard it must have been to hear.'

'But you don't understand,' he says, with a gentleness that breaks me. 'I know you'd like to. I know you think you do, but how can you? You say all these words, these things that I'm sure you think are the right things to say. Sometimes I'd listen and I'd really try, I'd really try to be okay. To let you pick up the extra work and not feel like a failure. To let you tell me we'd fix it together and not feel as though you were steamrollering me. And I could never explain how any of it made me feel, how it makes me feel still, because you've never stood in my shoes, you've never felt what I feel. How can you possibly know how I feel?'

All the conversations from the last week or two come to mind. The thoughts about how work, how providing, might be at the core of him. How his current situation might be breaking him. How it might not matter to me, but it clearly matters to him and a shame creeps in. Shame that I've talked about this, I've had people give me their opinions. I've listened and nodded and challenged and come away having changed nothing about how I might help.

'What can I do?' I ask, quietly, realising that perhaps this is the question I should have asked months ago.

He turns to face me. 'Honestly? I'm not sure. I'm not sure you *can* do anything because I'm not sure you have it in you.' I must look confused because he continues pretty quickly. 'I told you before that I needed space and you came up to smother me.'

'I came to hold you, to love you.'

'That's not giving me space.'

'I thought you needed affection, I thought you might just need to feel loved.'

'Like I've said, I don't know what I feel. One minute I need you to hold me and make it all better, the next I need you to leave me alone so I can work it out for myself. One minute I want to talk about everything, the next minute I don't know where to start. When I've offloaded, you've swooped in to fix it. I'd get cross, you'd tell me I was being unfair.'

'Maybe you are being unfair.'

'Maybe that's all I've got right now!'

I stare. At him. At the fire. At the photo he rescued of us, charred around the edges. I feel the loss of those days so physically, I want to wretch. Or scream out. Or hit something. I want to hit something so hard, time after time, until I'm as exhausted in my bones as I am in my heart. 'Helen…' He drops his head, his hands resting on tired hips. 'I don't think I can do this any more either.'

And as he heads up the stairs, I reach my hands out to stretch, then behind me, rubbing at my back. Something catches my hand, something inside a cushion. I pull it on to my lap, opening the zip to reach inside. And there it is. Months after it was lost. Moments after Alex has walked away from me, my wedding ring. And as I slip it on to my finger, letting it sit back in the groove it once made, I see a future I never dreamed of. A future where Alex doesn't factor.

Chapter Fifty-Nine

Geoff lay in the bed, a machine beside him beeped with each heartbeat. A light shone on paperwork in the corner of the room and the open door leaked sounds of Airedale Hospital into his psyche. He was awake but asleep. He was there but not. He was alive – thanks to Val popping over to apologise for their earlier conversation and finding him – but he was drifting. Fitful with dreams of his younger years. The cycle rides and picnics with Connie and friends. The homes they built. The lives they led. The purpose he had. The way it all led him so far away from the darker days of his childhood. His father, in a corner, 'no use to any of them', or so his mother would say as she gave him a job to do, his younger brothers looking innocently on.

To escape those things, he built a life based on purpose. On responsibility. On the pomp and circumstance of a man in charge. All pieces of a jigsaw that built the man he went on to become, Connie at the very centre, were gradually being picked apart and she didn't fit any more. She was lost between her health and his and he wondered what might become of the woman who he now realised, without question, had saved him. What would become of her if he were no longer here? And what if he pulled through, what then? The home would surely be inevitable. Then what would become of him when she went?

He was tired. He was confused. He was worn down by life.

Whatever Rosemary thought, Geoff didn't do vulnerable. It was not a word in his vocabulary. Until now. And now he wondered if in fact he'd been vulnerable all along. And if so, was it too late to change? For Connie's sake. For his own.

Chapter Sixty

Tom came back unexpectedly. Turns out I was right and he had met a girl and rather than going round to his mate's house, he had been on a date. Apparently his date didn't go according to plan. I may or may not have been a bit unfair in my response when I told him it served him right for being so bloody presumptuous and that I did not bring him up to assume he was going to get his end away at the first flash of interest from a girl. That maybe he should wait a while before planning to stay the night. That maybe she'd give him the signal when she was ready and until then, he'd have to put up and shut up. He sloped off to his room looking sheepish and I cried because I felt like a dick.

So this morning, I don't just feel like a dick – though I think I was probably right about Tom and his date – but a dick at work with a massive headache from all the tears and the knowing in the pit of my belly that my marriage is falling apart. Claire texted, asking me how I was. I haven't responded yet. She'll come over or gather the girls. They'll rally round and be brilliant and I don't think I can cope with that just yet.

I can't do this any more. That's what he said. Is that what he meant? It felt it, and that's why I'd put my wedding ring in my purse rather than keeping it on my finger. Somehow, it didn't feel like it belonged.

I slam the brakes on, the bus wheels skid slightly in the morning slush. The snow didn't turn heavy, instead rain followed and now we've a mixture of the two; but I should probably not be thinking about the state of my marriage, or Tom's teenage lusting, and instead focus on the road up ahead. I barely remember the last few miles. That's probably not okay for a bus driver, is it?

'Morning, on you come. Mind the step.'

A woman I don't recognise climbs on board, fumbling cash into the tray between us. 'A return to Bingley, please.'

I take her cash and give her the ticket and wonder what Alex is doing at home. He just needed space. Like I had once, back when we were kids finding our way through the early days of marriage. Asleep on an old IKEA futon because we didn't have a spare room and I was cross with him about something and probably nothing.

Except it's different. Back then, I found out I was pregnant that next morning. I realised that if we split up, our baby wouldn't know what we once were. In love. Passionately, completely. No matter how young. Alex begged for forgiveness for whatever it was he had done and I admitted it was likely just to be hormones and we made up, united in the fear of the fact we were about to become parents. We went for our first scan and I saw this tiny bean of a baby in my belly and I cried again because I was frightened we couldn't do it, I was frightened at the looming responsibility. And when I sat that August, after I had Tom, as dawn broke in an already stifling hot conservatory, I'd looked down at this bundle of beautiful joy and realised that this tiny version of us both, needed us both. Relied upon us both. And I knew, that no matter what might have happened before, or what could happen in the future, Alex and I were linked. Forever together. Connected.

It terrified me.

A ding of the stop bell makes me realise I've done another half of my route and still don't remember a thing and I'm one stop away from Geoff's. James sits up, peering out of the window. 'Isn't it Wednesday?'

'God knows, I've lost track.'

'It is, it's Wednesday and he's no' there again. Do ye think he's okay?'

'I dunno. I'm not sure he'd want me to knock again though, so I don't think there's anything we can do. Rosemary did say it might be a while 'til he got on the bus again.'

'Aye.'

'Apart from anything else, he's getting on. You know? He was old when he moved in next door, never mind now. He must be what? Late 80s, early 90s.'

'His daughter's car wasn't there though, either.'

James' arm is linked through the pole beside me. I pull up at the next stop, letting a passenger on whose aftershave smells just like something Alex used to wear when we were kids. Kouros, maybe? Can you still buy that stuff? I shove the bus in gear to move on but an angry toot of a car horn makes me slam on the brakes. James lurches forward. 'Shit! Sorry!' I say, spying the car I've just pulled out on in my wing mirror. I fling open the window to give an apologetic wave as the car pulls away, the driver shouting obscenities out of his window.

'Are you okay, Hel? You seem kinda distracted.'

'I'm fine, it's just… one of those days.' I point to the sign again and he takes the hint, retreating to the relative safety of one of the bench seats up front.

'Are you sure you're okay?' he shouts above the engine. 'How are… things?'

'Fine. I'm fine. It's fine.' I reply with a thumbs up. 'Now's probably not the time…' He nods a fair enough and I'm off and away back in my head. Picking last night's conversation apart. The thing is, you could be forgiven for accidentally falling asleep on the sofa, it happens. I've said as much to Tom when he's found me there from time to time these last few months. Usually after staying up to watch *Orange Is the New Black*. The spare room though? Where Alex fell asleep last night. That was a conscious decision on his part. A decision to stay away.

As we head down the back roads, driving deeper into the hills, a sleet starts and greasy spots land thickly on the windscreen. The faster my wipers go, the faster the sleet falls. I strain to see through the glass. Alex and I loved the rain, and the sleet. I remember one night, when we'd finally had sex, we couldn't get enough and would drive out to the hills and hide here, making the most of the privacy. I remember heavy rainfall and hot bodies. I remember needing him, he was my oxygen. I had to feel the closeness to breathe again. And if I think about it, if I really think, I can feel him. I can feel us. I can remember exactly what it was like to—

'HELEN!' James jumps up towards me. There follows a screech of slammed-on brakes, a shunt and a crash that deafens. A scream from passengers. James knocks his head against the Perspex between us and my neck pulls, kept in place by the seat belt.

Then it falls silent.

Slowly, I lift my head and look out of the window at a car, its front passenger wing completely folded in on itself, steam rising from the car bonnet.

'Shit!' I say, pulling at my neck.

Behind an inflated cushion of air, the face of a stunned driver stares back at me. 'Shit,' I say again, relieved to see that said driver is at least alive.

James coughs, rubbing at his arm, then his forehead. 'Are you okay,' I ask him, trying, but not quite able to free myself at first unclick of the belt. I adjust the rear-view mirror to look at the passengers. 'Is everyone okay?' I shout, as loudly as I can. There are some mumbles, but nobody outright says they're okay. I rub at my back to try and shift it, eventually unbuckling my seat belt and unpicking myself out of the driver's cabin.

'Is everyone okay?' I shout again, more urgently, steadying James down on a seat and picking up a bag of shopping that has fallen, emptied in the crash. The muttered response is slightly louder this time. The passengers look dazed, but all appear to be nodding, or answering with a quiet yes. I can't see any blood. There's no screaming. Everyone appears to be alive. 'Oh my God,' I start. 'I'm so… I just didn't… I was…' I stop talking. Nothing useful forming in my mind. I pull at my neck, my eyes closed to the sky and that is when I know that I'm going to cry a big sobbing ugly cry and there is nothing about my job as responsible for passengers can do to stop it.

Chapter Sixty-One

'Are you sure you're okay to wait?' asks Dave, one of the other drivers. He's brought the replacement bus and is apparently under orders to bring me back too, but I can't leave the bus until the recovery gets here. It feels wrong, like a captain letting his ship sink as he watches from a life raft. I don't know. I'm being ridiculous, but I can't go. What if James comes back? He wandered off. I didn't see which way. 'You look pretty shaken, Helen. You don't have to wait.'

'It's fine, go on. The paramedic checked me out after all the passengers. I've got a clean bill. Go on, get the passengers back home before anyone complains about us holding them up as well as them being in a road traffic accident.' I try to smile, letting my head rest against the side of the bus, exhausted.

'If you're sure. Janice did say—'

'Please, go on. Let Janice know I needed to stay. If she has a problem with that, it can't be any worse than the trouble I'm already in!'

'You're not in trouble, Helen. These things happen. It's life. Nobody was hurt.' He offers a sympathetic smile but my resolve can't quite handle the kindness. 'It's fine,' he insists.

'Roll on the whiplash claims.'

'That's what insurance is for.' I nod at Dave and wave a thank you to one of the first responders who sets off to another call-out.

'Look, as soon as you can. Get home, get a bath, get your fella to look after you.' I bite down on my bottom lip, which goes some way to distracting me from the hurt of knowing that my 'fella' probably won't be bothered, never mind look after me. No more tears. Dave searches out eye contact. 'Take a few days off, if I was you.'

'I'm rota'd off anyway tomorrow. It's fine.'

'Take longer, if you can. The shock'll kick in when you're least expecting it.' He gives me another nudge, northern man for *it'll be reight*, then jogs over to the replacement bus, quickly climbing on. I can just about hear him checking in, making sure everyone is okay again before the engine picks up and they all head off.

I'm alone.

The car I smashed into has been towed away. The woman driver taken in the ambulance as a precaution.

I'm on a smaller road now, the sleet has stopped but as I look around, I feel it in the air and shiver. Climbing back on the bus, I check up and down the aisle for rubbish as if it was the normal end of my shift. My back aches and my throat hurts and my head is banging. Not able to stand any longer, I drop into the driver's seat, leaning against the window. I pull at my neck and shoulders, adrenaline is seeping away leaving cold hard reality in the form of a body knotted tight with the jolt.

What have I done? Why wasn't I concentrating? Can I remember any of the driving this morning? I knew I was in no fit state. I knew I kept drifting off. How could I have been so careless?

I want to call Alex. I want to tell him what's happened and I want him to be the one to tell me it's going to be okay. I want him to comfort me, to take me in his arms. I need him…

I force the heel of my hand into my chest, then I drop it back down by my side. I squeeze my eyes shut then open them, seeing through temporary stars and as I look down, I see bits of my handbag strewn in the footwell, including the notebook. It must have fallen out of my bag in the shunt and now it is lying in a mucky puddle by my feet.

I wipe it down with the arm of my sleeve, trying to dry it off, trying not to let any muck or water get onto the pages and ruin the letters held between. Why do I still have this? Why have I held on to it? Why do I know the ins and outs of this person's feelings? I open the book, a few pages stick together, gently I peel them apart.

Chapter Sixty-Two

My love,

By leaving, I was to try and face up to the truth. My truth. It was to try and find a way to be okay, to talk about the things that stood in my way. The way I treated you, it was only half of the story. It's not that I didn't love you, or that I don't love you, I love you with every corner of my heart that is able, every part of my being that can. The problem is that I didn't love me and, for whatever reason, those two things were inextricably linked and fundamentally broken.

I always believed we'd be together until our last breath. Part of me still feels that but I know too much damage has been done, we've said too much. Yet as I write this, my life in a new phase, a new moon where I am full and life shines a pearlescent glow despite the circumstances I find myself in, the only person I want to know how my story ended, is you. The only fear I have is that you will never know the truth. You, the person who would plead with me, who'd beg me to talk or to get cross, to feel something. Anything. Anger, if that's what it took. I thought walking out was proof that I could feel something. I thought ignoring you, as you shouted down the lane after me, proved how strong I could be. That it broke you too, is my greatest regret.

And now, I live each day with the truth that you may never see the person I've become, the person you wished I could be. Perhaps that's karma's cruel hand but I'm doing it, my love, I'm here. I'm alive and I can feel. And it's because of you.

Maybe it's for the best that you don't see me. The twist in my tale may not be to your liking. I no longer listen to the thoughts of others for money, I do it simply because there was a time I wish I could have listened to myself. I have peace. I forgive me. I forgive us. I know now more than ever that I love you, because I feel it.

Life's pretty fast-paced these days, it's too much. It's all noise and instant gratification, even more than in our day. Sometimes, I see the look on someone's face and I know they're where I was. Or maybe where you were. They're struggling, drowning, being swept away.

Depression. Anxiety. Illnesses unseen. A cause of shame, of disdain. A cause of trauma to those who suffer and those around them. It needs love, it needs time, it needs respect, it needs support, it needs patience. It needs not to be hidden for fear of retribution, it needs talking about.

If only these lessons were a gift I could hand on. Instead, they're a gift only from oneself. These letters are, therefore, the most precious gift I can imagine. To me. To you. To anybody who reads them.

From,

The love you wished I could be.

Chapter Sixty-Three

I wipe my eyes clear of the tears. Tears that fell as I read the words and realised something I'd been ignoring because it didn't fit the narrative I chose to select. Even though he stood in front of me and all but said it himself. A narrative I built up in my mind because nothing else seemed to make sense and yet it could end my marriage because it being over might be easier than fighting for its survival. Easier for both of us.

Except that Alex doesn't hate me. Alex hates himself, his life. I don't know, maybe he doesn't even have the energy to hate. Maybe that's an emotion too far. A feeling too strong for his state of mind. Maybe he feels nothing, maybe he's numb. And I've been prodding, poking at the wound.

All the time, I've thought I was holding us together, stoically, if not piously, declaring it was all fine when that's the last thing he's been feeling. Those declarations have pushed him further away. All the times I've been angry as he's sat in that chair, day in, day out. Living inside his phone. Desperately searching to escape? Every time I've wanted to scream at him to get out of the house, to go meet people, to talk to people. Maybe he couldn't. Maybe he was bound. Invisibly tied. And then when he does go, I accuse him of the very thing he swore he'd never do.

Have I pushed him so far that he can never come back?

A knock on the bus window makes me jump. James peers at me through the glass. 'Can I come on?' he asks, smiling kindly.

I get up to open the door. 'Of course, come in.' I wipe my eyes. Sniffing back to refresh myself.

He looks down at the book in my hand. 'You found it.'

'This?'

'Aye.'

I look at it in my hands, the crutch, the thing that's kept me going, given me something to think about, to focus on. Is it his? Was I quoting his own words from it?

He takes it from my hands and flicks through the pages, the spine creaking as he does so. My palms are laced with the touch of his honesty and the revelations within.

'I did find it, yes. Just down there, by the doors and... I didn't mean to read it, I just... I didn't know who it belonged to and I tried to find out and then the words just meant so much and helped and I couldn't bear to be parted with it and I'm so sorry, I shouldn't have... I don't know what I was thinking—'

'It's fine,' he says, simply, placing it back in my hands. 'It turns out I didn't need it.'

'Pardon?'

'For so long, I've believed I needed it to survive and it turns out I can breathe with or without its words.'

'But it's so... personal. So raw. God, I'm so sorry, James.'

'It's okay.'

'But it's not, I crossed a line. I took advantage. I just saw so much that made a weird kind of sense, that I could relate to, and I kept reading when I should have made sure it got back to you.'

'But that's the point, Hel. I didnae need it to come back to me. Maybe it needed to be found, to be read.' Gently, I flick through the pages. 'All those words about forgiveness, about letting go, I was writing it, and maybe even feeling it, but I wasnae living it. Losing them meant I *had* te live it and, all of a sudden, I could look forward. I could see beyond the words and the heartbreak and the mistakes. Ye did me a favour, Hel.'

'Oh, James.'

He sits down, patting the bus seat for me to join him. So I do. In silence. His handwriting, his words, fresh in my mind. I let out a sigh, deep and prolonged. 'Ye need to be careful.' He roots round his pockets. 'Your blood sugar'll be low. The shock. Here, have this.' He hands me a Mars bar. 'I always have one, just in case. You never know when a chocolate fix might come in handy.'

I take it but my hands shake and I can't open it. James takes it and opens it for me.

'Share?' I offer.

'Nah, no' for me,' he says, pushing my hand back gently, waiting for me to take a bite. The chocolate cracks as I bite and pull away, leaving the characteristic drip of caramel to catch on my chin.

James pointed to his own. 'Ye've got…' he said, picking out a tissue from his pocket but sticking it back in when he saw how mucky it was.

We sit in silence for a moment, his book on his lap. He looks down at it, eventually breaking the pause. 'We'd been together for years,' he begins, quietly. Part of me wants to tell him he needn't do this. Another part of me wants to know, maybe needs to know. 'We both worked, busy lives. I was… well, we both worked. I said before that we came to Leeds for her job and I think, looking back, that's when it started.'

'You don't have to do this.'

'Not long after we moved, my father passed away. It was pretty sudden. Things were left unsaid. I was a long way from home. I was angry, angry that he'd died. Angry he didnae tell me he was ill. Angry he cheated me of a chance te tell him how I felt. I think, looking back, ah'd had lows before. But nothing was like this, nothing compared. To begin with, my wife was sympathetic, of course she was. But the longer my grief went untouched, the more I retreated. It changed shape. It was thick, dark, and suffocating. I should have known better, I had all the skills, all the training and yet I couldn't stop the spiral, the descent. Some days, I'd barely leave the house. I lost mah job. I wouldn't get up. I didnae eat. People would call the house and I'd ignore the phone.'

I remember all the times Alex didn't pick up when I called. When I knew that his phone would be in his hand, no matter where he was.

'That was her biggest bugbear, actually. The phone. That she could-nae call to talk to me when she needed to. I don't know, to tell me she was working late, or te ask me if I could do a job around the house, pick up some shopping or something. She suggested I go self-employed, then I wouldn't have to leave the house, so I tried it. And maybe that worked for a while, but ultimately the grief remained and the longer it went ignored, the more the pain increased. The louder it got. The need to step back from life was all-consuming and I stopped answering my phone again, and soon, it just stopped ringing. I wasn't there for my clients. I wasn't focused. I wasn't emotionally robust enough.'

I wonder what kind of job he had. I can't imagine him doing anything because I'd only ever seen him as the traveller. The homeless man on my bus. I've never looked beyond the man I see before me and maybe that's the reason I'm in this situation... my inability to see beyond that which stares me in the face.

'You don't have to tell me any of this, James.'

'Of course I don't. But what if I had an experience that could change somebody else's life and I said nothing? What if I did to somebody else what society had done to me?'

'What do you mean?'

'I felt gagged. I felt like I couldnae talk about it, and no' just because that meant I wasn't the person people expected of me, but because I couldn't explain why. I didnae understand it, despite all of my training, all the books I'd read and the reports I'd written, I didn't get it. Because all the books in the world mean nothing when you're in its midst. I was lucky, somehow, through a combination of time and medication and talking and…' he nods down to the notebook '… and writing. Those are the things that saved me and could be the things to save someone else, and to not speak up… well, that makes me complicit.'

'In what?'

'In a society that doesn't take this stuff seriously. A society that tells us to man up. A society that, by and large, has no idea how to deal with the reality of broken minds.'

'Broken minds?'

'Absolutely. And it's so widespread, Helen, so typical. So prevalent. I'd like te bet, there are few people who don't know someone whose suffered some kind of mental health challenge. I'd like te bet this goes back years. Generations even. Look at the war heroes, First and Second world wars, where was their post-traumatic stress diagnosis? The women who stayed at home and held it all together, not knowing if their loved ones would return. Where's their anxiety diagnosis? This isn't a new thing, maybe life today makes it a bigger thing, more widespread, or maybe life today just breeds different triggers. Or maybe we just recognise it more.'

I look to the floor. The sleet ramps up, turning more hail like, battering the side of the bus windows, almost deafening.

'These letters were my coping strategy. They're the thing I wrote to the one person I wish I could've told. Who I will never be able to tell and who is the sole reason I am still alive, because I realised that my love for her was the smallest spark of hope that gave me the will to carry on. Even after I left. I couldn't do it when she was by my side, maybe I didn't feel that I needed to. But something snapped and I knew I had to leave. For her sake as well as mine. I knew I had to do something and the book, the letters, they were part of it... There is no right way te deal with any of this, Helen. Maybe that's better, we can find something that fits the individual. But only when they're ready.'

'I don't think he's ready, James. And certainly not for me to help him. We're too far apart, so much has been said.'

James sighs. 'Then it's time to deal with you, Helen. With how you cope, how you survive whilst he fades. And then you have to wait, and hope that he comes back when he's ready. You know, for some, a relationship keeps them afloat, for others it's a millstone. Maybe your Alex needs the space, the time to breathe.'

'How much time? How long can that take?'

James smiles, with a shake of his head. 'Days, weeks, months, years. There's no formula. And that's the hardest thing.'

Chapter Sixty-Four

'Dad, you need to rest. You need to let the nurses care for you. You can't rush this.'

'I need to get home for your mother,' Geoff answered, breathless from shifting to sit up in bed.

'She's fine, Dad. She went into the home again. I called this morning and she was settled in. Eating breakfast. She's fine.' Rosemary plumped his pillows up.

'Your mother doesn't like it there,' he said, resisting putting his pillows back exactly as they were.

'Dad... *you* don't like it there. Mum... well...'

'She doesn't like it there and she is supposed to be with me. I am her carer.'

'You're her husband, Dad,' said Rosemary. 'A husband who's just had a heart attack. You're also my dad and I'm worried about you.'

'It was mild. The doctor said so.'

'Dad, you're in your nineties, however mild it may be, you don't have a heart attack at your age then jump out of bed and carry on as normal. You've got to slow down. All the trips into town, the hours walking around with shopping and whatever else you do when you're there. You can't keep living like it's twenty years ago.'

'I can't live like an old man.'

'But, Dad!' Rosemary paused, before seemingly deciding she had nothing to lose. 'You ARE an old man, Dad!' she said, quietly. 'An old man and, right now, a stubborn old boot!'

'Rosemary!' Geoff looked stunned.

'Sorry but…' Rosemary sighed, before pulling up a chair beside him. She put her hand on his, he couldn't remember the last time she'd done that, years probably. 'Dad, I know you hate it, I know you want to look after yourself and Mum, but this has to be a signal, a warning. You're allowed to ask for more help. You're allowed to tell us it's hard. Nobody would judge you. Nobody would think less of you or the love you have for her. She's… she's more demanding these days. I know she is. I see how much you're doing when I visit.'

'Val helps, too.'

'Of course she does, but Mum needs more and more care and that's not getting any easier. Places in good homes are not there just whenever we want them, Dad. People have to wait, especially for placements that can cater for Mum's particular needs.' Geoff's eyes glistened with sadness. Rosemary stroked his hand with her thumb. 'I understand this is hard, Dad. I promise you I do, but… it's necessary. It's time to accept the help. It's not a weakness, it's not a bad thing. You're not letting anybody down.' Geoff moved his hands from her hold. 'God…' she says, not quite under her breath. 'Now I know where I get it from.'

'Get what from?'

'Stubbornness! The need for things to be done a certain way. Mum always said we were very alike and I never believed her, but I get it now. I am. We are. It's like we don't think anybody else is capable, but we hide behind it. It's protection. It keeps us in control of our environment and do you know something? We've never been in control. Not now, not in the past. We're all just travelling along, doing our best. The carers, that's what they're doing. They're doing their best and that's all Mum needs. And you need to let them, you need to…' Geoff looked at Rosemary. 'I get it, Dad. I do. Maybe these next few days will be good for you. Make you sit for a bit. Let Mum settle in. Rest. You can work it out then, what's best for you both.'

'Maybe I already know what's best,' he said.

'No, Dad…' she paused. 'You know what's best for you. At least, you think you do. I just… I don't think it is any more. I don't think it's good for either of you.'

Geoff wiped a tear. Though he didn't want to let on to Rosemary, he knew that she was right. He knew what he needed to do. In fact, he'd known it since last night. He'd known it since he'd realised that he had survived and thrived in his life because of Connie. She had made him the man he was today and she believed in him, always. Even when he found that so hard himself. She saw through the pomp and the status and she still believed in him because she knew his approach to life was about self-protection, it was a framework he'd created to function. To live with the things he'd seen and done. And because she loved him without question, she let him be who he was and because of her, he thrived.

'I think it's time to let her go, Dad,' said Rosemary. But Geoff had already worked that one out.

Chapter Sixty-Five

'Helen, the only thing Alex needs, is to know that he's not alone. That whatever he is feeling, is no' unusual. Women struggle too, I know that, but I think maybe you're better equipped to deal with it. Maybe your support network is better. You have friends you can talk to.'

'Sometimes… sometimes I don't wanna talk.'

'Aye, I accept not always, but generally, society encourages you to talk, you're allowed. Men though? So often they can't, so often it's no' okay… I mean, of course, it is okay, it should be okay, but it's no' easy. In some worlds, in some environments, in some situations, it's just not the sort of thing you talk about down the pub.'

'Surely that's a cliché?'

'No, I really don't think it is. There are statistics. There are facts.'

'You seem to know a lot.'

James half smiles, looking to his shoes. 'I used te know a lot.' He moves towards the door. 'The old me, he knew more.'

'The old you? How?'

James shuffles on the spot. 'Well, I was… I was a psychotherapist,' he says, reluctantly. Before I realise I've done it, my mouth drops open and my eyebrows shoot up, which is awful because it's obvious I've just assumed he's never really done anything other than wander the streets day in, day out. 'Surprising, isn't it.'

'Oh God, sorry. Yes, but it shouldn't be. I'm sorry, this says more about me than you.'

'Dinnae worry. We all judge, we all assume. It's natural. We dinnae all let people ride the bus for free te keep warm, so you know, you're forgiven.'

'But how… I don't understand.'

'What? That I'm here, like this.' He picks at his clothes. 'It can happen te anyone. Some of us are lucky and can rely on the kindness of strangers to survive.' He holds my gaze and I'm touched by the sense that maybe I have helped and maybe I'm not all bad, despite how things are unfolding with Alex. 'Look, you cannae fix it, remember. You cannae help until he's ready and asks you for it. This is his journey, you have your own. A different one.'

He steps down off the bus and I follow him. 'But if he's not ready… how can I… I don't know how much longer I can do this for. This functioning. He's already told me he needs space, I don't want to lose him. If he's not ready, I may break.' The shivers come thicker, faster. The wind whips up and the sleet shifts to snow. 'I don't know if I'm strong enough, James.'

'You are absolutely strong enough, Helen. No question whatsoever. You just need to believe it, then feel it… then live it.' The recovery truck pulls up. 'Here, have this. Take it. Read it. Don't think about me, think about the person who wrote it, who was learning. Who was fighting the fight. You are strong enough,' he says again and the look in his eye makes me think maybe he's right. If I stop thinking about me, if I think about us. About Alex. About the future instead of looking in the past. Maybe I am strong enough.

I dig out my phone.

Had a bit of a bump in the bus. Am fine but coming home early. Just want to let you know. Hope you're okay. X

I click send, look up, and James is nowhere to be seen.

Chapter Sixty-Six

It's nearly two hours before I make my way home after hopping in the recovery truck and seeing my bus delivered back to the depot. I'm on high alert as I drive my little car back through the streets. I mirror, signal and manoeuvre the whole way. My hands are at ten to two and my rear-view mirror gets more action than it's had in years. I ignore the urge to go over past conversations with Alex in my head. Instead, I focus on the future. All that we have worth fighting for, not least, Alex's health. His happiness. Maybe, hopefully, that will lead to our happiness. And if that means we have to be apart, I will learn to take it because I love him.

His car is parked on the drive when I pull down our lane and my heart jumps a little. Beside it is Claire's. As I go to open the front door, she comes out.

'Helen, hey.'

'Hi, lovely, how are you? I didn't know you were popping round?'

She groans. 'Hmmm, well, I thought I'd come talk to him about the job.'

'And?'

'I tried, Hel. He's not interested. In fact, he was bloody rude, to be honest. He took ages to answer the door, and when he did, finally, he just walked off up the hallway, leaving me to come in on my own. He obviously didn't want small talk so I went straight into it and told him about the job. He told me he's not interested, that he'd prefer it if people didn't meddle in his career, then invited me to leave.'

'Claire, he's not—'

'What?'

'I don't think he's in a good place at the moment.'

'No shit, Sherlock. The problem is, he won't get in a good place if he doesn't change his attitude.'

'What if he can't just change his attitude?'

'Then… I don't know.' Claire looks back inside the house, then to me. 'Look, maybe I was a bit gung-ho, maybe he needs time to think and I know I have a habit of steamrollering. Tell him I'm sorry, tell him I'll leave the job open for a few days before advertising. Just… look after yourself, okay.'

'I will. Don't worry.'

'Promise?'

'Promise. Look, thanks for trying. I appreciate it. Love you.'

She moves down to her car, unblipping and letting herself in. 'You haven't forgotten about tomorrow, have you?' she asks, slinging her bag on the passenger seat. I guess I have a blank expression because she answers her own question. 'Finlay's fourth birthday party. '

'Oh erm, yes! I had forgotten, but it's fine. I'll be there! I can't believe he's four already!'

'You and me both. And Zoe has gone a bit crazy with the planning, something about pissing on Felicity Hedgefund's mum's last party.'

'Felicity Hedgefund?'

'That's what Zo calls her. Somebody in Finlay's nursery group. Their last party was a bit flash and when I told Zoe about it, she decided her godson was going to have the mutha of all parties and, frankly, I'm regretting saying she could organise it!'

'I'm coming. I'll be there.'

'Great, and…' she pauses, hanging her arms over the car door. 'Call me. If you need anything, okay? Promise?'

I give her the brownie promise and watch as she drives away.

Inside, I head into the lounge. Alex isn't in his chair. 'Hello? Are you there? Did you get my message?' Alex comes down the stairs, a packed bag slung over his shoulder. 'What's that? What's happening?' I ask, as he collects a book and a charger from the side of his chair. 'Alex?'

'I didn't think you'd be home 'til later.'

'I had an accident. At work. I texted, did you get it?' Alex shakes his head. 'I'm okay, I'm fine. I just…' but Alex moves to the kitchen, flicking through some post and binning whatever he doesn't want. 'Alex, I've been talking to someone, I realise something. I know you're struggling. I know I've not helped.'

He stops still.

'It's okay, Alex. I know. I get it. I'm sorry if I've got it all wrong until now but I've never been around someone who's suffering like this, like you are. I just… I thought I was doing the right thing and I can see now that I wasn't. Or maybe that there is no right thing because how you feel changes. What you need changes. I just want you to know that I'm ready to learn, to take your lead. I've been reading something, it's helped give me some perspective, maybe it would help you too?' I rummage in my bag. 'I want to give you all the support you need to help you through this, not the support I think you want. You'll be okay, Alex… we'll be okay, one way or another.' I pull out the notebook.

'How do you know I'll be okay? How do we know we'll be okay? Too much has passed, it's gone too far. I'm broken… we're broken.'

All breath leaves my body as he slings his bag on his shoulder and I can feel something coming that I'm powerless to stop.

'I went to Wigsy's because he thought his wife could help. He understood. He understands. He's been there. And it did help, on some level. It did because it made me realise that the only thing I know now, with absolute certainty, is that this… us… it's not helping.' He stares but I can't look back because this hurts too much and I don't want him to see. I don't want him to feel worse. 'I'm sorry,' he says, taking his house key off the bunch with his car keys. He places it on the kitchen side. 'I'm sorry,' he says again. 'I wish this wasn't happening.' He steps towards me. It's as if he's about to reach out to me, yet he stops himself and I know better than to force it. And I know better than to argue. I have to let him do this. I have to let him go and it has to be as painless as it can be for him.

He takes an envelope out of his back pocket. 'I thought I'd be gone before you came back. I was going to leave this on the side.' He hands me a letter. Our fingers brush for the briefest moment, where he holds my gaze and deep in his eyes I see what used to be. The man that I love is still in there somewhere. And then he leaves.

A car horn sounds outside. A tractor bumbles along. I stare at the kitchen floor, the tiles we laid together, reclaimed terracotta, set down with love. They blur as I slide down the cupboards to the floor. I try to breathe through it, but there is nothing to stop the pain swelling from stomach to chest, to eyes. Piercing and stinging the back of my throat. This isn't a text message to say he's popping away for a few days. This is Alex, leaving. And this time, I don't think he's coming back.

Chapter Sixty-Seven

My love,

There's something that happens in a marriage. A moment, maybe something as significant as childbirth or as seemingly insignificant as a cup of tea brought up to bed when you're least expecting it. Whatever the moment, you realise that you've spent all your lives learning and growing as people. You've seen each other at your worst and your very best. You've heard anger and you've felt disappointment. You've let them down or you've been let down. You've judged and been judged. You've detached, yet always, you've reunited. You've returned to the one person who forgives all those choices and more. And that is the moment when you realise, above all else, that this person you love and who has loved you in return, means more to you than you ever thought possible. And life without them seems unspeakable. Unbearable.

I loved you, I love you. And that can never be undone. No matter how far apart we are. No matter what our future holds.

From,

The love you wished I could be.

Chapter Sixty-Eight

Geoff lay awake, his eyes fixed on a point on the ceiling. The ward was dark, which seemed to make the hushed tones of nurses on change-over even louder, the patients pressing buzzers for help, a toilet flush, a cry. Normally, such darkness and such noises brought about his anxieties, his memories. They'd fill him with anxious tension, worse if he was tired or stressed. He was both of those things now and yet he felt neither anxious nor tense.

In the past, when the terrors took hold, Connie would hold him close, she'd let him cry without asking him what the matter was, without forcing him to speak of what he saw: the prisoners in the camp next door, painfully thin and ghostlike, here one day, gone the next. The men, his friends, shot down at his feet by snipers. The torture of fellow prisoners, the fears they would share. The mixed emotions over the days they'd play football, or perform a pantomime, all for their captors' entertainment. Sometimes they'd even share laughter and though it passed the hours the very thought brought about guilt and shame. They were, on balance, some of the lucky ones. Another thing to feel guilt about. As was the years he missed out on Rosemary growing up because he was so focused on work, on being the breadwinner for the family. On being the man of the house, as was expected. Post-traumatic stress? Is that what they'd call it now? He'd heard it talked about, when serving soldiers returned from Iraq or Afghanistan. But it wasn't something he'd considered for himself. Or maybe he hadn't dared admit it. To admit was to be weak? Or so he'd been raised to believe. Instead, Geoff had packed away his heart to save himself the same fate as his own father, a life drowning in grief and pain. And all that time, all those years, Connie had patiently, quietly, steadfastly let Geoff be Geoff. And all that time, he had no idea that in so doing, she'd patiently, quietly and steadfastly rebuilt him. He survived because of her. If it was time to let her go, he would continue to survive. Because of her.

Chapter Sixty-Nine

'Mum? Mum!'

I hear Tom's voice whilst still asleep. I'm dreaming of him as a young boy, we're at the park. He's running up to me, arms aloft, waiting for me to scoop him up into a hug. It's only when he comes into the bedroom that I wake up fully.

'Mum! Are you okay? I've just spoken to Dad. What's going on?'

'You spoke to your dad?' I pull the covers around me, my knees nestled into my chest. 'What did he say?'

'He rang from Uncle Rob's, asked to meet me, he wants to talk. He said he'd packed a few things and was stopping there. What's going on?'

'I don't know, Tom. I don't know. Your dad's... he's not well.'

'What do you mean he's not well? What's wrong with him? Is he going to die?'

'What? No! No. It's not that, it's...' I can't help wondering if it's my place to say and realise I feel ill-equipped to deal with any questions he might have. How much does Alex want to tell him? How much does he truly understand for himself? 'He's just... he's struggling. Let him talk to you himself. I think he needs space. I don't know how long for, or if it will help, but we have to let him do what he needs to do... because we love him.'

'If he's struggling, surely here is the best place for him? At home with us.'

'I don't think it's that simple. I've tried but maybe I've not handled things well, love. I don't think I've helped him. He needs to do this his way.' I look to the bedside table, James' notebook is there, face down on a page I must have been reading when I came upstairs. Alex's letter is within the pages too. I've still not read it. I couldn't. I came to bed, I looked through James' book. The more of his letters I read, the more I feel I know what Alex might be going through. The loss. The darkness. The despair, even.

Tom climbs in bed beside me. 'Are you splitting up?' he asks, gently.

'No! I don't know… I don't think so, I don't… I don't know what's happening, to be honest. I just need to wait, I need to leave your dad to work out what he wants and how he feels.'

'And what do you do whilst that's happening?'

'Wait?'

'For how long?' he asks and part of me wants to tell him as long as it takes. 'What do I say to him about it?'

I look at my boy, the man he's now become is in hiding. His face is fraught, nervous, young again. You think about the kids when they're little, if you have an argument or hit a rough patch, you imagine what it would do to them to split up, but when they're older it's not the same. And yet, it's clear it is exactly the same for him. 'Come here.' I pull him into me, tucking the duvet around his back and kissing him on top of his head. 'You do and say whatever feels right and know that it can't be wrong if you're doing your best. You just have to wait and see if it's what Dad needs.'

'I don't understand.'

'I don't think any of us do, not really. We're all just trying our best. Wishing we knew more than we do. Wishing a grown-up might tell us what's right.'

'You are the grown-ups,' he says.

'Doesn't always feel like that.' I stroke his head and he relaxes into me. 'I love your dad. I always have, and I always will. No matter what happens.'

'I don't want to go.'

'Tom, you need to. He's your dad. He'll want to talk to you. We need to be there for him, on his terms.'

'What about my terms? What about what I want?'

'Well…'

'I'm not going. Not tonight. If he needs space, maybe so do I.'

'Well then you need to call him.' Tom buries his head further into the bedding with a groan. 'Come on, please, love, you must. Don't be angry with him, this isn't his fault.' Tom doesn't move. 'Shall I call him for you?'

'No.'

'Come on then.'

Reluctantly, Tom pulls out his phone and dials his dad's number. There's a pause, before the line connects. And something inside the drawer on Alex's side of the bed rings out. Tom looks at me and I do everything in my power not to let on how much it hurts that the one thing he's lived with, by, practically inside of, is his phone. He didn't just leave me, or Tom for that matter, he left everything.

Chapter Seventy

Tom sleeps beside me. I called Rob in the end, asked him to pass a message on to Alex that Tom couldn't meet him as planned. I mentioned the phone, as casually as I could, just in case it was a mistake to leave it behind. It probably wasn't very casual at all because Rob just said he'd pass the message on and sounded all older brother protective, like I was some mad, crazy stalker woman, not Alex's partner of two decades.

Tom went through several phases of upset, anger, disappointment, disbelief. He kept asking if we'd get back together. If I'd stay at the house. He told me he wouldn't move out after all, I told him he had to. That it is important. That this situation should not mean he has to change his plans. That we haven't split up and I am staying in the house. Only some of which is true given that I don't actually know about any of these things right now. Whatever happens, I'm still taking the *Rocky* box set. Some things are non-negotiable.

So now that he's asleep, I keep looking over at James' book. Alex's letter within. I reach for it, his block capital handwriting. The pen had run out before making it to the end of my name so he's replaced it with red biro instead. He used to write notes to me all the time, his writing hasn't changed. The paper was always scruffy, ripped in haste because he was hiding it beneath the sandwich of a packed lunch I'd made to take to work. I'd get to the shops sometimes, pulling out a list taken on the back of an old birthday card. There'd be doodles, or requests for food, drink or (more often than not) sexual favours. At the back of the loft, in an old briefcase, there's a bundle of them. Each kept and occasionally read when I've gone up for a suitcase or the Christmas decorations. So many times, I've sat amongst the boxes and cold of our loft, warming my heart with the memories each note would bring. The letters he'd write when we first met, the notes round the house when we first moved in. The cards and photos we'd each leave for the other in micro acts of romance. I'd pulled them together one day, wrapping them up with the piece of ribbon he'd used to dangle my engagement ring from the Christmas tree, back in the days when we both made an effort to surprise and woo each other.

I never minded that romance, the kind you'd find in a book, had long gone. That the surprises were no longer tickets to the theatre, a map for a walk that he loved, rose petals in the bath or a mystery tour to his favourite pubs; that those things fizzled out didn't matter. They'd been replaced with cups of tea in bed, a piece of toast or an egg wrap on the weekend. A pesto pan washed up even when it was my turn to do the dishes, because he knew how I hated the smell. It was still romance of sorts, just a different kind. The longevity of our marriage might have erased the surprises of new love, but it had replaced them with a comforting shorthand. A shorthand I miss.

I unfold the letter. Swallowing back a nip of disappointment that there's no nickname, or kiss, or anything to ease the formality. I grit my teeth…

Dear Helen,

I don't know what went wrong. Or why. I've spent so many months trying to work out how to fix it and it's clear to me now

that I can't. We can't. You were the love of my life and yet I find I
have no feelings. Not for you, not for me… not for anyone.

I wish things were different, I really do.

I'll talk to Tom. I'll be in touch when I've found somewhere to
go of my own.

I'm sorry,

Alex.

Breath shallow, teeth clenched, I reread the words. Words of singular
dimension. No sub-message, no hidden meaning, no glimmer of who
we used to be amongst the pain. All our years together and he goes,
leaving this. It might as well be a note for the postie, or the milkman.
No milk today.

I stare at the wall, lost without thought, until they arrive, noisily,
pushing their way to the front, tiny ideas jostling, eager for attention.
How will I keep paying the bills all alone? How can I manage the
house? When Tom leaves, I'll rattle around. Will I be on my own
forever? Will Alex meet somebody else? Each anxious thought is like
a primary schoolchild, hand thrust in the air, bouncing on the carpet
in desperate bid for attention. Thoughts and words that pour into my
heart like setting concrete. If I'd seen this coming, like, really seen it
coming, I might have been better prepared. I know he said he needed
space, I know I could see a future unfolding that didn't have him in
it but I've been hanging on to a shred of hope that maybe I was over-
reacting, that it really is just space. This letter though, and leaving his
phone. It's more than space. It's an ending.

I stop. I breathe. I fix my eyes on a tiny spot on the wall. A spot
representing my future. Maybe he's right. Maybe this is best for us both
and I've just not been able to see it. Maybe, if I think about it properly,

maybe this is the first thing we can agree on for a while. Because the man who could leave behind everything he once held dear, is not the man I want in my life. That's not the man I signed up with till death do us part. Just as all the notes before had opened up my love for him, this one zips me right up. It locks my heart. I just wish I knew what to do with the key.

Almost twenty years. One man. One son. One life, together, done. It wasn't supposed to be this way.

Chapter Seventy-One

A nurse wheeled the ward payphone into Geoff's room. 'Here you go, love.'

'Thank you.'

Geoff dialled the number for the home, just to check in. He wanted to know for himself that Connie was okay. 'Good morning,' he said, when the phone was eventually picked up. 'It's Mr Steele, Connie's husband. I was just calling to find out how she was?'

'Ah, Mr Steele, how are you? Are you feeling any better? Bless you, you must have been so frightened, but it's all fine, she's in good hands, as are you.'

'Erm, yes, thank you.' Geoff didn't know how to take the lady's tone, she was sympathetic, but he couldn't help feeling as though she talked down to him. Like he was one of those old people that people bend down to, or talk louder to, as if he was deaf and old and a child, all rolled into one. 'I shall be coming home soon, hopefully before the weekend. Will it be okay for me to let you know so that we can organise things for Connie?'

'Oh! Well, there's no rush, Mr Steele, I mean, she's perfectly fine here. Maybe it would be better for you to have a few days at home to rest up before she gets back?'

'It may be. It depends how she is too. I'd just like to be certain,' said Geoff.

There were voices in the background, the phone line was muffled and the lady he was talking to spoke to somebody else. He couldn't make out the detail. 'Sorry, Mr Steele, I'm going to have to call you back. There's been—'

'But Connie, I'd like to organise—'

'I'm terribly sorry, Mr Steele, I'll call you as soon as I can.'

And with that, the lady hung up.

Geoff looked across to the side of his bed and a photo of Connie, brought in by Rosemary. He had taken it on an old camera he'd borrowed from one of the elders in the church. They were at a picnic on the beach with friends. She stared into the lens, seeing through it, seeing into his soul as he captured the moment. She loved him. Against all she'd said of him not being mature enough, against her own mothers' protest at the time, against the advice of the elders in their church. Advice that said they were too young for such intense feelings, that it would never last. That they should concentrate on work not on each other. But she loved him. And he her. Her face was fresh, he'd captured that moment. He could close his eyes and see her still. After the click of the camera, she lay back with her hands behind her head, her body melting into the sand with late summer heat and overwhelming happiness. His charm and dedication had finally won her over.

Had he repaid her? Had he been a good husband? Lord knows, he'd tried his very best. He just wanted to do that one last time, go see her in the home, make sure her staying there was going to be in her best interests, irrespective of what he might prefer.

Chapter Seventy-Two

I think I finally dropped off around four this morning, so Zoe's 7 a.m. text message of *Are you still coming today? The rocket is late, so I can't pick up the artisan chocolates, Claire's having a meltdown, can you help?* wasn't necessarily met with the all the positivity in the world.

I mean, a rocket for Christ's sake? What world is this? Real Housewives of Bingley? After being mardy about it, I dutifully text her back, *Of course, tell me where and how much.*

They're from …And Chocolate, Main Street, Haworth. All paid for. Need them by 11. Mwoah!

Stretching, I groan, my body aching. I don't know if that's the accident yesterday, when your muscles all tighten and everything locks up. Or stress. Both, probably.

Tom got up and gave me a hug this morning, told me it was all going to be okay, that we were going to be okay. That he'd help out with the bills because he was earning decent money and wanted to pay his way. His demonstration of unity threatened to undermine my resolve, so I told him I had an eyelash in my eye and rubbed so hard they couldn't help but water.

Downstairs, as the kettle boils, another message comes through. This time from Claire. *Zoe is driving me crazy! Send help! And gin!*

The mental image of Claire lugging a child on each hip, whilst preparing the house for a million four-year-olds comes to mind. Bets on Zoe being busy with the finishing touches around Claire's house and that she hasn't even noticed she's on the edge of a meltdown. It's probably a good thing that I have this on today. The noise will drown out whatever thoroughly depressing inner monologue my subconscious is peddling. Time to pause life for a few hours.

Chapter Seventy-Three

I lift a stack of beautifully wrapped chocolates out of the boot of my car, just as a minibus arrives with about thirty toddlers and their parents. The minibus has been decorated to look like a dinosaur, which I can't be certain is entirely road legal, but the kids are delighted and I suspect that's all that matters to Zoe. As they get off and file into the house, one of the mums looks scornfully at the replica rocket, now nestled in a makeshift launcher in the garden, and I put a secret bet on with myself that she's Felicity Hedgefund's mum. I nip through the crowds, hands aloft with chocolates, ditching into the kitchen.

'Quickly, quickly, this way,' says Zoe, ushering me in. Claire is in the kitchen, too, leant against the Aga with a large coffee and a dazed expression. She doesn't look ready to host her son's fourth birthday party. She barely looks human. Zoe continues buzzing about, barking instructions. 'Helen, dig around in the bottom of my handbag, you'll find some candles along with one of those indoor fireworks. I'm just going to set the children up with pass the parcel, you should see the gift, a miniature Gucci wallet!'

'Zoe!' exclaims Claire in total despair.

'What?' She says it with all the innocence of a lump hammer. 'It was at the back of my wardrobe! I think I probably bought it as a present for someone who I've no interest in seeing again and, let's face it, the kids won't know it's last season.'

'They won't know 'cause they're children and don't need a Gucci wallet!'

Zoe steps in closer to her. 'You wanted to nip this nonsense in the bud, didn't you?'

'Well, yes, but… I'm not sure this isn't adding fuel to an already well-flaming, designer party fire!'

'No. I've got the Gucci wallet pass the parcel, a lucky dip involving a weekend away which is hidden amongst the quinoa, and the entertainer may or may not have been a runner up on *Britain's Got Talent*.'

'Zoe! How much has all this cost you?' asks Claire.

'Never you mind. Nothing is too much for my Finlay. Especially not if it fucks off the Hedgefunds,' she says, before realising a parent with toddler balanced on hip has just wandered in behind her. 'Apologies. Potty mouth. Now come on!' She sweeps them away from the kitchen with an authoritative clap of her hands, taking the pass the parcel with her as she passes me by.

Claire gives me a look of abject horror and I roll my eyes. I was right, this is exactly what I needed. How can anyone not be distracted by this car crash playing out?

'Let's peek,' I say, dragging Claire behind me.

'Sit in a circle, come on.' Zoe claps her hands again. 'Babies on laps, please, that's it. Toddlers beside you, they're old enough to unwrap for themselves. Now, NO CHEATING!' she instructs, as Katy Perry starts singing something about a plastic bag. 'If I see you hanging on to the package waiting for me to stop the music you will be disqualified. No arguments. There's something in there for everyone so let's get passing!' She whoops, turning up the music and jigging about like only a woman without children to give her a disdainful look ever could.

'Wow,' I say to Claire. 'Now I get why you look like you've been steamrollered!'

'Since 6.30 a.m.!' says Claire, wiping her knackered face. 'She arrived with a helium balloon filler and three hundred multi-coloured balloons that needed blowing up before 9 a.m.'

'9 a.m.?' I follow her back into the kitchen.

'I don't know why. Apparently they needed several hours to settle into place and she had a million other things to do as well. I am literally running on caffeine!' She flicks the kettle on whilst reaching into the fridge for the coffee. 'You having one?'

'Thanks.'

I take the milk out the fridge, passing it to Claire, enjoying the noise. Katy Perry gets frequently interrupted and replaced with a hurried rip of paper and a chorus of oooohs. Claire pours steaming hot water on ground coffee, sniffing deeply to smell it. 'God, that smells so good. Let's take a moment.'

'Some kid's just been sick on your carpet, have you got any wipes?' interrupts Zoe, her head poking around the door whilst looking back at the action.

'How's someone been sick already? The buffet hasn't started yet!'

'I may have handed out unlimited yum yum's on the party bus over here. No! Mario! Leave it!' she shouts and I dread to think what this Mario kid is doing.

Claire gets out a pack of wipes, then throws them back in the cupboard, heading to the drawer for a different pack instead. 'Organic!'

'Of course, God forbid we should landfill with anything else!' Zoe disappears again and, after a few moments, the music ramps back up again forcing Claire to squeeze her eyes together with thumb and forefinger before looking back at me in desperation.

'You look like I feel,' I say. 'Quick, grab the biscuits, then follow me.' I wink. She follows, somewhat surprised as I crouch down and crawl beneath the table, hiding within the draped tablecloth that protects us from view. Whilst three sides of the table are hidden by the cloth, one is exposed, looking through vast glass doors and out onto their acres of neatly clipped garden. 'And relax,' I say, dunking a chocolate Hobnob into my coffee and sucking off the chocolate.

'Oh my goodness, can we stop here for the rest of the day?' Claire asks, through biscuit crumbs and descending joy. 'I love Zoe, but she is hellish at a party!' she says, popping the rest of the biscuit into her mouth and taking a good slug of coffee.

'Bless her. I can't decide if you are crazy or genius for letting her do this.'

'Claire?' booms Zoe's voice and we hold our breath, eyes wide. It goes quiet for a second then Zoe mutters something sweary yet unintelligible before moving from fridge to pantry to the table we are hiding under, then back out of the kitchen saying something about the Heimlich manoeuvre.

Waiting until she's out of earshot, we both fall about laughing. 'Jesus, I needed this!' I reach for another biscuit, stacking two on my kneecap.

'How are things? How's Alex? Did you tell him about the job or had I pissed him off too much to mention it?'

'I don't think you pissed him off. No more than I already had. No more than it appears I have been doing for months. God, where do I start? No, I don't think it was you specifically, so much as life at the moment. I was home early 'cos I crashed the bus.'

'Shit!'

'I know, right. That's me out of the Bus Driver of the Year Award.'

'That's a thing?'

'Of course! I've a long held ambition to be the first woman to win it.'

'Of course you have,' says Claire in a way that makes me laugh. 'That's not it though, is it? What's really bothering you?'

'Alex left.'

'Left? Where to? Did he say who the message was for? Jesus, what is going on with him?'

'The message was for his counsellor.'

'His counsellor?'

I nod.

'And he's gone.'

I nod again.

'Gone, gone?'

I try not to cry. I don't want to cry.

'Shit.'

'I know,' I sniff.

'We need to get the girls together.'

'I don't think I want to—'

'Nonsense. This is a crisis, we always need each other in a crisis.'

'What crisis?' asks Zoe. 'And where the fuck are you two?'

Claire lifts the tablecloth, shoving her head from beneath it. 'We're hiding from you. And children. And life.'

'Can I come in?'

'No! You've got a party to host! It was your idea.'

Zoe groans. 'Jesus, I am literally never doing this again!' She notices my face. 'Oh, love! What's the matter?'

We crawl out from beneath the table. 'It's Alex,' answers Claire on my behalf.

'I knew it!' she says.

'No, no. Not that. He's not been right for months. I think it's serious. I think he needs to see someone, talk to someone, I don't know – get medication.'

'He's depressed?'

'James thinks it's everywhere. He suffered. Turns out the notebook, with the letters, that was his.'

'James? As in freerider James?'

'What notebook and who the fuck is freerider James?' A dad walks in with a toddler, interrupting Zoe momentarily. 'Christ, every time, sorry – potty mouth. Okay, hold these thoughts, we need to talk. When the kids have all gone home and I can swear freely! Call Vicky, see if she can come round after school.' She turns to the dad. 'Can I help you?'

'You don't all have to do this,' I say to Claire.

'Do what? Look after our best mate when she needs us? Get the girls together to make sure you're okay? Do everything we need to to keep your spirits up as you fight whatever fight you need to fight? That's what friends do, Helen. That's what you'd do for us. Now, grab some party food. The sooner we can get this lot fed and every last game played, the sooner we can get them out of my house!'

Chapter Seventy-Four

The smell of cleaning fluid wafted through the corridors, seeping into Geoff's room. The ssht, ssht sound of liberal anti-bacteria spraying was swiftly followed by the rattle of bracelets as the cleaner wiped down doors and handles, before heading into his room.

'Afternoon, Mr Steele, you all right? I'm just going to give the room a quick once-over, if that's okay.'

'Good afternoon, yes of course, no problem.'

'Have you seen outside? The snowdrops are peeking through, bitterly cold, but there they are, happily popping up all over. It must take the gardeners hours, planting all of those bulbs. Do they need planting each year? I'm not much of a gardener, I'm afraid.'

Sssht. Sssht. Rattle rattle.

'I think they're perennials,' said Geoff. 'They grow and multiply each year.'

'Oh. Isn't that amazing. And so lovely when you're stuck in here to be able to see nature growing out of the window and so on.' She gets out an extendable duster, reaching up with a stretch to sweep along the length of the windows. There was no dust, like there might have been at home. 'You in for long?' she asked, reverting back to the spray as she moved round to the sink.

'I hope not, no. I'm feeling much better already,' he said. Which wasn't a total lie. He was nervous, of going home and his future being taken out of his hands, but he'd had time to think in the hospital. Time to look at the photo of Connie and realise she needed him to be okay with whatever the authorities felt was the best thing for her. They were paid professionals. They knew their jobs. Who was he to challenge them; if Connie needed to be in a home, then he would find a way to put his feelings aside, just as she had for him over the years. Connie's needs must come first.

'Mr Steele?' There was a tap on glass and a young woman appeared in the doorway. 'Would you have a moment?'

'Of course,' he answered.

She looked to the cleaner who gave a nod and left the room, pulling the door to. 'I'm Jessica, I'm from the pastoral care team.' She pulled up a chair and Geoff felt time stop. 'It's Connie,' she said, solemnly. 'The home called us, your wife has had a bad fall, Mr Steele.' Geoff tried to sit up but the young woman moved to keep him where he was. 'Please, be careful, Mr Steele.'

'What happened? Is she okay?'

'She's been admitted here. She's still in emergency at the moment. They're trying to establish the extent of her injuries.'

'But… she was in the home. They were supposed to look after her. They keep telling me they can do it better than me, that she needs their care. She's never fallen at home.' Geoff grew increasingly distressed and breathless.

'Please, be careful, Mr Steele. You're not well yourself and I'd hate this to make things worse, I understand you're on the mend and hoping to be released soon.'

'Yes. I was hoping to go home today, tomorrow maybe. I was hoping to have Connie back for a few days before she… well, she can't go there now, she has to stay with me.'

The young woman stood up to help shuffle Geoff into a more comfortable position.

'I knew she was better with me,' he said and coughed. 'I told everybody…' Geoff coughed again, sitting back, trying to catch his breath. Eventually, he said, 'They were supposed to look after her.'

'I understand, Mr Steele. I'm sure they were doing their very best, Connie could have fallen at any time.'

'She's never fallen at home.'

The young woman looked down at her hands. 'They may need to operate on her, Mr Steele. So they are having to do a number of scans and tests to understand the extent of any damage, eliminate the threat of internal bleeds, and establish how strong she is to cope with the trauma of any necessary treatment.'

'The trauma?'

'It was a bad fall, Mr Steele.'

'When can I see her? I need to see her. She will need me there.' Geoff tried to swing his legs round but the bedding had been so tightly pin-tucked, just the way Connie hated, yet she wasn't here to untuck him as he had her. He couldn't move quickly enough. He couldn't escape.

The young woman stood, placing her hand on his leg. 'You need to let the team do what they have to do, first. Please, Mr Steele, I understand how distressing this is for you. She won't be aware of anything at the moment, the medication she's been administered will keep her body calm whilst we treat her. Your daughter is on her way, she will be able to liaise between yourself and the ward Connie's on.'

'She's never fallen at home,' repeated Geoff, his voice faltering now. 'They told me it was in her best interests. I was about to let her go.'

'I can assure you she's in excellent hands with us,' the young woman said, looking down at her pager as it buzzed in her hand. 'I'm afraid I… I need to go. I'll come back and see you shortly. I'll try to get an update for you. Please try not to worry, Mr Steele, we will do everything we can for her.'

We will do everything we can for her. He thought. How bad is she? How quickly will she recover? Why couldn't he see her? Why did Rosemary let them take her in when he became ill? Why couldn't anyone see that she was better off with him? They were better off together. They always had been, for more than seventy years.

Chapter Seventy-Five

My love,

When I left, I don't think I imagined it would be forever. Maybe I didn't think at all. I just needed to get away, I felt suffocated, stifled. I could hear what you were saying, and I guess I could probably understand, maybe even agree with some of it, but I just couldn't do it. I couldn't live it. I couldn't change. And each day I felt the same, was a day my guilt would increase as you'd tiptoed around me.

I remember the conversations, us sitting, you with your hands upon mine, asking me to talk to you, to talk to somebody else. Asking me to consider medication, or exercise, or some kind of spiritual therapy you'd come across and thought might help.

I remember how you looked each day, I could see it. Maybe you thought I couldn't. But I could, I could see how tired you were, how frustrated you grew. How angry at times. How alone you felt, how distracted. I could see it and, yet, I was powerless. All strength was gone and I couldn't find any way to reach out so that you didn't feel so alone.

I remember hushed conversations with friends. I remember the sighs. I remember the moments of hope if I had a good day, and how much harder you seemed to fall when things went back, often further, darker each time.

I remember hearing you cry.

How I wish you knew I made it in the end. How I wish you could see me now.

From,

The love you wished I could be.

Chapter Seventy-Six

I close James' book. There's something about reading such personal thoughts, you start to picture yourself in their world. You wonder how it relates and now, I find myself torn. How much of what I'm reading is Alex and how much is me? How much am I living day-to-day as James' wife did? Is there a part of this situation that places me between the two? Am I part fixer, part broken? There must be something broken to think lunch with Martin was a good idea. To talk that explicitly. I was playing at it, I was pretending to be somebody I'll never be. That I don't want to be. And in the process, I hurt the person I love the most.

God, I did that. To Alex. To Martin. What was I thinking? It was embarrassing. It was desperate.

The girls rallied round this afternoon. Even Zoe put her own prejudice to one side to listen and offer up advice. I told them about Martin, about Alex seeing us. About thinking I could get back at him. They didn't judge. In fact, Zoe said it was a shame I hadn't had a chance to have a fling before the truth came out. Claire shot her a warning look and we all agreed that was bad advice. By the time Vicky joined us, we'd sunk two bottles of Prosecco and Claire had brought the gin out. I left my car there but avoided having too much more to drink. I'm not sure alcohol helps my mood just at the moment.

So now I'm back home. Just me and James' book, tucked up on the sofa. The front door slams, Tom calls out and disappointment floods my bones. I knew it wouldn't be Alex but for a split second I hoped. I wonder how long it will take for that to pass. Will it ever?

'You in, Mum?' he shouts, clattering through the hall and into the kitchen. Doors and drawers are flung open then shut again, bags rustling and the tap running.

'Through here.'

'Tea?' He sticks his head around the kitchen door. He's much brighter than the last time I saw him.

'Oh, I don't know if we have milk.' I do know. And I know it's off.

'I've bought some, and a few other bits and bobs. I wasn't sure what we had in, if you'd had time to go to the shops.' He's unpacking shopping. Putting bread away, teabags. A few more Pot Noodles in his special cupboard along with beans, pasta and tins of tuna. 'You had tea?'

'Erm, no. Not yet.' I step towards him, trying to intercept as he reaches for two mugs as the kettle boils. 'Are you okay, love? You seem…'

'I'm fine.'

'It's just… you were so upset last night, and now you're all…'

'Well, what can I do? I can't mope around about it all. I can't change what's happening. I just figured, I might as well man up.'

Helen cringed. 'I hate that phrase. What does man up even mean? We're your parents, you're allowed to be upset about the situation.'

'Okay, sorry. You know what I mean though.' He pours hot water on the tea bags, reaching for the milk with his free hand.

'I suppose so.' My little boy busies around the kitchen, wiping down the surface after passing me my drink. 'Thank you for this.'

'It's just a cup of tea, Mum.'

'And the shopping.'

'I was passing the Co-op. It's fine.'

I reach for my purse, pulling out a tenner and stuffing it in his hand. 'Here, have this.'

'I don't need it, Mum. I got paid. Besides, most stuff has gone in my cupboard so, you know… it's for me.' He throws me a wink. 'No nicking my Pot Noodles!' He pulls a bag of crisps from a bag in his cupboard, along with a banana and a bag of biscuits. I resist pointing out that these items do not exactly constitute a healthy, balanced meal.

'Oh, Mum,' he says, one foot perched on the bottom step of the back stairs. 'Dad called.' My heart skips. 'He says he's going to stay at Uncle Rob's for the foreseeable.'

'Right.'

'I thought I might swing over tomorrow, after work. If you didn't mind.'

'Why would I mind?'

'Well… you know.'

I go over to him, planting a kiss on his cheek. 'Of course I don't mind. He's your father. He needs to see you, and I'm sure you need to see him.'

'Yeah… I just… I don't want you to think I'm taking sides or anything. I'm not, I mean, I'm still cross with him. Frustrated. But, I thought I could talk to him. It might help.'

'Of course. It's fine, love. Honestly.'

He smiles at me and despite all the grown-up stuff, I can still see the tiny baby who'd roll on his play mat when I was on maternity leave, the toddler that would run to my arms if I ever went away, the young teenager, his voice squeaking, his chin breaking out in a complex mixture of stubble and spots. 'I love you,' I say to his retreating back.

'Love you too,' he answers, before closing his door behind him.

So Alex is with his brother. I guess that's a good thing. I suppose I'm pleased, that he's turned to family. He and his brother have never been close, but maybe that helps. Maybe he can get Alex back.

Maybe I should take some time to get me back in the meantime. I step closer to the mirror in the lounge. I look tired, drawn even. The fullness of my slightly overweight, kissing forty, cheeks, has gone. I have cheekbones, not seen since my teens. Pre-Tom. But I also have bags, dark circles, fine lines, the telltale signs of the years that I smoked, just at the edges of my mouth. I peer closer, realising I've not looked at myself in detail for months. Years even. I've not paid attention to the woman staring back at me. I'm worn, ragged, I look like I'm carrying the weight of the world and, in truth, that is what it feels like. Did James' wife get to a point where she saw it was time to let go? And if so, what was her turning point?

Chapter Seventy-Seven

When a porter wheeled Geoff into Connie's room, his heart broke at the sight of her. Tiny, wrapped up in the crisp white sheets, the left-hand side of her face black and purple, a little swollen. 'How is she?' he had asked.

'She's…' the nurse had paused. She looked to her feet. To her knees. She'd smoothed down her skirt. 'She's not well, Mr Steele,' was pretty much all she could offer, but he could see that for himself, he still can, looking at her now.

They thought she'd had a stroke. They couldn't be sure what damage had been done yet. There was a knot in his stomach, a hole in his chest. He'd been sat for a while, Rosemary still on her way having been caught up in horrendous traffic on the M62.

A nurse came into the room. 'It's past six,' Geoff said. 'She likes to eat at six. She gets distressed if she doesn't eat at six.' The nurse did one of those sympathy smiles, as if Geoff hadn't realised his wife couldn't eat in her current condition.

He swallowed. He resisted rubbing at his chest, where the hole was being replaced by a deep ache that suffocated. He found himself wishing she looked like the Connie she'd gradually become, heavy rouged cheeks and all. Where once she'd roll her hair, then release sometime later, using her pink comb to tease the curls into a soft covering across her head, she'd started asking him to put the curlers in, and when she took them out, she'd leave the tight lines of twisted hair across her head. What he wouldn't give to have her look that way now. In that bed. Instead, Geoff's wife had almost gone. And Geoff could feel his future arriving. He could see the end. He wasn't sure when it would come exactly, but it was close. And he didn't know what he was going to do. He'd thought he was prepared, he'd thought he was ready for the next part of their story. He knew it was the final act, he knew they were both nearing their natural end, but he hadn't realised how much it would hurt to see that in front of him, in reality. In that bed. All he did know was that there were things in his life, in their life, that he'd been avoiding. Things he'd never told her. Things he had only just accepted himself. And he was tired of keeping up the pretence. He wanted to change that. He wanted to tell people how she was because ignoring the truth helped nobody. He wanted to admit to the people he knew cared, that life had taken a dark turn. Connie was gravely ill.

He needed to address it with the people who cared: Rosemary, Helen, Ruby up at the post office. Bill at the pub. The people in the bank. The last remaining friends up at chapel. Geoff had spent a life pretending to be something and somebody that he wanted everyone to believe him to be. It was easy that way, it meant he could pretend he was fearless, he could detach himself from the eleven-year-old who'd had to grow up. From the eighteen-year-old who fought for his country. The twenty-one-year-old prisoner of war. The man in his nineties who was so frightened of being alone, he'd pushed real connections away... with everyone, except his wife.

And that was why he'd pretended.

And she was the reason he had to stop.

Chapter Seventy-Eight

I've been hiding. Sleeping when I wanted. Eating when I could be bothered. Pretending I was fine whenever Tom came home and embracing the hot mess I was when he left. I kept wanting to switch Alex's phone on, just to see if anyone had been in touch with him. I didn't, obviously; instead, I scrolled through our old conversations on my phone. If I scrolled far enough, I'd get to a time when we were still friends. A text just to say he loved me. A photo of the hotel room he was staying in whilst away on business. A single kiss.

It didn't take me long before I realised I needed to come back to work. I needed to stop wallowing. I needed to get the fight back. I needed the money.

'Are you sure you're ready?' asks Janice, holding her pen between thumb and forefingers, twisting it. She's studying me, her eyes narrowed, her chin high. It probably isn't supposed to be intimidating, Janice isn't really like that. 'It's only been a few days and, of course, we know it wasn't your fault. The conditions were terrible, that corner in that snow and sleet, the other driver just lost control but still, it's only been a few days.'

'I'm positive.' I smile. 'I feel fine.' I resist the urge to rub the small of my back, which has been niggling since I got up this morning. When I creaked out of bed like a woman in need of new hips, I did take a moment to stretch it out. I even did a downward dog because Vicky said they help. I think she was suggesting I take up regular yoga, not just do the occasional dog. And I guess if I did them a little more often, I probably wouldn't get stuck and then have to point the hot jets on it in the shower. Then take extra paracetamol. Yoga's not really my thing.

'I promise you, I'm fine. I wouldn't come back if I wasn't.' I didn't mention that I kept thinking about James whilst I've been off, and if he's been able to persuade anyone to let him on. And Geoff? Was Geoff okay? I didn't tell Janice that, in fact, I needed this job and all it gave me, just to get through these next few months of uncertainty.

Janice makes a note of something in her diary. 'Everything else okay?' she asks, taking great interest in the circle she's drawing around a date. She flips the pages, making marks that don't look like anything in particular. She doesn't look up. 'I mean, in general, are you okay? You know, in yourself?'

I shift in my seat. I don't talk about my life at work. I don't talk about home. Never have, it's just a rule.

'Only… well… I don't like to pry… but…' Janice flips her diary shut. 'Okay, look, so we had a phone call. Someone called Martin? He was asking if you were okay. And if he could have your number. Obviously, I didn't give it to him, but he did try a couple of times before I eventually said I'd take his number and pass it on to you.' She passes me a piece of paper with numbers scrawled on it. My face is getting undermined by the polyester jumper again, I don't even need to see in a mirror to know what colour purple it is.

'So there you go.' She points at the paper. 'There's his number. I should say that this is not appropriate, Mr Ali wouldn't like to think of us… having relations with our passengers… it's not…' I think she may now be as embarrassed as I am. 'I'm giving you the benefit of the doubt, that this is something entirely innocent. Okay?'

'Erm, yes… I mean, I wasn't. There isn't anything going on… Well, we had lunch and he did bring me flowers, but he didn't realise I was married and, anyway, he's just a friend.' I feel like that last bit is a lie.

'Right. Well. Good.' The chair leg scrapes as I move to stand. 'How's Alex?' she asks, her face buried back in her diary.

'Yes, yes. He's good, he's…' I search for the right word before dropping against the door frame and fessing up. 'Okay, no, he's not great. *We're* not great at the moment.' Janice looks up. 'Don't get me wrong, Martin has nothing to do with that!' I add in, quickly. 'It's just… a bit of a tricky period.'

'But you're sure you're okay to work? I don't want you driving when you're distracted.'

'I promise. I'm here. I'm focused…' I leave a pause because I don't know if I should admit how I feel, but figure I've nothing to lose? 'I need this, Janice.' I hold her gaze.

'Of course, of course you do, love. I'm sorry, I didn't mean to pry. If you need anything, give me a shout. Do you still want extra shifts? Mo has pulled his back so will be out of action for a little while.'

'Thank you. Yes, that would be great. Thanks, Janice.'

By the time I pull out of the station and along the road, I've settled back into my routine. I know where every single other car in my vicinity is, and I am not going to lose focus. I pull up to the traffic lights in town and it's reassuring to see James up ahead, making his way to the bus stop. When he sees the bus move on from the lights, I give him a flash and he sticks his arm out for me to stop.

'Helen!' he says, his face wide in smile, his eyes warm.

'James, it's so good to see you. Have you been okay? I came back as soon as I could.'

He grins at me. 'Ahm fine, cheers, Hel. How are you?'

'Yeah, yeah… not bad,' I say. 'I'm okay.'

'Sure?'

'Well, you know… I will be.' James gives me a wink then sits in his usual spot up front. I look up at the road ahead and realise there is nowhere else I want to be right now. Here, my job, I am going to be okay. I am.

Chapter Seventy-Nine

Geoff had set his alarm for the morning, just as he had for each morning since he came home from hospital. This last bout of illness had taken its toll and each day it took longer to come round, he was a little slower to get up. He was slower to make his way downstairs, often taking advantage of Connie's stairlift to take him. He ate breakfast, absentmindedly taking a bowl out for Connie, before realising and placing it on her place mat anyway, though of course she wasn't there. He listened to the news on the local radio, paying careful attention to the weather. He'd decided, last night, that today he would make a start on putting things right. Which is why he stood, waiting for the bus, ready for Helen's arrival.

At exactly 9.35 a.m. the bus turned the corner, as usual in perfect-precision time. As usual, he thought approvingly, thrusting a straight arm out for her to clearly see. Today, more than most days, he was grateful she flaunted the rules for him.

'Geoff!' she squeaked, as the doors bounced open. 'It's so lovely to see you!'

'Helen,' he replied, his formality coming more naturally than anything else.

'How are you? We've been worried about you both, haven't we, James?'

James nodded in agreement. 'Aye, we have. It's good te see you, Geoff.'

'How is Connie?'

'Well,' began Geoff, a little uncomfortable with the truth, but aware of the purpose of today's trip. 'To be honest, Helen, she's not so good, I'm sad to say.'

'Oh, Geoff…?' Helen put the handbrake on whilst Geoff found coins in his wallet, handing them over. James sat forward on his chair a little, listening. 'I was in Airedale Hospital for a few days, I had a… well…' Being honest was one thing, giving the detail was slightly trickier. 'I had a heart attack.'

'Oh, Geoff!'

'It's okay, I'm okay. I just have to be careful, take things steady.'

'And Connie?'

'Connie hasn't been well for a while. She has… Connie has Alzheimer's, Helen, James. It's… well, it's quite advanced now. So, when I was taken in, they had to move her to a care home.'

'Oh, Geoff.'

'Unfortunately, she had a fall there so she's now up at the hospital, too. It's… a difficult time. We're…'

'You don't have to talk about it, Geoff, we understand, don't we, James? Just, please do say… if there's anything at all that we can do. For you or for Connie. I have plenty of time, outside of work. I'd be happy to help out. Please, just ask.'

'Thank you, Helen.'

'So, where to today?'

'Just to the post office, please.'

And with that, it was over. The very thing Geoff had been so protective of, the information he'd sought to hide had been taken and handled with care and respect. No details were required, no analysing of his role in it all. Instead, it was simply taken as difficult, and kindness was offered. And neither Helen nor James looked at Geoff in any way other than that which they had always done. He didn't become a different person. He was not pitied or judged. He was simply a man who'd been ill. With a wife who was ill. Helen hadn't needed the detail, she hadn't needed the facts because she knew. And Geoff realised Helen knew just like Connie always knew. All the things he'd never said, all the fears he'd buried deep, the persona he created and why he lived that life. Connie had always known about everything, all along. Always.

Geoff took up his seat. He nodded to Helen when he was comfortable for her to move on, and up the hill they drove and Geoff soon realised that nothing had happened. Nobody judged. He'd told them the truth, and he didn't change. He was still Geoffrey Steele. A man they cared for. Husband of a woman they loved. And so the world kept turning.

Rosemary was on her way back over. She said she'd get there for around quarter past ten, so Geoff had asked her to pick him up from the post office. When she told him he wasn't well enough to be out and about, he let her rattle off her concerns, but stuck to his guns. He had five minutes on the bus, ten minutes in the post office, ten minutes to knock on Bill's door at the pub, five to wait patiently for his lift back home. And then it was time to go back to the hospital and see Connie, see if anything had changed at all. Change was happening, for him at least. And it was because of her; now, he could only pray that change was God's plan for her too.

Chapter Eighty

Who knew that normality can bring such relief to a weary mind? I wanted to hug James when he got on the bus this morning with his cheery smile. He asked me if I was okay but he didn't push for detail, he wasn't rushing to my rescue, he was just checking in then hanging about. It made me see why Alex might have needed that.

Poor Geoff though, all those years with Connie, they've been through it all. They were always so connected, so together. And to think that all this time Geoff has hidden her illness from us. Was it to protect her? I suppose I was an old neighbour, a bus driver, not a confidante. It's not my business, but I'm glad he opened up. Childhood sweethearts, that's how Connie described the two of them. She was the first to tell me to ignore the naysayers when Alex and I got together. I wonder what she'd say now? I wonder what she'd think about Martin? About what I did? Which I've been able to pretend not to think about for the most part until I drove up through Crossflatts first thing and feared Martin might be waiting. His phone number remains in my pocket. I don't think I'll call.

'Here you go, Geoff,' I say, pulling up at the post office. 'Take your time.'

'Thank you,' he says, moving down the bus.

'No problem. Go steady, I won't be offended if you end up getting a taxi for a while.'

'They'd never drive me as nicely as you do. And if I did that, I wouldn't see you or James. You brighten my day, you do.'

'And you brighten ours,' says James.

'Don't you worry, if we didn't see you on the bus, we can always pop round to brighten your day. I make a mean cuppa and I reckon I can just about remember where you keep your teabags.'

Geoff smiles. 'Oh, that won't be necessary, I can manage,' he said, taking each step slowly and carefully. At the bottom, he steadies himself, his hand gripping the handle firmly. He pauses before turning back to face me. 'What am I saying? Of course you can pop round, any time you like. I can't promise Connie will know who you are, but I will, and it would be lovely to see you both.'

I watch him as I drive away. He looks different, older and tired, but resolved, somehow. Not quite so buttoned up. We journey on, and the further along the route I get, the more I relax into my chair. The comfort I've always had driving the bus is still there. I love this job. Always have. The people, the travelling around town, the hills and the dales. At this time of year there's a real beauty to the winter bleakness, and spring will be here soon. Then the lush green fields of summer, the rich reds of autumn. It's fine, I'm where I'm supposed to be, no matter how things turn out at home, I have this. And it's good to be back.

I pull up at some lights, looking around me whilst waiting for them to change. The out-of-town offices that had been built some years back are crammed full of cars, multiple buildings with corporate logos on signage. There's not many people about, presumably because they're all being super-busy and important inside. A car turns into the car park closest to me, swinging into one of the few spaces left. The doors on either side of the car open and out of the passenger side climbs Alex.

Alex?

Except, it doesn't look like the Alex I've come to recognise of late. The joggers he's lived in for months have gone. So has his hair. Hair that had taken on a life of its own is now cropped short and neat. Maybe I'm mistaken. Again. Maybe it's not him. A car horn beeps behind me and I realise the lights are green. Trying to watch where he goes, but careful to check around me before pulling I way, I lose sight of him as I turn a corner. I should be glad that he's up and out and has had a haircut. It shows more motivation than he's displayed in months, but shit – why can he do that now? Has Rob made this happen? And if so, what did he say that I didn't?

'Left here!' shouts James down the bus.

I manage to take the turning, ensuring we keep on the right route, but I can feel myself getting distracted again and begin to wonder if maybe I have come back too soon after all.

Chapter Eighty-One

Geoff didn't sleep. Yesterday, after seeing Helen and James, he'd talked to Ruby who'd been devastated to learn how ill Connie was. She insisted on dropping by with dinner for him and Rosemary that evening, shepherd's pie, and an apple crumble from Beryl. She left her number in case he needed anything after Rosemary had gone back home. Then Bill at the pub. Bill shook his head, offered him a handshake and said, 'There but for the grace of God.' He had a quick coffee in the pub and by the time he'd finished, Rosemary was there to pick him up and take him back home again. He sat for the rest of the afternoon, jiggered from the talking, from the being vulnerable.

And here he was now, vulnerable again. Sat by Connie's bed. The hospital called at six this morning and asked him to come in. It was now eleven. Rosemary had gone for coffee for them both and there was something serene about Connie, something he couldn't take his eyes off. It was just him and her, alone, together. He reached down to her hand, taking hold of her bony fingers in his own. He stroked the side of her thumb. There was a whistling outside, a porter perhaps. Geoff half smiled. 'Can you hear that?' he asked her. 'That whistle? You used to grumble about my whistle. Too blowy, you said. Maybe if I'd whistled like that,' he said, still stroking the side of her hand. He listened to the whistling, trying to detect the song. 'Is it Johnnie Ray?'

he asked. '"Just Walking in the Rain"?' And then softly, he joined in. Just the hook, over and over. A key change. Then he started to sing. Serenading Connie like he had back when they first met. The night they went dancing and he surprised her by sweeping her off her feet. 'Do you remember how I sang to you that night? "Our Love", by Frank Sinatra. Our song for evermore. You complained I was tickling your ear,' he laughed. 'As God was my witness, that night was the most perfect of my life… you were the most perfect…' As his words ran out, Connie's hand flickered.

'Connie?' he asked, his eyes fixed on her tiny, crooked fingers. They flinched again. 'You were the making of me, Connie Steele. I only wish I could have told you that before. I only wish I could have spoken about the things that truly frightened me, but maybe I didn't have to. Maybe you didn't need the detail because it changed nothing for you. I was the man you loved just as you were the woman I adored.' Connie's tiny hand tightened around his, just the slightest movement, a moment's squeeze, a sign that she understood, just like she always had. He looked from her eyes, still closed, then back to her hand, one final squeeze. And as he began to whistle their song, Connie let out a breath, and the moment they shared, the serenity he had sensed wrapped around her body and his. Geoff held on for as long as he could, he daren't breathe, he daren't let go, he was desperate to hang on to their final moment for as long as was humanly possible.

As a child, when his father fell ill and his mother demanded he became the man of the house, he would creep downstairs in a morning, to light the fire in the scullery. It would be black and cold in there. Empty. And sometimes, his hands wouldn't work. His young fingers failing him as he tried to click at the coal to get the fire to light. He'd sit back on his heels, feeling empty and useless, knowing he had let his mother down.

As Connie took her final breath to his whistle, Geoff had felt purposeful. He'd held her, he'd sung her a song he knew she loved. He'd been there as she had for him.

The longer he held her hand, knowing he'd have to let go, the closer he was to being back in the scullery, a place he swore he'd never return. His only question being, could he survive without the very person who had rescued him?

Chapter Eighty-Two

Geoff sat in Connie's chair, the same place he'd sat since Rosemary reluctantly left him the day before. He'd ignored the first knock at the door, and the second and third. By the fourth, a voice was calling through the letterbox. It was Val. 'Geoff, Geoff, are you okay?' He didn't respond so she started leaning across from the top step to try and peer in through the window, but lost her balance, pulling the trellis that Connie's climbing rose grew up against. It was enough to give Geoff the energy to get up and open the door.

'Oh, thank God you're okay,' she said, leaning against the front door, one hand on her hip, her head bowed as if she'd just run a marathon. 'I thought I was going to have to call the police! Geoff, why haven't you answered the door? Or the phone?' she asked.

Geoff moved back to sit in Connie's chair.

'Have you eaten?' Val asked, standing in the lounge in front of the electric fire. 'Have you had anything to drink?' She looked around the room for any evidence of food or water. 'Geoff, love. Are these… you haven't changed, have you?' she said, of his clothes. Geoff looked down to the shoes and the trousers and the jacket he still hadn't taken off. 'Oh, Geoff.' She wiped a tear away before he noticed. He noticed.

'I've had a bit of toast. Some water. I'm not really hungry.'

'You've got to eat, love.'

'Perhaps I'll have a little more,' he said, pulling himself up to stand. As he did so, he lost his balance slightly, knocking an empty glass from Connie's side table. The one he'd collected for himself as the clock chimed four a.m.

'Come, sit back down,' said Val, taking his arm and letting him drop back into the chair.

'I'm fine,' he said, flatly.

'I know you are,' she answered, knowing him well enough not to suggest otherwise. 'I know you are, but I'm not. So let me help you and that will help me.' She went into the kitchen, her shoes peeling on the lino. 'I'll just wash up, shall I?' she shouted through, running the tap before he could answer. He stared at the wall before him, cars passing, the bus. He listened to her washing the pots. Just the single plate and a coffee cup from days ago now. Before he went into hospital. Before all this happened. When life still had purpose. Like when he was back in the hospital, noises seemed louder. The tap. The pots. The loading of them on the drainer. The sound of her shoes on the floor.

'I'll make you a sandwich. You need to keep your strength up. What time's the vicar coming? Rosemary called me earlier, said she'd be here by one o'clock.'

He listened to the sound of the fridge opening then closing. Drawers. Cutlery. The click of the kettle. Connie used to make a lovely sandwich. She always knew just how much butter and how much cheese to use. In fact, it was only really ever the gooseberry crumble that she got wrong, when he thought about it, not enough sugar. He'd eat it without pulling a face if it brought her back. If they could have a few more years. If she were still here.

Val brought a plate and his cup of tea through to the lounge. Habit made her almost place it down on the side table by his chair before she remembered herself and placed it on Connie's instead. She moved to sit on the sofa, taking up the space next to Geoff's usual spot. She sat on the edge, her feet together, her arms hugging her knees.

The phone rang. Geoff froze.

'Would you like me to—'

'No it's fine, I'll…' Geoff thought again. 'Although, perhaps you could, if you don't mind?'

'Of course not.'

Geoff reached down to his sandwich, taking a bite. He realised he hadn't brushed his teeth in days, he couldn't taste the sandwich. Or the coffee when he drank it.

'It was the vicar, he's running late. He'll be here by four.' Geoff nodded. 'And Rosemary will be here by then, won't she?' Geoff nodded again. 'Shall I stay with you, until she gets here?'

Geoff thought for a moment, he'd been on his own for days now. Months, if you included the times Connie wasn't really there. The loneliness though, this time, it was bigger than he could have imagined. Too big. It was too much. It was too noisy. So Geoff nodded for a third time. 'Thank you, Val. If you don't mind staying for a while, I'd appreciate it,' he said, quietly.

When he got upstairs, he paused in their room. He laid his hand on her wardrobe to steady himself. He glanced over to the photos. He looked out of their window, over the houses to the Yorkshire hills beyond. He looked into the sky, thick clouds rolling by. And he knew, with total certainty, that if he was any kind of a husband, today was the day he should find the strength to be the man Connie needed in death, as in life. And if he could do it, it would be because of her.

Chapter Eighty-Three

I shuffle down into my pillow, studying James' handwriting. It's no longer just somebody's notebook so much as a guide, a sense of love and loss. I notice everything about it now, the neat loops and flicks, beautifully written in a blue fountain ink. There's a poetry and articulation that I didn't appreciate when simply looking at how it might help me. My connection to the words is deeper now. As I read, I can hear him, his accent, the Glaswegian vowels. I scrutinise the choice of words, the depth of feeling. Sometimes, there's a dot of ink, fuller than a full stop, maybe where he's paused, pen poised, wondering what to write next. I wonder how long he waited to find the right words.

Alex's letter is now a bookmark, nestled in the pages that I take out and lay across my chest as I read James' words.

My love,

I saw you today. I read about Julian's passing in the paper. I wanted to pay my respects too, his friendship over the years meant such a lot to me, and I know he was there for you when I left. I kept my distance because I didn't want to cause you any further distress on what must already have been a painful day, though it was hard. I just wanted to tell you I'm sorry, as I have for so many years now. I just wanted to let you know that I made it. That in spite of how our story fractured, you taught me everything and I made it. I survived. Perhaps not the way you'd have imagined, or even would like, but I'm here. And I'm thankful. How I wish I could tell you.

Later, as dusk fell, I sat by the tree to the right of his grave, fresh soil piled upon him. I told him all about the man I am today, how I learnt from my mistakes, how you were the reason I survived and how grateful I was to those around you who rallied when I walked. I hoped, on some level, that he might have heard me. The need to make amends with those I wronged grows stronger with each day. I fight the sense that, perhaps, that need is selfish. Self- interest. You've all moved on, after all. What does it matter to you that I survived? What does it matter to any of you? And yet, it was because of you, and that's why it feels important.

Maybe one day, I'll find the right way to do it.

From, the man you wished I could be. The man I am.

I can't bear it. I can't bear the hint of despair. The love in the pages that she'll never see, the truth, as he has unwound it, a truth she'll never know. I wipe my chin of tears and wish James had never had to write such letters. And I wish, more than anything else in this world, that Alex could see and hear the stories in these pages, maybe even learn from them. That our fate would not be the same as theirs. I want to lead the life we worked for, the one we committed to, not the one some twisted road has taken us down. I run my hand along the pages of James' book and wonder if he has regrets about his life, about all of these things he's learnt but never shared with the only person it seems he's ever loved.

What are the things we'd say to each other? What are our truths? What are the things I'd like to say to him? Maybe sorry for losing my wedding ring, but yay! I found it. Sorry for always being the practical one. Sorry for rarely reciprocating his gestures of romance… sorry for not stepping back, sorry for being impatient, sorry for making wild assumptions that must have been so hurtful at a time he needed my love, my support, my patience and time. I reach for a pen and a piece of paper from my bedside table. And I start writing…

Chapter Eighty-Four

Dear Alex

I don't know where to start and yet I feel like I have to write this. I have so much I want to say, though no idea if it will make sense. If it will be welcome. If it can make a difference. Would I write anyway, if I knew for certain that it changed nothing? Yes, I think the answer is yes, because it might be the only way to say what I actually feel. When we talk, my thoughts muddle and the emotions manipulate everything I want to say and before I've even realised, what I wanted to say has been confused with anger or frustration.

How did this happen, Alex? How did we come to this? When I think of how far we've travelled together, in spite of all those who told us we'd never make it, I can't bear that we've stumbled. That we've come to a standstill. I don't feel like our story is over. I don't feel as if this is it for us and maybe I'm foolish because I don't know how we get through it, but I know that I want to. I want to, so much. I can see us, through the other side of this, together in the knowledge that no matter what life throws at us, we can make it. Because of love.

I've had time to think, these last few days. I've picked apart every chat, argument or look we've shared. Every moment, every atmosphere. All the things we've said and everything else that we haven't, and I can see why you left. I see what you need to do, and I see that I wasn't helping. I tried, I tried so hard, but I just didn't have it in me. I was clumsy, impatient, perhaps even thoughtless or cruel at times. You weren't ungrateful. You weren't lazy. You did care, I knew it even when I said it. You cared as much as you were able, that you couldn't act upon that feeling was no more your fault than mine. I lurched from trying to push you into life, to retreating and leaving you to it. I nagged to try and inspire you, I told you it was all fine to take off the pressure. I told you I loved you because I did. I do. Did I ever ask how you were feeling? Or what you needed from me? I don't remember, maybe you couldn't have told me, but still, I should have asked.

I love you, Alex, I always have. Even when things have been tough, you've been the only one I've ever wanted to be around. To have on my side. To stand up for. To be with.

Take whatever time you need, and if this is it, the end of our days, know that I will always love you. Let's hope we both find happiness, in whatever shape that may be.

Love, Helen. X

Chapter Eighty-Five

The vicar sat in Connie's chair. He was using her table. He was systematically, albeit unintentionally, erasing Geoff's memories of her in her own space. Whenever Geoff looked over to that chair from this day forward, would he see the reflection of his wife of seventy-odd years or the vicar, smiling as he dunked a custard cream?

Geoff was beginning to realise that the problem with this kind of meeting, this sort of conversation, is how perfunctory it becomes. The vicar was fact finding, trying to establish the kind of person Connie was so that he could piece together a fitting eulogy. But, of course, he already knew her, she worshipped at the chapel regularly, right up to the point she no longer remembered her faith, or the role it played in her life. She helped out at church fetes, she baked gooseberry tarts that sent the congregation into as much of a sour spin as Geoff. She knelt to pray on the cushions she helped the Sunday school decorate when the old ones got too threadbare. The vicar knew her and yet he still sat before Geoff and Rosemary now, asking them to regale stories of the woman she once was.

'You flew Concorde once, tell him about that, Dad.'

'We did.' Geoff smiled, determined to give the vicar what he needed despite how superficial the process seemed. 'I made Connie laugh by telling her it was the only time I ever landed in a plane.' The vicar looked up, confused. 'Instead of jumping out. I was a paratrooper,' explained Geoff. 'Connie laughed, then pulled me in to give me a squeeze, maybe because it was one of the only times I mentioned the war.'

'Of course,' said the vicar. He made more notes, perhaps for Geoff, further down the line.

'She was like a child in the seat of that plane. She looked out of the window then over to me, her shoulders practically pinned to her ears in anticipation; pure excitement etched across her face.' Geoff could still see the look in her eyes when he closed his.

'I remember how giddy she was,' said Rosemary, smiling sadly. 'She had a sense of wonder, didn't she, Dad?'

'She did, she really did. She taught me that wonder, that sense of play.'

'Did she?' asked the vicar.

'Yes. Well, she tried. I think sometimes, I wore life a little too heavily, but she never gave up, on me or on fun. Even when I made that hard for her.'

'Couples can make things hard for each other,' said the vicar.

'Indeed. They can also make things better, and she did, for me, every day. I don't know if I returned the favour.' Rosemary took Geoff's hand and he looked over to her. 'But I tried my best. Every single day of our lives, I did the very best I ever could.'

'You had a good life together, Dad. You did.'

Geoff looked around the room, Connie was everywhere. The photos, the paintings she'd chosen, the wallpaper. The flowers she nurtured and the fire she lit. On a shelf, Connie's teddy bear sat upright beside a photo of the grandkids. Geoff stood up, stretching out the pain in his heart, before taking three steps to the other side of the room, reaching for the little bear on the shelf above the rented television.

'This,' he said, handing the bear to the vicar, 'was the only one she ever had, her parents died when she was very young. It was a gift from the family for her seventieth birthday. She loved that bear. It summed up her life, the childlike wonder she'd kept despite living some of the darkest moments in life. The sense of fun and light, even when the world seemed to fight against her joy. The love and patience she showed to others, despite never having been taught that herself, it was limitless. Without question. Even to me, despite all the times I must have made it hard for her, I never once felt that she did not love me and for that reason, I could not have loved her more. Perhaps…' Geoff looked down at the bear, fondly. 'Perhaps she could take that with her,' he said, handing it over.

The vicar took the bear, smiling at its little black eyes and cuddly belly. 'She could, undoubtedly, but perhaps it would be better for you to keep it. As a reminder of all she taught you?'

Rosemary saw the vicar out to the car before popping over to see Val. Geoff watched, holding the bear. The vicar's car lights disappeared down the hill and the clock chimed six. Bear clutched under his arm, Geoff crossed the room, lifting the clock off the wall. He reached inside and silenced the chimes. 'There, love,' he said to the photo, placing the bear beside it. 'That's better, isn't it?'

Connie's face beamed back at him, just as it always had, and exhausted from fighting the sadness, Geoff dropped into his chair and started to cry. But as he did, an icy breeze blew across his face. It surrounded him, enveloped him. It crawled inside his aching heart and lifted him. It gave him the strength to stand, it breathed a peace into his soul and it made Geoff wonder if Connie was, in fact, still somehow with him. Just as she'd always been. She'd given him love, life, a family, a home. She'd given him the strength to survive even when he thought he couldn't. Whilst she may no longer have been there in person, Geoff felt Connie's love for him remained in his very bones, and that would be how he'd survive.

Chapter Eighty-Six

THREE MONTHS LATER

The timer goes off in the kitchen so I switch off *The Real Housewives* and set about the dinner. The smell of roast chicken and garlic fills the house making my mouth water. I wasn't sure I could still do this, it's been so long. Tom will be here any moment, James and Geoff in tow. I take the meat out to rest and whack the oven up for the Yorkshires. There's a nut roast and the potatoes in the top oven, and a pavlova on the side. I'm basically Mary Berry. When the oven's at peak temperature, and the oil has heated through, I pour batter into the muffin tins, enjoying each satisfying sizzle.

As I kick the oven door shut, James wanders in, Geoff behind him. 'Oh, doesnae that smell good, Geoff?'

'Certainly does, are there Yorkshire puddings too?' Geoff peers into the oven.

'Mum's Yorkshire's are the best!' Tom leans down to give me a kiss on the cheek. I grin up at him.

'How did he do then?' I ask, straightening Tom's hair. 'How was his driving?'

'Spot on,' says Geoff. 'I felt very relaxed in the front there with him, he's very careful.'

'Well, that's a relief. I suppose him paying a fortune out for his own car probably helps!' Tom grins at me. 'You had a good week?'

'Yeah, not bad. Work's good. And at the flat, the other lads have finally agreed to do their fair share of the housework so we're not living in a pit now.'

'Great.' I switch the veg on. 'Now, can you sort out drinks for us all, there's white in the fridge. Red on the table. And juice on the side.'

Tom busies about, taking drinks orders, getting James and Geoff settled in the dining room. 'How's your dad?' I ask, when he pops back in with James' coat. 'Did you get a chance to catch up properly?'

'He's good. Yeah. He's doing well, in fact. He's...' Tom pauses, picking at the chicken until I playfully smack his fingers away. 'He's got a job... actually.'

My heart both explodes and sucker punches at the same time. 'Has he? Oh! Wow! I mean, that's amazing! Brilliant! Where?' I turn away, plating up roast potatoes, checking in the Yorkshires, carving the nut roast. I'm happy for him. I'm happy for him.

'I think Uncle Rob helped in the end, something in IT. I'm not exactly sure. But he seems really chuffed. He starts next week.'

'Oh, I am so pleased for him. What a brilliant thing. He has waited so long.' I want to call him and congratulate him. I want to take him in my arms and squeeze him tight. I want to ask him why he could do it with Rob's help but not mine. I want to punch myself in the face for being so self-absorbed.

'Well, tell him congratulations from me. When you see him next. Now, come on, we have guests. Let's get them fed and watered. Let's start taking things through.' I point to the various plates of food and Tom picks up a couple of plates and heads into the dining room. I brace myself against the kitchen side for a moment, take a deep breath, then pick up the chicken and paint on a smile.

'Now, come on then, dig in. Don't let it go cold. Yorkshires are just coming. James, do you want to carve? Geoff, pass us your plate, let's get you some roasties on.' I load his plate up with meat and roast potatoes. 'Tom, can I have a wine please, red? Thanks, love.' Tom fills me up and I take a sip before fetching the Yorkshire puddings.

'Now come on, there's two each.'

'Connie made the best Yorkshires,' said Geoff, fondly. 'They were huge, it's a real treat to have them again.'

'Do you know, I remember them. I remember coming round for lunch once, not long after you'd moved in. I think it might be when my love affair with them began.' Geoff smiled, proudly. 'I can't promise they'll be as good as hers, but I give 'em a good go.'

Food is passed about, gravy is poured, and within a few minutes, we've all settled down to eat.

'It's so lovely to have you all here, nice to have people to cook for. Thanks for coming.'

'Well, I cannae speak fo' Geoff, but ahm very grateful. I cannae remember the last time I had a Sunday dinner like this.'

'Rosemary sometimes takes me for a carvery up at the East Morton Inn, or out in the Dales somewhere. They're lovely, but…'

'It's no' a home-made one, eh?' James shoves a potato in his mouth, making appreciative noises as he chews.

'No. Not a home-made one.'

'How is Rosemary?' I ask. 'I saw her car last week.'

'Yes, she's good, thank you. Comes up every other week, just to check in and see how I'm getting on.'

'And how are you getting on?' I pour more gravy on my plate, offering it to Tom to put the other side of the table. 'If you don't mind my asking?'

Geoff takes a sip of his juice. 'Well, I'm okay. All things considered. I always thought I couldn't cope without Connie.' Geoff puts his knife and fork down for a moment. 'You learn a lot about yourself when everything you thought makes up who you are is stripped away.' I concentrate on my dinner, focusing on getting the crispy bits from my potatoes loaded up on top of some veg. 'Well, it turns out that as painful as it is, losing someone you have loved since you were a teenager, you can survive.'

'Of course ye can,' agrees James.

'But I never knew. I didn't believe it. She…' Geoff's eyes glisten. 'She was my purpose in life for so long, I didn't know what purpose I'd have when she'd gone.'

'And yet, here ye are.'

'Yes.' Geoff takes out a handkerchief and dabs his eyes. 'Here I am.'

Tom looks at me and I give him a wink, he squeezes my hand no doubt because he's seen my own eyes fill up a little. 'To Connie,' I say, lifting my glass. 'And all those who teach us to be the very best versions of ourselves.' I wonder if either of them have any idea how much I include them in that sentiment.

'To Connie.' Our glasses chink, we each take a sip, and settle back into eating our dinner.

Three hours later, I thank them again for coming and let Tom take them home on his way back to his flat. I clear up, fill the dishwasher, save the leftovers, wipe the table down, and finally flop into the sofa.

I turn *The Real Housewives* back on and reach for my phone. I open up messages, search for Alex's number, and type: *Well done on the job, Tom told me the great news. I'm so proud of you. X* I click send and pray it's received the way it's intended. Seconds later, a response arrives.

Thanks. I appreciate that. Means I can finally get my own place and find my feet. X

I read it a few times over. I remind myself that this is good news. That him moving on and finding his feet is exactly what he needs. That if I really love him, I have to let him go. And if I really love me, I have to let 'us' go. A new place? He's moving on. Maybe it's time I did too. If James and Geoff can survive, then so can I.

Chapter Eighty-Seven

SIX MONTHS LATER

The sun is warm, the birds are singing, there's late summer green in the trees, casting a dappled shadow across the driveway from the crematorium. Beauty is all around me and although I'm sad that we've had to say goodbye to Geoff, I feel like he made it. He survived. When I dropped by his house two weeks ago, he made me a cuppa. He shared photos of his grandchildren. He talked about Connie as if she were still around, not in a way that told me he'd forgotten she'd died, or hadn't accepted the truth, but in a way that kept her alive in his heart, which kept him alive too. Until eventually, he simply passed away peacefully in his sleep.

Walking back up towards my car, James is standing beside it. He nods to the paratrooper who walks just up ahead of me. When he'd arrived in full dress, red beret and medals, paying his respects to a fellow serviceman, I wasn't sure I'd be able to hold it together.

'How'd it go?'

'You could have come in, you know. Rosemary did say so.'

'Nah, I'm no religious. I went and had a cuppa and a slice of cake over at the coffee shop instead. I dinnae think he'd mind.'

'Come on,' I say to him, unlocking the car so he can climb in. 'Shall I drop you in town?'

'Aye, if ye don't mind.'

'Of course not.'

We drive in silence, I don't know about James, but I'm recounting my memories of Geoff from back when I was a kid, right up to now. Funny what an impact some people can have on your lives. We drive past the street I think Alex is renting in now. He moved out of the first flat and into a house. Apparently, he's doing really well, the job suits him, he's reconnected with friends, he feels like he has purpose. At least, that's what he's told Tom who told me, then said he felt bad because it made me upset. I told him not to be silly, that I was happy for his dad. I am. I really am.

'What are you up te fo' the rest o' the day?' asks James.

Instantly, I colour at the question. 'Oh, well… I've got some jobs to do round the house, clear up a bit. I think I'm going to put the house on the market. It's too big for me on my own. Alex has just got a new place, he's settled in his new life, there's no point in me sitting waiting for him to come back, you know?'

'Ah. Tough, but a good move.'

'I think so.'

'Though… if that's all yer doing, I cannae see why you'd turn pink?'

'Oh.' I let out a nervous laugh. 'Well… I have a sort of date too.'

'Ahhhh, that makes more sense! A sort o' date, you say?'

'Agh, I don't know. It's a blind date set up by one of the girls.' Vicky, in fact. Someone she teaches with. Apparently he is a lovely, gentle soul. Two young kids. His wife passed away and he's been on his own with them for a few years now. 'I don't know if I'm ready really.'

'Oh?'

'Well... I know it's not been that long since Alex and I split up, but he's moved into a new place, he's loving his job. He's not coming back, I can see that now so... I mean, it's not that I want to replace him. I'm fine on my own, it's just that Vicky thought this guy was nice and the girls think I should at least try and get out there, meet people, that sort of thing.' I pull up into a side road in town, pulling the handbrake on. 'Silly really.'

'No' silly. You cannae put your life on hold.'

'I know, that's what the girls said. That's why I'm going. It's also why I brought this for you.' I pull out the notebook, holding on to it for one last time before handing it back. 'I think it's time you had this back. Thank you, so much. I wish it could have helped Alex, but it definitely helped me. I think it's time I focused on who I am and what I want out of life now. Reading this... I guess it just makes me sad because I can see how I might have done things differently, but I can't turn back the time.'

James takes the notebook with a smile. 'I'm sorry it couldnae fix everything, but I'm glad it helped in some way.'

'It did. It really did. Thank you.'

'It's no bother. Actually, it's serendipitous timing. I wanted to say thank you to you, too.'

'It's all right, can't have you walking back into town.'

'No... I mean fe looking out fo' me these last few years. I've appreciated it.'

'Oh, no. Anytime. That's just... you're always welcome, you know that. I'm back on on Monday, see you then?'

'Erm... actually, no...' James moves to face me. 'You're not the only one to make some changes.'

'What do you mean?'

'Ahm going home this weekend.'

'Home?'

'Glasgow, it's time I went back. I've wandered fe too long. I've meandered the streets, I've sought shelter, I've hidden from life. I've buried ma head in those letters I wrote. I've watched other people living their lives, whilst I've avoided my own. It's time to stop doing that. When you found those letters, I had no idea that it'd help me too. I have te live fe today, no' yesterday, Hel. I've been hiding from life, I need to stop. So, I'm going home. I've an old friend with a flat that he says I can stay in for a while, he knows people who might be able to get me in to some kind of work. I'm no' sure what exactly, but anything's a bonus when you've been wandering for so long. So yeah, I'll be heading off.'

I don't know if it's the fact I'm already on the edge following Geoff's funeral this morning, but James' news seems to tip me over and I find myself struggling to hold back the tears. 'Oh, James! I don't know what to say!'

'Good luck? Travel safe? Be happy?'

'Yes! Of course, all of that, but…' and I realise I'm about to tell him how this makes me feel instead of encouraging him to follow what's important for his own life, so I stop. I don't say it. If he's taught me anything it's that sometimes other people have to do what they have to do, no matter how it affects me and my life, my feelings. 'James, I think that is brilliant and I am so chuffed for you.' God, I'll miss him though.

'Thanks.'

'So… I guess this is it then. Goodbye.'

'Well… not quite, ye see… I did wonder if before I go, you might help me with something?'

'Of course, anything.'

'Before I go, I want to see my ex-wife. I saw a mutual friend last week, they said that she still talks about me. That she's sad she couldn't save me. I just need her to know that I don't need saving, then we can both move on fully, ye know?' I nod, because by God do I know. 'She lives in Pudsey now. Would you take me?'

'Of course, of course I can.'

'One last bus ride.' He winks.

'One last bus ride. It'll be in the car, but let's not split hairs.'

'Perfect.' He looks down at his notebook, stuffed full, held together with an elastic band. 'I wondered if I should give her these, since I wrote them for her in the first place.'

'Oh, James…'

'And then I wondered if that was a bit… self-indulgent, you know?'

'She might love to read them.'

'She might not.'

'You've taught me many things, James. I don't think you realise, but you have. And one of those things is that we can't make decisions for other people. We can't assume to know what they want, or how they want to deal with things, or what's in their best interests. They're beautiful, and full of love, and full of gratitude. They're a love story. They're proof that we can learn to love ourselves no matter what. They're precious. She might not want to read them, but maybe that's a decision for her to make?'

'Do ye think?'

'I do.'

James runs his thumb across the pages, thoughtfully. 'Can you do it tomorrow? Say, two-ish?'

'I'll pick you up by the station.'

'Thanks, Helen, who knows, maybe she'll find a way to forgive me.'

'Maybe,' I say as he climbs out of the car. 'Maybe she did that years ago.'

James closes the door and heads off down the street. And as he turns the corner, there's a tiny part of me that wonders what she will say, and how she'll feel about seeing him. And perhaps it's the old romantic in me, but I can't help daydreaming what it might be like if they fell in love all over again.

Chapter Eighty-Eight

'Do you remember when Claire was seeing that bloke, the one who worked in the bookies, oh… what was his name?'

'Sleazy Simon!' shouts Zoe, quick as a flash.

'Yes! Oh my God! He of the Brylcreemed quiff and questionable taste in jeans,' adds Claire. The girls squeal with laughter and though I join in, my nerves are stopping any full-on engagement in the banter. I take a sip of my drink, my hands shake. 'I mean, I know it was the nineties, but seriously, white jeans? What was he thinking?' she grimaces.

'It wasn't the colour so much as the tightness that distressed me,' says Zoe. 'I never knew where to look. You could practically see it twitch!' We all fall about laughing.

'I used to love those days, back in the nineties. Alex and I would get a pass out, one of our mums babysitting for Tom. We'd head out to meet all you lot down the local pub on balmy summer nights. God, it feels like we'd just sit outside drinking, laughing, having fun like everyone else our age.'

'You did go for it those nights, we remember.' Zoe lifts her pint glass. 'I reckon you could have even drunk me under the table.'

'Could you do parenting on a hangover when you were young?' asks Claire.

'I don't think we got hangovers! We'd just stay until night fell and the fairy lights kicked in.'

'I loved those fairy lights,' says Vicky, dreamily. 'Metres and metres strung around the beer garden.'

'Yeah, until the pub was bought by a chain and all charm was replaced by mock industrial décor.' We mumble in agreement.

'I think I'd rather remember patronising textile industry references over Sleazy Simon's twitching trousers.' Vicky sips at her wine. 'Anyway, should we be talking about penises when we're about to wave Helen off on her hot date.'

'It's not a hot date!' I protest. 'It's just a drink and some food.'

'That's where it starts!' nudges Zoe. 'First it's a drink, next it's twitching trousers.'

'Oh my God,' Claire looks at Zoe. 'Are you not getting enough, or something?'

'The more you get the more you want and I am getting A LOT!' She winks.

'Where from?' I ask, because we all know Zoe is mad busy at work and totally single. 'Have you met someone?'

'Nah, course not. Can't be doing with that. And why bother when Tinder is still available to me. Now don't deflect. What time are you meeting him?'

I groan. 'In half an hour.'

'Right, is he coming here?'

'Bloody hell, no! As if I'd throw him into this pack of lions.'

'I prefer the term cougar,' says Zoe.

'You do not!' I say. 'He's meeting me outside the restaurant. So I'd better finish this up and head off.'

'And have you planned what you're going to say? What you'll talk about? And have you got new underwear?'

'Claire, I don't think Andrew's like that,' says Vicky. 'He'll be as nervous as Hel is, no new underwear required.' She looks at me. 'Not today, anyway.'

I bury my head in my hands. 'I can't even think about that. Sex with someone who isn't Alex? I don't even know... I've never... Oh God, I can't do this. I can't go. I can't...'

Vicky jumps up. 'Come on, yes you can! Up you get.' She passes me my drink. 'Finish that.' I do as instructed. 'Give us a kiss.' She pulls me in, plants a kiss on my cheek then turns me round. 'Now, go, get over there. You don't want to keep him waiting. Remember, he's lovely. You're great. It's all going to be just fine.'

Butterflies in my stomach and a sudden urge to go to the toilet, I ignore all of those feelings and make my way out of the pub. I blow the girls a kiss and they all respond with massive thumbs ups. Zoe makes a lewd gesture and Vicky slaps her arm.

I push the pub door open and head out into the evening. The sun has started to set, but it's still mild outside. A taxi pulls up, a young couple get out. The girl sees some friends and pushes past me to run over and say hi as her suitor pays the cab. 'I'll have that,' I say, hanging on to the door. The guy stands up.

'Martin!'

'Helen!' he says, looking as startled to see me as I am him. 'Wow, you look...' He looks me up and down. It's fair to say I've made an effort today, I had my hair cut, apparently it's a long, wavy bob. Apparently that's on trend. I've no idea. I've got tailored trousers on, a white shirt half tucked in. Claire lent me a statement necklace and I tried to put a bit of make-up on. I don't know that I feel like me, but I suppose I do feel okay. Maybe better than that. My feet hurt in these stupid heels though. 'Wow,' he says again.

'Erm, thanks.' We stand for a moment, he's giving me the look he gave me back in The Potting Shed. It makes my tummy go funny again. 'Well, I'd better be…'

'Sure, date night with the husband?'

'Oh no, I… we… Well, anyway…'

The girl Martin arrived in the taxi with shouts over that she's going in, she asks him if he wants his usual. She doesn't give me a second glance. I guess I'm no threat to a gorgeous young woman like her. 'I'd better go,' he says. 'Have a good night, he's a lucky guy. You look hot.' He gives me a confident wink then saunters off, holding the door open for a couple before giving me one last glance and going inside. That's when I realise it's definitely Alex he reminds me of. A young Alex, with all the swagger and charm of someone with youth and opportunity on his side. With the intensity of a look and a grin that could render me putty in his hands. A look and a grin that noticed how I'd dressed and complimented me on it. And whilst the need for his, or any male, approval is surplus to requirements, I can't help but appreciate it. Maybe I *do* feel okay. Maybe I *can* do this. Maybe I'm not on the shelf just yet.

Chapter Eighty-Nine

The taxi pulls up outside the restaurant. I see who I assume must be Andrew at the door. I'm almost tempted to tell the cabby to drive on because seeing him makes this whole thing real. I've never been on a date with anyone but Alex. I've never even kissed anyone, but Alex. I've certainly never—

'Four pounds thirty, please,' says the driver.

'Oh! Of course, yes. Here you go.' I hand over the money, dropping it between the car seats. 'Shit! Sorry, I've got...' I rummage around in my purse for more money.

'Don't worry, it's fine. I'll find it.'

'Okay, sorry. Yes. Thanks.' The driver looks at me as if I've lost my mind. I sit in the car looking out of the window. Andrew looks up and down the street, then nervously at his watch. He steps away as if about to leave, then stops and stands again. Is he as nervous as me? The driver resets the clock then clears his throat. 'Oh, sorry. Right. Thanks.'

I climb out of the car, adjusting the collar on my shirt and fixing my hair. Andrew sees me and smiles just a little, like he isn't sure if I'm really his date or not. I walk over. Think confident. Be confident. This is just a meal. It's no big deal. 'Hi,' I say, smiling widely.

'Hi. Helen?' he checks.

'Yes. Andrew?'

He laughs, gently. 'That's me. I think. Though I don't feel like me, I feel nervous… terrified, in fact.'

'You too? Thank God it's not just me.' He visibly relaxes at my confession and I think that maybe this will be okay.

'After you.' He holds open the door for me.

'Thank you.'

Our meal comes and goes in a blur. We talk the whole time, I laugh, often. He compliments me frequently and it feels nice to be the focus of someone's attention… someone more my age. I insist on us going halves with the bill and he doesn't get all blokey and offended about it, which I appreciate. Mostly because, whilst I've had a lovely time, I know that nothing can come of this. He is lovely, Vicky was right about that. He is smart, and funny, he is kind. He clearly adores his children and he's worked hard to balance work with home life whilst dealing with his own loss. Which sounds like it was horrendous for him. No, he's lovely but something is missing. The spark? People talk about that, the magical ingredient. I've seen them talk about it on *First Dates* whenever I've watched that and wondered if I will ever feel those first flushes of new love again. He's attractive, as we walk out of the restaurant and holds the door for me again, I can see that. He's got a lovely smile. Gorgeous hazel eyes. He is attractive, I just… He holds his arm out for me to hook mine through. 'Would you like a drink?' he asks. But I don't want to. And I feel bad.

'I should get back.'

'Oh. Okay.' I can sense his disappointment. 'Let me walk you for a cab then,' he says, heading down the flagstoned street towards the taxi rank. 'I had a great time,' he says, eyes up ahead.

'Yes... me too...'

We get to the cabs, I reach for the door handle.

'Helen,' he says, taking my hand. He holds it in his, taking a step closer. Oh God. 'I've really loved this. It's my first date. In years. I was really nervous, but... you made it really easy and...' Oh no. He leans in, his beard tickles my face as he kisses me softly and I kiss him back because I don't want to be rude or make him feel bad. And it's perfectly pleasant. It's sweet. It's mouth closed, but lingering. And it's not Alex. 'Good night,' he says, his hand over mine to open the door for me. 'Thank you.'

I swallow, hard. 'Thank you,' I say, then climb into the cab and shut the door before he can say anything else.

When I get home, I see Tom's car on the drive. I pay the cab driver and run up to the front door. Tom gets out of his car. 'Tom, love. Hi! Are you picking up those bits I sorted? You can still let yourself in you know.'

'Well, when I saw the taxi pulling up, I didn't want to interrupt. Just in case.'

'What do you mean?'

'I didn't know if you'd be bringing him home.' He gives me a pointed look as I unlock the front door.

'Who?'

'The guy you were kissing in the street. I didn't know if that was a kiss goodbye, or the starter for ten.'

'Tom!'

'What? You're single, I guess.' Am I? Is that how he sees it? 'It's up to you what you do with your Friday evenings.'

'He kissed *me*!'

'It's fine, Mum.' I fling my bag on the side, not sure what to say. 'You're a grown woman. Still married, but a grown woman.'

'Still married to a man who is moving on, Tom.'

He opens up the box I left out on the side for him, all his old school books piled up within. 'Dad still cares, Mum.'

'I care about him, but that doesn't mean much really.'

'No, I mean he really cares.'

I pause, my hand on the fridge door. 'Does he?'

'Of course he does.' My heart jumps. 'He always will, you were his wife for a long time. You two made me. You will always be an important part of his life.'

I'll always be important. Words that sum up what it seems Tom has already got his head round. Always important. Were his wife. I should have given Andrew more time. I pour myself a wine.

'So was he nice?' Tom packs the books back in the box, then leans against the worktop.

'He was.' Not your father is probably the wrong answer. 'He was lovely. I just don't think I'm quite there yet, you know? I mean, I'd like to be. I may seem ancient to you, but I'm not. I've got my whole life ahead of me and I don't want to spend it waiting, just in case your father decides to come back. I don't want to rush into anything either, I'm fine as I am, it's just…' Tom reaches for my wine, taking a sip. 'It's just that it's nice to be part of a team. That's all.'

'Of course it is. And if that's what you want, I'm sure you will be again.' He pulls me into a hug. 'You just might need to give these guys more than one date, that's all.' I bury my face into his chest because I can't believe I'm taking life advice from my almost eighteen-year-old son.

Chapter Ninety

I keep thinking about what Tom said. I did more sorting after he left, actually, that's not true. I sat with the rest of the wine and all our photo albums, poring over the past. I shed a few tears and got quite snotty, but then I realised something: I'm okay. I can be alone. I've done it since Alex left and I didn't crumble. I've been strong. I've got on with life. I've not sat pining.

I mean sure, if I had my way, we'd be back together. If I had my way, none of this would have happened, but actually, I can manage. I've never been alone before, we got together when I was seventeen and I've never been with anybody else. When things got tough before, I stayed because Alex opened up and told me how he felt. I stayed because of Tom. I stayed because I loved him, and I felt there were two sides to the story, and maybe we both needed to learn from it and grow as human beings, as young people, as parents. And this time is different. So, I'm going to be fine. I just might have to remind myself of that each time I pack away another piece of the house. But I will be fine.

My head, on the other hand, is not. All the wine, and maybe some of the pent-up stress from the date with Andrew, and the upset from Geoff's funeral, which I know was a celebration of a life well served, but still made me feel sad. Then the shock at hearing James was heading back to Glasgow, my head feels like it's been steamrollered. Hence feeling the need to take a walk, to get some fresh air, maybe it'll clear my head.

I pull up at the car park by the canal. I sit for a moment, it's early. A few dog walkers go past, a jogger. It's cool, this morning. I can see my breath as I climb out of the car. I wrap my shawl around me, then my arms, around my waist. And I walk. I admire the boats, I pass a lock and remember the photo of Alex and me on the canal and I feel a bit of a cry coming on so I stuff my hands into the pocket of my hoody. My fingers meet from either side, amongst ragged tissues that disintegrate in my fumbling fingers, nothing useful enough to wipe my nose on, so obviously I opt for my sleeve. A dog scampers up to me, wagging its tail, its breath hot and cloudy in the air. His dog walker utters a polite 'good morning' and the dog follows on.

I come to a bench. Alex and I sat here in the prickling heat of an August day when I was three days overdue with Tom. My ankles were roughly the size of my thighs and my belly felt like it might explode. I'd leant against Alex, the heat making the previous few days so uncomfortable yet as we giggled and chatted, his hand on my belly, we felt like we could take on the world. Warriors.

And after Tom arrived, we would bring him down here to splash in puddles on rainy days. We called each other Mummy and Daddy, like we'd lost our own identity when parenthood arrived, but it was okay, because we were okay. I wonder if I'll always miss him?

I reach inside my bag, rooting for my purse. I take my wedding ring out of the zipped pocket, holding it between both thumbs and forefingers. I wonder what his grandma would think of us, her own long and happy marriage woven into the history of its eternal circle. A shadow casts across my hands.

'Is there anyone sat here?'

Chapter Ninety-One

I look up sharply, a familiar stranger stands before me. Neatly shaven, hair short and styled, a new coat, not that dissimilar to the one I bought him that ended up with James. 'Alex…' I can't take my eyes off his, they're focused, clear. Familiar and unfamiliar in equal measure. When was the last time he looked me in the eye without hatred or at the very least, disdain. I make room for him beside me on the bench, eyes still fixed on him, heart in mouth as he settles in beside me. Our knees touch and it sends an electric shock of warmth through my body. I can't speak.

'You found it.'

'I did. It was in the cushion cover. On the sofa. It must have been there all along.'

We fall silent and I twist the ring around, not daring to put it back on.

'Come here often?' he jokes, stuffing hands into his pockets, his body crouched over to keep warm. 'Sorry.'

'It's okay,' I say, my voice breaking, uncertain what it is he's apologising for.

He sighs, stretching his legs out before him. 'I've been walking down here most days these last few months.'

'Have you?'

'Memories… lots of memories…' I nod. I don't know what to say, though maybe I don't care about finding the right words. Maybe that was always my problem when, in fact, there aren't right words, maybe there aren't even any words. Not from me, at least. He keeps on looking at me. Searching. Familiarising. Reconnecting? 'I remember that time before Tom, was it this bench? The Braxton Hicks, I was convinced you were going into labour.'

I remember, too.

'God, we were just kids.' He lets out a long sigh. 'We've made a mess of things…'

'Have we?' I ask, because I think I've realised we've only ever done what we thought was best. We just haven't always got it right.

'Haven't we?'

'I don't know that that's fair. On us. On me. On you.' I fiddle with the tissue bits, trying to focus my mind. 'I mean, when I think about it, I don't really know what we've done or how we got here, I just know that it's not where I hoped we'd be.' He looks over to the other side of the canal. A swan glides past. 'I know it's not where I want us to be.' His eyes drop. 'You know, if it was my choice. If we had our time again.'

'What would you do differently?'

'I don't know. Think. Listen. Wait. Watch. Learn more about myself and how I respond to the things life throws at you.' I let out a sad laugh. 'Do you remember Geoff? My old neighbour.'

'And Connie?'

'Yeah. He passed away, it was his funeral yesterday. Connie died around the time you… well… he didn't think he could cope without her. He didn't know who he was, if she wasn't there. And James, the guy on the bus, he was the same, though different in lots of ways… but neither understood who they were, or what they wanted for so long in their lives and that impacted on the choices they made. The things they did. The way they lived their lives, and I've realised, over these last few months, how important it is to understand ourselves. To know ourselves. To work out what makes us up, how we identify. Like… that day you walked in on me talking to Martin.' I feel Alex prickle. 'It really wasn't what you thought; in fact, I don't think I knew what it was, except that I was cross. I felt let down. I felt lost. There was this split second where I thought I could feel better if everything was completely different, you know?' Alex softens a little. 'I don't know, maybe it was like that when—' and then I stop myself, because I don't know if I want to mention what happened with him and Amanda Hobson. Except that I'm tired of the eggshells and they've never served me well before. 'When you went off to Amanda's back in the early days. I sort of think it had nothing to do with wanting to be with someone else. Or not wanting to be with me. I think you just wanted something different, somebody else to talk to, and I get that.'

Another dog walker goes past and his greyhound trots, stops, and sniffs at Alex. He gives it a fuss before it trots off again, bouncing behind its owner, down the towpath.

'I never stopped loving you,' says Alex, his eyes fixed forward. 'When I walked away. I never stopped loving you. I'd hear what you'd say about jobs, about being kind to myself, about pushing myself, about getting up off my arse, or taking my time. Whatever message it was you'd selected on any given day. All so mixed because you were mixed and so was I. I'd hear them, and I desperately wanted to act on them. To do something that proved to you I was worth loving, or being patient with, or supporting. But I was helpless. I couldn't move. I couldn't find the will to do any of those things. To begin with I wanted to ask for your help. I wanted to tell you how I was feeling. After a while, I didn't want to talk about it because I couldn't face it. I was powerless, Helen. Utterly, utterly, powerless.'

We fall silent. I can feel myself begin to cry and I've no energy to fight it. This time when I look up, Alex is looking at me. He has tears running down his cheeks, too. I hold the ring and my hands together hidden in my pocket, desperate to wipe his away. I'm wrapped up in confusion, my body is swaddled in doubt. All I want to do is read his thoughts.

Our breath twists together in the cold air.

He wipes away my tears and gently, I lean into his hand.

'I was broken,' he whispers. And I nod, because I know it now. I can see the traces of it. I can feel it. He may look smart, clean, focused even, but there's still a shade of sadness beneath it. 'I didn't know what to do, how to cope. I didn't want to talk. I didn't want the help. I didn't want…'

'It's fine,' I say, seeing him struggle to explain. 'I don't need you to explain. 'Maybe we were both broken. Independently? Together? I'm glad Rob helped.'

'It wasn't just Rob. Don't think that I left and he fixed it all, that's not… that's not how it was. I mean, yes, Rob got me job interviews, he was the one to drag me out of the house. He made me wear his suits and get my hair cut.' He moves his hand to his head, ruffling his fingers through the dark waves, the cut making them tighter. 'I walked the walk, and I thought maybe eventually I'd feel it too. That's why I got the new house. I thought that if I was to move on and build a new life, now I had the new job, it would all become clear. I thought I had to find my own way. And that when I did, I'd finally feel like it was right. Like, maybe I'd feel a sadness that we hadn't made it, but I'd know in my heart it was right that we split. I'd read your letter.'

'You got it then.'

He pulls it out of his pocket. 'I've carried it with me every day. I tried being alone because I thought I should, but it didn't feel right… it doesn't feel right. This…' he holds up the letter. 'This feels right. And I couldn't work out how to tell you, or if I even deserved to, after everything I put you through.' He leans forward, letter in his hands, head bowed.

I pull a hand free of my hoodie, placing it on his. He turns his hand round so our palms meet, and our fingers entwine. 'I went to the doctors. I got tablets, antidepressants. It took a while for them to kick in, longer than I would have liked. In fact, I almost came off them because I thought they weren't working, but Rob persuaded me to stick with it. I remembered what you'd said about them once. So I waited.'

'And?'

'I'm here. I'm talking. I'm not fixed, but I'm fixing.'

A narrowboat slowly moves through the water. The wake it leaves behind rolls out to the edge, causing water to bounce back off the towpath and back. Ripples.

'I wasn't myself,' he whispers. 'I need you to know that. I couldn't see what to do, I couldn't see a future, I couldn't see a way out.' He reaches to lift my chin, searching out my eyes once again. 'I couldn't, but I can now. I can see it. It's a future I want… if you want it too.' My heart quickens. 'And you don't have to tell me now. And I'd understand, if you didn't want it. I know I hurt you. Before. This time. I know it's been hard on you, an understatement probably.'

'It has been hard. For both of us though.'

'Helen, I would understand if too much has been said or done. I'd understand.' He takes both my hands in his and this time, his touch dissolves me. 'I love you, Helen, I always have. I always will. No matter how this ends.' I crumble into his chest and I hear him crumble too. I feel his heart beating and I feel him wrap his arms around me. I feel him holding me as tight as he used to when we first fell in love. When we were invincible. When the world was our playground. When we believed we'd be together forever. And I am terrified, and nervous, and overwhelmed by the love that I feel for him.

I think about James missing out on a lifetime with the only person he loved, and I think about Geoff and Connie – in love until the end. And even though I know that I could survive without Alex – I've proven that these last few months – I know that I don't want to. As Alex rests his head on top of mine, and whispers that he loves me, I know that I don't have to. And together, we hurt, but together we'll survive. Because that's what we signed up for that day down here, back when we were kids.

'I love you too, Alex. More than I could ever say.'

Sometime later, I don't know how long, we release each other from our tight hold. We stand. He takes the ring from my hand, fumbling to place it back on my finger, which makes us both laugh a little. Then he looks up towards the car park, then down towards the path we've walked so many times before; together, as a two, arm in arm. And instinctively, we walk in time, together, towards our past, ready to reclaim it as our future.

'Till death us do part.

Epilogue

My love,

It's cold. Colder than ever. But I'm back home in Glasgow, so what do you expect? I wanted to write to you one last time, close the loop, you know?

When I knocked on your door, I didn't know if you'd see it was me. I made an effort, I cut my hair, I trimmed my beard, I put on the cleanest clothes I had, but I knew that I looked nothing like the man who walked out on you, all those years before. That you didn't hesitate filled me with love. That you didn't close the door allowed me to forgive the person I was before. I had wanted to tell you everything but, in truth, the moment overwhelmed me. When I told you that I had walked and thought non-stop since the day I left you, there was sadness in you that I hadn't anticipated. When I told you that I had learnt from every one of those walks and thoughts, and you told me how much that meant to you to hear, you could never have known how my heart sang. How it still sings. Because all I ever wanted was for you to know that our past was not your fault. Nor, in fact, was it mine. We were victims of circumstance, of a world that didn't know what to do with me, of a time in our lives when we could do nothing but walk away.

Each day I wrote sharing my thoughts, my observations. Each letter allowed me to consider what had happened. To think about what you might be doing, about what might have been. But then I lost them and I didn't know what to do. I feared what might become of me without them. But I soon realised, it was okay. I was okay. Helen, the woman who brought me to see you, she had found the letters, and when I realised that they'd helped her, I let her keep them longer because what I had learnt had a chance to help someone else. And through sharing, by handing them over and no longer having to write to you, I was set free.

Sometimes, you meet people in life and they've no idea that they can change your world. Not having those letters meant I stopped looking for words to prove to you how much I had changed. Instead, I searched for life in my days. I searched for connections. I searched for warmth. I searched for myself and I realised I'd been there all along.

That you smiled at me, when I told you how things had changed, meant I could let go. And whilst a day will never pass where I do not think of you, my love, the days will also be full of the life I have left to lead.

You called me last night, told me it was time for you to return to Glasgow too. You asked if we could meet up, if we could be friends, and I wanted to shout out because I could not imagine anything more beautiful from you. And if all we have left is friendship, it will be the brightest gift you ever gave me. I am now, and will always be, the love you wanted me to be. And I will cherish that fact, as I cherish you.

So, thank you, for everything you've taught me. Here's to us, however our story ends.

From,

James… the love you wished I could be.

A Letter from Anna

Dear Reader,

I want to say a huge thank you for choosing to read *I Wanted to Tell You*. If you did enjoy it and want to keep up to date with all my latest releases, just sign up at the following link. Your email address will never be shared and you can unsubscribe at any time.

www.bookouture.com/anna-mansell

I Wanted to Tell You is a story I've wanted to write for years and I think I had to wait until I'd written a few other books before I knew how to approach it. Funnily enough, the character of James has appeared in every story I've ever written, and until now, has always been cut. In How to Mend a Broken Heart, he was on a bench in the park by Susan's tree. In *The Lost Wife*, he was on a bus that was taking Rachel away from Nottingham. Both times he had words of wisdom that neither character expected to come from him and both times he was cut because he was in the wrong place at the wrong time. It makes me smile to think he was just waiting around for me to write this story, just as the story was waiting until I found the headspace to write it. Maybe there's something in that, you know, if you've a story, or a character in your head. Just thinking out loud…

This story covers many aspects: friendship, marriage, love, truths, secrets, personal growth, depression. Depression and wider mental health issues, in particular, are around us all the time. If it's not us suffering, it will be someone we know. I am lucky in that I've never felt any shame around my own mental health challenges. When well, I am open to talking about how it affects me, about how it affects those around me. It's something I live with on the daily and warrior through because I know no other way and I am privileged in that I have access to the support of specialists, friends and family who understand what I need, when I need it. I recognise, however, that not everyone is in the same position. There are numerous charities supporting mental health work, the NHS is deeply underfunded in this area, yet still strives to do its best for those of us who are able to ask for help. If you can't ask for help, know that you are not alone. You are not weak and you are not at fault. There is no shame: 1 in 4 of us suffer and there is help available. Time-to-change.org.uk is a great online resource with lots of pointers, lots of people talking about their own journeys, and lots of useful advice on what to do if you are suffering, or caring for someone who is. Don't be afraid to reach out, you'll be amazed what a difference it can make.

I hope you have enjoyed *I Wanted to Tell You*. If you did, I would be very grateful if you could write a review. I'd love to hear what you think, and it makes such a difference helping new readers to discover one of my books for the first time.

I love hearing from my readers – you can get in touch on my Facebook page, through Twitter, Goodreads or my website.

Thanks,

Anna x

 AnnaMansellAuthor

 @annamansell

 www.feelthefearandwriteitanyway.com

Acknowledgements

Hello? Hello? Are you still here? Did you read the entire book and now this is wrapping everything up or have you skipped to this before you read the book itself? Either way, thank you! Thank you, thank you, thank you. You are the first and most important group of people I want to acknowledge. I know authors always say this, I'm not exactly trailblazing, but you are literally making my dreams come true. Literally. If you didn't read it, I couldn't write it. I mean, I could probably try writing it, but it's a tough gig and if nobody picked it up it would feel like a very long and torturous process for no real reason. I've written books before that nobody read, in fact I've written books before that not many people have read, and even the not-very-many is better than none. Does this make sense? Possibly it's rambly, I blame the fact I've just typed The End on a book that has been a very long time in the making. Bear with…

I actually started writing it back in 2015, inspired by the longevity of my grandparents' marriage. At the time, my him indoors and I were soon to celebrate our tenth anniversary. The timing made me reflect on how we'd made it that far; a mere seventh of the time Nana and Grandpa had been married. I thought about what him indoors has had to live with, supporting me through my mental health journey; something that I know has made me incredibly difficult to live with at times. That is where the story came from, that idea of how we each warrior our own fights, how mental health affects those around us as much as it does those of us suffering. Mental health manifests in lots of different ways for lots of different people and the only thing I truly believe, is that for me, talking is important. Seeing mental health portrayed in film, TV, books and so on, that is the thing that reminds us it can happen to any of us, at any time. And most importantly, that there is no shame in it, there is nothing to hide… and whilst having things to be thankful for is no protection from depression or anxiety, for me, there is still a lot to be thankful for, particularly when it comes to my him indoors.

So who else should I thank? Well, it would be remiss if I didn't say a massive thank you to the book bloggers who have been so blooming lovely and supportive to me over the last couple of years since my debut came out. They read so much, talk with such passion and work tirelessly to support and promote our work. They make a real difference and I am very grateful to them all!

The team at Bookouture continue to be a marvel. My new editor, Isobel, has been patient and supportive and full of ideas and guidance and genuine love for the story. She has understood what I wanted to say and has, without doubt, helped me to get the story as right as I possibly could. Thank you Isobel, I really appreciate your time and insight. Publicity Queens, Kim and Noelle, continue to amaze me with their total commitment to our books and our work. I am looking forward to working more closely with them over the months leading up to publication and will definitely owe them a large G&T and a big hug at the end of it, so in advance of that, thank you both. Truly. On Bookouture, one of the best things about being one of their authors is the Lounge. An online watercooler of a space that we can all congregate in to celebrate, commiserate, complain, belly laugh, and generally live to fight another day with bums in seats, working to deadline. I swear down, I've no idea where I'd be without you all… under my desk, rocking, possibly.

Authors in general are blooming lovely and really do make a difference. Being able to chat with people who know what it's like and support one another with generosity and a knowing Twitter GIF, in particular, people like Miranda Dickinson, Joanne Millington, Florence Keeling, and not forgetting Keris Stainton, whose #DailyHarry GIFs were golden when writing this.

In this story, Helen survives not least because of three brilliant friends. Brilliant friends inspired by my own brilliant friends. I'm lucky to have more than just three, so to those women who I consider my closest, thank you for always seeming to know the right thing to say or do at exactly the right time. Ones I've known for twenty years or maybe more, and ones I've known only a few, I hope that you know who you are and how important you are to me.

Finally, as always, a big thank you to my husband and children. In the depths of a structural edit I am a pretty lame wife and mother. The only upside for them being that the guilt I feel is equal to the number of Cornish pasties they consume. I know a traditional pasty goes no way to replacing a wife and mother's love, but I hope that one day you'll see it has always all been worth it.

With love, and thanks, and appreciation in abundance,

Anna